Better Homes and Gardens

SLOW COOKER FAVORITES
★ made ★
Healthy

Meredith® Books
Des Moines, Iowa

Project Editor: Joyce Trollope
Contributing Editors: Linda J. Henry, Winifred Moranville, Spectrum Communication Services, Inc.
Associate Design Director: Som Inthalangsy
Copy Chief: Terri Fredrickson
Publishing Operations Manager: Karen Schirm
Senior Editor, Asset and Information Manager: Phillip Morgan
Edit and Design Production Coordinator: Mary Lee Gavin
Editorial Assistant: Cheryl Eckert
Book Production Managers: Pam Kvitne, Marjorie J. Schenkelberg, Rick von Holdt, Mark Weaver
Contributing Copy Editor: Sarah Oliver Watson
Contributing Proofreaders: Alison Crouch, Gretchen Kauffman, Michael Maine, Candy Meier
Indexer: Elizabeth Parson
Test Kitchen Director: Lynn Blanchard
Test Kitchen Product Supervisor: Marilyn Cornelius
Test Kitchen Home Economists: Juliana Hale; Laura Harms, R.D.; Jennifer Kalinowski, R.D.; Maryellyn Krantz;
    Jill Moberly; Dianna Nolin; Colleen Weeden; Lori Wilson; Charles Worthington

Meredith® Books
Executive Director, Editorial: Gregory H. Kayko
Executive Director, Design: Matt Strelecki
Senior Editor/Group Manager: Jan Miller
Senior Associate Design Director: Ken Carlson
Marketing Product Manager: Gina Rickert

Publisher and Editor in Chief: James D. Blume
Editorial Director: Linda Raglan Cunningham
Executive Director, New Business Development: Todd M. Davis
Executive Director, Sales: Ken Zagor
Director, Operations: George A. Susral
Director, Production: Douglas M. Johnston
Director, Marketing: Amy Nichols
Business Director: Jim Leonard

Vice President and General Manager: Douglas J. Guendel

Better Homes and Gardens® **Magazine**
Editor in Chief: Karol DeWulf Nickell
Deputy Editor, Food and Entertaining: Nancy Hopkins

Meredith Publishing Group
President: Jack Griffin
Executive Vice President: Bob Mate

Meredith Corporation
Chairman and Chief Executive Officer: William T. Kerr
President and Chief Operating Officer: Stephen M. Lacy

In Memoriam: E.T. Meredith III (1933-2003)

All of us at Meredith® Books are dedicated to providing you with the information and ideas you need to create delicious foods. We welcome your comments and suggestions. Write to us at: Meredith Books, Cookbook Editorial Department, 1716 Locust St., Des Moines, IA 50309-3023.

If you would like to purchase any of our cooking, crafts, gardening, home improvement, or home decorating and design books, check wherever quality books are sold. Or visit us at: meredithbooks.com

Our seal on the back cover assures you that every recipe in *Slow Cooker Favorites Made Healthy* has been tested in the Better Homes and Gardens® Test Kitchen. This means that each recipe is practical and reliable, and meets our high standards of taste appeal. We guarantee your satisfaction with this book for as long as you own it.

TABLE OF CONTENTS

INTRODUCTION

YOU ALREADY KNOW THAT WHEN IT COMES TO PROVIDING family-pleasing meals despite long hours away from home, the slow cooker is just the ticket. Perhaps on your way home from work, you smile as you drive right past the drive-through, knowing that a better, more wholesome meal is simmering away at home and that it will be ready and waiting.

What you might not know is that you can also call on your slow cooker to make good-for-you meals that can help you maintain a desirable weight, feel good, and stay healthy. This book includes 229 slow cooker recipes that fit into a healthful eating plan. For each recipe, the calories, fat, saturated fat, cholesterol, and sodium have been kept in check, while ensuring the recipe offers the convenience and satisfaction you've come to expect from slow-cooked meals.

Don't think of this book as yet another "diet" book; instead, think of it as a resource to call on again and again for healthful eating in years to come. These nutritious recipes are one step on a path to a healthy lifestyle. Read on for further pointers to help you find your way on this merry path.

SLOW COOKER BASICS

AS WITH ANY APPLIANCE, IT IS BEST TO READ THE MANUFACTURER'S USE AND care booklet for specific instructions when using your slow cooker. The following tips are general guidelines you also might find helpful.

SIZE MATTERS

Slow cookers range in size from 1½ to 6 quarts. Each recipe in this book lists the recommended size or sizes that will accommodate that recipe. Check the capacity of your cooker to see whether it fits the recommendation. In general, cookers must be at least half full but no more than three-fourths full for best results.

COOK UNDER COVER

Removing the lid during cooking can dramatically reduce the interior temperature inside the cooker. When you lift the cover to stir or add ingredients, replace the lid as quickly as possible, especially when cooking at the low-heat setting. And if you have no reason to peek—don't!

CARE FOR YOUR SLOW COOKER

To keep your slow cooker in good condition and extend its life, follow these tips:
• Do not put cold food into a hot cooker or place the cooker in the refrigerator. Sudden temperature changes can crack ceramic liners.
• Do not immerse the cooker or cord in water.
• Clean the ceramic liner with a soft cloth and soapy water only; avoid using abrasive cleaners and cleansing pads.
• Wash removable ceramic liners in a dishwasher or by hand.

HEALTHY EATING FROM YOUR SLOW COOKER

IT'S BY NO MEANS A STRETCH TO COOK HEALTHFULLY FROM YOUR SLOW COOKER. In fact, the low, moist heat of the cooker lends itself well to cooking with very little fat. To help cut fat in your slow cooking even more, and to add flavor, enjoyment, and good nutrients to your slow-cooked meals, follow these tips:

• Remove skin from poultry or all visible fat from meats.
• When browning meats, coat a skillet with nonstick cooking spray or, if oil is needed, use as little as possible. Drain off excess fat before adding to cooker.
• Skim off fat from sauces and mixtures before serving.
• Substitute lighter ingredients for their high-fat, high-calorie counterparts whenever possible. For example, as a finishing touch to chilies and stews, replace high-fat sour cream with light or fat-free yogurt or sour cream.
• Call on fat-free touches to boost the enjoyment of healthful recipes. For example, serve salsas, chutneys, fresh or canned chile peppers, mustards, fruit spreads, and citrus slices alongside main dishes to flavor-up foods. Finely shredded citrus peel, grated fresh ginger and horseradish, fresh minced garlic, flavored vinegars, blended salt-free seasonings, herbs and dried herb mixtures, and onions can all be called on to increase flavor in recipes—as toppings or stir-ins—without adding extra fat.
• To healthfully round out slow-cooked menus, choose fruit salads, fresh or frozen vegetables, vegetable salads with healthful dressings, and whole-grain breads.

LIVE A HEALTHFUL LIFESTYLE

THE RECIPES IN THIS BOOK ARE DESIGNED TO HELP YOU USE YOUR
slow cooker to make healthful, wholesome meals that fit into overall habits of good nutrition. Here are further steps you can take on your route to lifelong good health and well-being.

- Be calorie-conscious. Controlling calories is a major key to controlling weight, so it's useful to learn how many calories are in the foods you eat. Checking nutrition labels on foods you purchase will help, as will the nutrition facts with our recipes.
- Eat a variety of nutrient-packed foods every day. In its 2005 Dietary Guidelines for Americans, the U.S. Department of Agriculture and Health and Human Services recommends an eating plan that emphasizes fruits, vegetables, whole grains, and fat-free or low-fat milk and milk products. The guidelines also recommend including lean meats, poultry, fish, beans, eggs, and nuts. You should also strive for a diet low in saturated fats, trans fats, cholesterol, salt (sodium), and added sugars.
- Live an active life. Physical activity is also key to a healthful lifestyle. The Dietary Guidelines for Americans recommend that adults be physically active at least 30 minutes on most days. Activities such as walking, jogging, swimming, biking, and exercise classes are terrific ways to meet your quota. Remember that you can break the 30 minutes into shorter chunks of time (10 minutes here, 20 minutes there) and that many daily activities count too. So go ahead—climb the stairs, garden, rake leaves, shovel snow, dance, run with the kids—all can count as moderate physical activity.
- Ramp up your exercise routine. The more you increase the intensity or amount of time you exercise, the greater the health benefits. People who maintain a healthy weight tend to get at least one hour of moderate-intensity physical activity daily. According to the American Council on Exercise (ACE), a complete fitness program includes three components: aerobic exercise, muscular strength and endurance conditioning, and flexibility exercise. To find out more, go to their website at www.acefitness.org.
- Control portion sizes. Spoon reasonable portions onto plates rather than putting serving bowls on the table. Family members can always request seconds if their hunger persists. Put snacks into a bowl instead of eating out of the box or bag. At fast-food restaurants, shun super sizes in favor of smaller options. In sit-down restaurants, ask for a take-home container before you start eating so you can immediately put half of your meal away for the next day.
- Read the facts. Use the Nutrition Facts labels on food packaging to learn about the nutritional value of foods, to make comparisons between products, and to plan your family's meals and snacks.

How recipes are analyzed
- The Better Homes and Gardens Test Kitchen uses nutrition analysis software to determine the nutritional value of a single serving of a recipe. The analyses do not include optional ingredients. The first serving size listed is analyzed when a range is given. When ingredient choices appear in a recipe, the first one mentioned is used for analysis.
- The exchanges, listed with the Nutrition Facts, are based on the exchange list developed by the American Dietetic Association and the American Diabetes Association.

CALORIE TALLY

A–B

American cheese, processed, 1 ounce	106
Angel food cake, 1 piece	161
Apple, 1 medium	81
Apple juice, 8 ounces	116
Applesauce, sweetened, ½ cup	97
Applesauce, unsweetened, ½ cup	53
Apricots, 3 medium	51
Apricots, canned in light syrup, 3 halves	54
Apricots, dried, 10 halves	83
Artichoke, 1 medium	60
Artichoke hearts, cooked, ½ cup	37
Asparagus, cooked, ½ cup or 6 spears	22
Avocado, 1 medium	339
Bacon, Canadian-style, cooked, 2 slices	86
Bacon, cooked, 3 slices	109
Bagel, 1 (2-ounce)	163
Baked beans (canned), ½ cup	282
Banana, 1 medium	105
Barley, cooked, 1 cup	193
Beans (dried), cooked, 1 cup	
Garbanzo	269
Great Northern	210
Kidney	225
Navy	259
Beans, refried (canned), ½ cup	270
Beef broth, 1 cup	16
Beef, cooked, 3 ounces	
Flank steak, lean only	194
Ground beef, lean	240
Ground beef, regular	250
Pot roast, chuck, lean only	188
Rib roast, lean only	208
Round steak, lean only	162
Sirloin steak, lean only	171
Biscuit, 1	103
Blueberries, 1 cup	82
Blue cheese, 1 ounce	100
Bread, 1 slice	
French	81
Italian	78
Pumpernickel	82
Raisin	70
Rye	66
White	64
Whole wheat	65
Breadsticks, 2	77
Broccoli, cooked, ½ cup	22
Broccoli, raw, 1 cup	24
Brussels sprouts, cooked, ½ cup	30
Bulgur, cooked, 1 cup	152
Butter, 1 tablespoon	108

C

Cabbage, raw, shredded, ½ cup	8
Cantaloupe, 1 cup	57
Carambola (starfruit), 1 medium	42
Carrot, raw, 1 medium	31
Carrots, cooked, ½ cup	35
Cauliflower, cooked, ½ cup	15
Celery, raw, 1 stalk	6
Cheddar cheese, 1 ounce	
Fat-free	41
Reduced-fat	90
Regular-fat	114
Cherries, sweet, 10	49
Chicken	
Breast, without skin, roasted, ½ breast	142
Dark meat, without skin, roasted, 3 ounces	176
Drumstick, without skin, roasted, 1	76
Light meat, without skin, roasted, 3 ounces	148
Chicken broth, 1 cup	24
Chocolate	
Milk, 1.55-ounce bar	226
Semisweet, 1 ounce	134
Unsweetened, 1 ounce	148
Clams, cooked, 3 ounces	126
Coconut, flaked and sweetened, 1 tablespoon	22
Colby cheese, 1 ounce	112
Corn bread, 1 piece	198
Corn chips, 1 ounce	153
Corn, cream-style, cooked, ½ cup	110
Corn, whole kernel, cooked, ½ cup	67

Rice, cooked, 1 cup

Brown	216
White	205
Wild	166

Ricotta cheese, ½ cup

Part skim	171
Whole	216

Rolls, 1

Dinner	84
Hamburger or hot dog	123
Hard, kaiser	167
Whole wheat	105

S

Salad dressings (low-calorie), 1 tablespoon

Blue cheese	15
French	22
Italian	16
Mayonnaise-type	49
Thousand Island	24

Salad dressings (regular), 1 tablespoon

Blue cheese	77
French	67
Italian	69
Mayonnaise-type	99
Thousand Island	59
Salsa, ½ cup	29
Saltine crackers, 2	26
Sauerkraut, canned, ½ cup	22
Sausage, pork, cooked, 1 link	48
Scallops, raw, 3 ounces	75
Sherbet, orange, ½ cup	132
Shrimp, cooked, 3 ounces	84

Sour cream, 1 tablespoon

Fat-free	12
Light	20
Regular	26
Spaghetti, cooked, 1 cup	197
Spinach, ½ cup chopped, boiled	21
Spinach, ½ cup chopped, raw	6

Squash, ½ cup

Acorn, baked	57
Spaghetti squash, cooked	23
Yellow summer, raw	12
Zucchini, raw	9
Strawberries, 1 cup sliced	45

Sugar, 1 tablespoon

Brown	52
Granulated	48
Sweet potato, mashed, ½ cup	172
Swiss cheese, 1 ounce	107

T-Y

Tomato, 1	26
Tomatoes, dried and packed in oil, 1 piece	6
Tomato juice, ½ cup	21
Tortilla chips, baked, 10 chips	54
Tortilla chips, regular, 1 ounce	142
Tortilla, corn, 1	58
Tortilla, flour, 1	104

Turkey

Bacon, cooked, 2 slices	68
Dark meat, without skin, roasted, 3 ounces	159
Ground, cooked, 3 ounces	193
Light meat, without skin, roasted, 3 ounces	133
Veal, round, cooked, 3 ounces	129
Vegetable juice, ½ cup	23
Waffle, 1 (4-inch diameter)	87
Watermelon, 1 cup pieces	50

Whipped dessert topping, frozen, 1 tablespoon

Light	10
Regular	15
Whole-grain rye wafer, 1	37
Whole wheat crackers, 4	71

Wine, 3.5 fluid ounces

Red	74
White	70

Yogurt

Frozen, soft-serve, ½ cup	115
Fruit-flavored, fat-free, with nonnutritive sweetener, 8 ounces	98
Fruit-flavored, low-fat, 8 ounces	231
Plain, low-fat, 8 ounces	144

Chapter 1

APPETIZERS & Beverages

Here's a slick trick for uniformly shaped meatballs: Pat the meat mixture into a 6×5-inch rectangle on a piece of waxed paper. Cut the meat into 1-inch cubes; use your hands to roll each cube into a ball.

APRICOT–GLAZED HAM BALLS

Prep:
20 minutes

Bake:
20 minutes

Cook:
Low 4 hours,
High 1 1/2 hours

Oven:
350°F

Makes:
30 meatballs

Slow Cooker Size:
3 1/2- to 4-quart

1   egg, beaten
1/2   cup graham cracker crumbs
2   tablespoons unsweetened pineapple juice
1   teaspoon dry mustard
1/4   teaspoon salt
8   ounces ground cooked ham
8   ounces ground pork
1/2   cup snipped dried apricots
1   18-ounce jar apricot preserves
1/3   cup unsweetened pineapple juice
1   tablespoon cider vinegar
1/2   teaspoon ground ginger

1. For meatballs, in a large bowl combine egg, graham cracker crumbs, the 2 tablespoons pineapple juice, mustard, and salt. Add ham, pork, and apricots; mix well. Shape into 30 meatballs. In a 15×10×1-inch baking pan place meatballs in a single layer. Bake, uncovered, in a 350° oven for 20 minutes. Drain well. Place cooked meatballs in a 3 1/2- to 4-quart slow cooker.

2. For sauce, in a small bowl combine apricot preserves, the 1/3 cup pineapple juice, vinegar, and ginger. Pour sauce over meatballs.

3. Cover and cook on low-heat setting for 4 to 5 hours or on high-heat setting for 1 1/2 to 2 hours.

4. Serve immediately or keep warm on low-heat setting for up to 2 hours. Gently stir just before serving. Serve with toothpicks.

Nutrition Facts per meatball: 86 cal., 2 g total fat (1 g sat. fat), 15 mg chol., 151 mg sodium, 15 g carbo., 0 g fiber, 3 g pro.
Daily Values: 3% vit. A, 3% vit. C, 1% calcium, 2% iron
Exchanges: 1 Other Carbo., 1/2 Lean Meat

Make the meatballs ahead of time and stash them in your freezer. On party day, it will take only minutes to combine the fixings in your slow cooker.

PINEAPPLE MEATBALLS AND SAUSAGES

1   egg, beaten
½   cup finely chopped onion (1 medium)
⅓   cup finely chopped green sweet pepper
¼   cup fine dry bread crumbs
3   tablespoons soy sauce
1   pound ground beef
1   16-ounce package small cooked smoked sausage links
1   cup chopped green sweet pepper
1   12-ounce jar pineapple ice cream topping or pineapple or apricot preserves
1   cup hot-style or regular vegetable juice
1   tablespoon quick-cooking tapioca
½   to 1 teaspoon crushed red pepper

Prep:
35 minutes

Bake:
15 minutes

Cook:
High 2 hours

Oven:
350°F

Makes:
30 appetizer servings

Slow Cooker Size:
3 ½- to 5-quart

1. In a large bowl combine egg, onion, the ⅓ cup sweet pepper, the bread crumbs, and 1 tablespoon of the soy sauce. Add ground beef; mix well. Shape into 1-inch meatballs. Place meatballs in a single layer in a 15×10×1-inch baking pan. Bake, uncovered, in a 350° oven for 15 to 18 minutes or until done. Drain well.

2. Place cooked meatballs in a 3½- to 5-quart slow cooker. Add sausage links and 1 cup sweet pepper. In a bowl combine ice cream topping, vegetable juice, remaining 2 tablespoons soy sauce, the tapioca, and crushed red pepper. Pour over meatballs and sausages; stir gently to coat.

3. Cover and cook on high-heat setting for 2 to 3 hours. Serve immediately or keep warm on low-heat setting for up to 2 hours more. Serve with toothpicks.

Nutrition Facts per serving: 124 cal., 7 g total fat (3 g sat. fat), 27 mg chol., 274 mg sodium, 10 g carbo., 0 g fiber, 5 g pro.
Daily Values: 2% vit. A, 11% vit. C, 1% calcium, 3% iron
Exchanges: ½ Other Carbo., 1 High-Fat Meat

You'll love the combination of spicy and sweet in this updated version of cocktail wieners. Orange marmalade, chipotle peppers, and tomato sauce make up the sauce. Use cocktail wieners or small smoked sausage links—or both.

HOT AND SWEET COCKTAIL WIENERS

Prep:
5 minutes

Cook:
Low 4 hours, High 2 hours

Makes:
16 appetizer servings

Slow Cooker Size:
1½-quart

1　16-ounce package cocktail wieners or small cooked smoked sausage links
1　8-ounce can no-salt-added tomato sauce
¼　cup low-sugar orange marmalade or apricot spread
1　to 2 tablespoons canned chipotle peppers in adobo sauce, chopped

1. In a 1½-quart slow cooker combine cocktail wieners, tomato sauce, orange marmalade, and chipotle peppers.

2. Cover and cook on low-heat setting for 4 hours or on high-heat setting for 2 hours. If no heat setting is available, cook for 3 hours. Serve with toothpicks.

Nutrition Facts per serving (about 3 wieners): 101 cal., 8 g total fat (3 g sat. fat), 17 mg chol., 293 mg sodium, 3 g carbo., 0 g fiber, 3 g pro.
Daily Values: 1% vit. A, 2% vit. C, 3% iron
Exchanges: ½ High-Fat Meat, 1 Fat

Vary the flavor of this party starter with your favorite-style barbecue sauce. Have plenty of napkins on hand!

CHICKEN WINGS WITH BARBECUE SAUCE

3 pounds chicken wings (14 to 16)
1½ cups bottled barbecue sauce
¼ cup honey
2 teaspoons prepared mustard
1½ teaspoons Worcestershire sauce

1. Use a sharp knife to carefully cut off tips of the wings; discard wing tips. Cut each wing at joint to make 2 sections.

2. Place wing pieces on the unheated rack of a broiler pan in a single layer. Broil 4 to 5 inches from the heat for 15 to 20 minutes or until chicken is brown, turning once. Transfer chicken to a 3½- to 4-quart slow cooker.

3. For sauce, in a bowl combine barbecue sauce, honey, mustard, and Worcestershire sauce; pour mixture over chicken wings. Cover and cook on low-heat setting for 3 to 4 hours or on high-heat setting for 1½ to 2 hours.

Nutrition Facts per appetizer: 83 cal., 4 g total fat (1 g sat. fat), 20 mg chol., 197 mg sodium, 6 g carbo., 0 g fiber, 5 g pro.
Daily Values: 1% vit. A, 1% iron
Exchanges: ½ Other Carbo., ½ Medium-Fat Meat, ½ Fat

Prep:
15 minutes

Cook:
Low 3 hours,
High 1½ hours

Broil:
15 minutes

Makes:
28 to 32 appetizers

Slow Cooker Size:
3½- to 4-quart

Five-spice powder is a blend often used in Asian cooking, especially Chinese-inspired dishes such as these tantalizing appetizer wings. Look for five-spice powder on your supermarket spice shelf.

FIVE-SPICE CHICKEN WINGS

Prep:
20 minutes

Bake:
20 minutes

Cook:
Low 4 hours, High 2 hours

Oven:
375°F

Makes:
about 32 appetizers

Slow Cooker Size:
3 ½- to 4-quart

3 pounds chicken wings (about 16)
1 cup bottled plum sauce
2 tablespoons butter, melted
1 teaspoon five-spice powder
  Thin orange wedges and pineapple slices (optional)

1. Use a sharp knife to carefully cut off tips of the wings; discard wing tips. Cut each wing at joint to make 2 sections.

2. In a foil-lined 15×10×1-inch baking pan arrange wing pieces in a single layer. Bake in a 375° oven for 20 minutes. Drain well.

3. For sauce, in a 3½- to 4-quart slow cooker combine plum sauce, butter, and five-spice powder. Add wing pieces, stirring to coat with sauce. Cover and cook on low-heat setting for 4 to 5 hours or on high-heat setting for 2 to 2½ hours.

4. Serve immediately or keep covered on low-heat setting for up to 2 hours. If desired, garnish with orange and pineapple.

Nutrition Facts per appetizer: 88 cal., 6 g total fat (2 g sat. fat), 35 mg chol., 41 mg sodium, 3 g carbo., 0 g fiber, 6 g pro.
Daily Values: 1% vit. A, 1% calcium
Exchanges: ½ Medium-Fat Meat, 1 Fat

Cooked in hoisin sauce with garlic and red pepper flakes, bite-size button mushrooms pack a surprisingly large amount of flavor.

HOISIN–GARLIC MUSHROOM APPETIZERS

½ cup bottled hoisin sauce
¼ cup water
2 tablespoons bottled minced garlic
¼ to ½ teaspoon crushed red pepper
24 ounces whole fresh button mushrooms, trimmed

1. In a 3½- to 4-quart slow cooker combine hoisin sauce, water, garlic, and crushed red pepper. Add mushrooms, stirring to coat with sauce.

2. Cover and cook on low-heat setting for 5 to 6 hours or on high-heat setting for 2½ to 3 hours. To serve, remove mushrooms from cooker with a slotted spoon. Discard cooking liquid. Serve warm mushrooms with toothpicks.

Nutrition Facts per serving: 39 cal., 1 g total fat (0 g sat. fat), 0 mg chol., 107 mg sodium, 6 g carbo., 1 g fiber, 3 g pro.
Daily Values: 2% vit. C, 1% calcium, 3% iron
Exchanges: 1½ Vegetable

Prep:
15 minutes

Cook:
Low 5 hours,
High 2 ½ hours

Makes:
10 appetizer servings

Slow Cooker Size:
3 ½- to 4-quart

Vegetables, spices, and sweet mango contribute big taste to these beefy mini tacos.

ZESTY BEEF–FILLED TACOS

Prep:
25 minutes

Cook:
Low 7 hours, High 4 hours;
plus 15 minutes on High

Makes:
24 appetizer servings

Slow Cooker Size:
3 1/2- to 4-quart

1 medium onion, cut into wedges
1 medium carrot, quartered
12 ounces beef flank steak
¼ cup snipped fresh cilantro
½ to 1 teaspoon crushed red pepper
½ teaspoon salt
1 14½-ounce can diced tomatoes with roasted garlic, undrained
½ cup water
24 miniature taco shells
Finely chopped mango (about 1 cup)
Toppings, such as snipped fresh cilantro, sliced green onion, chopped tomato, and/or finely shredded lettuce

1. Place onion and carrot in a 3½- to 4-quart slow cooker. Place beef over vegetables. Sprinkle with ¼ cup cilantro, crushed red pepper, and salt; add the undrained tomatoes and water. Cover and cook on low-heat setting for 7 to 9 hours or on high-heat setting for 4 to 5 hours.

2. Remove meat from cooker. Shred meat with a fork, cutting into shorter shreds, if desired. Drain vegetable mixture well; discard liquid. Transfer vegetable mixture to a food processor or blender. Cover; process or blend with several on/off turns until chopped.

3. Return meat and chopped vegetable mixture to slow cooker. If using low-heat setting, turn to high-heat setting. Cover and cook for 15 to 30 minutes more or until heated through. Spoon mixture into taco shells. Top with mango and desired toppings.

Nutrition Facts per serving: 53 cal., 2 g total fat (1 g sat. fat),
6 mg chol., 145 mg sodium, 5 g carbo., 1 g fiber, 4 g pro.
Daily Values: 14% vit. A, 5% vit. C, 1% calcium, 2% iron
Exchanges: ½ Other Carbo., ½ Lean Meat

Your guests will feel truly treated to something special when they taste this spicy and warm shrimp dip.

CAJUN SPINACH–SHRIMP DIP

1   10¾-ounce can condensed cream of shrimp or cream of chicken soup
1   10-ounce package frozen chopped spinach, thawed and well drained
1   8-ounce package cream cheese, cubed
1   4-ounce can tiny shrimp, drained
¼   cup finely chopped onion
¼   to ½ teaspoon Cajun seasoning
2   cloves garlic, minced
    Celery sticks, sweet pepper strips, and/or crackers

1. In a 1½-quart slow cooker combine soup, spinach, cream cheese, drained shrimp, onion, Cajun seasoning, and garlic. Cover and cook, on low-heat setting if available,* for 2 to 3 hours.

2. Stir before serving. Serve dip with vegetables and/or crackers.

*Note: Not all 1½-quart slow cookers have heat setting options.

Nutrition Facts per serving (dip only): 52 cal., 4 g total fat (2 g sat. fat), 21 mg chol., 144 mg sodium, 2 g carbo., 0 g fiber, 2 g pro.
Daily Values: 37% vit. A, 2% vit. C, 2% calcium, 2% iron
Exchanges: 1 Fat

Prep:
15 minutes

Cook:
Low 2 hours

Makes:
24 (2-tablespoon) servings

Slow Cooker Size:
1½-quart

Hot enough for you? If you like your snacks on the spicy side, use hot salsa or Monterey Jack cheese with jalapeño peppers.

RIO GRANDE DIP

Prep:
15 minutes

Cook:
Low 3 hours,
High 1½ hours

Makes:
48 (2-tablespoon) servings

Slow Cooker Size:
3½- to 4-quart

8	ounces bulk Italian sausage
⅓	cup finely chopped onion (1 small)
2	15-ounce cans refried black beans
1½	cups bottled salsa
1	4-ounce can diced green chile peppers, undrained
1½	cups shredded Monterey Jack cheese (6 ounces)
	Baked tortilla chips or corn chips

1. In a large skillet cook sausage and onion until meat is brown. Drain off fat. In a 3½- to 4-quart slow cooker combine meat mixture, refried beans, salsa, and undrained peppers. Stir in cheese.

2. Cover and cook on low-heat setting for 3 to 4 hours or on high-heat setting for 1½ to 2 hours.

3. Serve immediately or keep covered on low-heat setting for up to 2 hours. Stir just before serving. Serve with tortilla chips.

Nutrition Facts per serving (dip only): 45 cal., 2 g total fat (1 g sat. fat), 6 mg chol., 119 mg sodium, 3 g carbo., 1 g fiber, 3 g pro.
Daily Values: 1% vit. A, 2% vit. C, 4% calcium, 2% iron
Exchanges: ½ Medium-Fat Meat

Few hot party dips are easier—and few will disappear more quickly than this fantastic four-ingredient crowd-pleaser.

SUPERSIMPLE BEAN DIP

2   15-ounce cans refried beans
1   11-ounce can condensed nacho cheese soup
½   cup bottled salsa
¼   cup sliced green onions (2)
    Tortilla chips

1. In a 1½-quart slow cooker combine refried beans, soup, and salsa. Cover and cook, on low-heat setting if available,* for 3½ to 4 hours.

2. Sprinkle with green onions. Serve dip with tortilla chips.

*Note: Not all 1½-quart slow cookers have heat setting options.

Nutrition Facts per serving (dip only): 24 cal., 1 g total fat (0 g sat. fat), 1 mg chol., 143 mg sodium, 3 g carbo., 1 g fiber, 1 g pro.
Daily Values: 1% vit. A, 1% vit. C, 1% calcium, 2% iron
Exchanges: ½ Fat

Prep:
10 minutes
Cook:
Low 3 ½ hours
Makes:
44 (2-tablespoon) servings
Slow Cooker Size:
1½-quart

Garlic, onion, tomatoes, and meat are the basic picadillo quartet; this sassy pita dip takes on Mediterranean flair by mingling with olives, almonds, and raisins.

PICADILLO PITA WEDGES

Prep:
20 minutes

Cook:
Low 6 hours, High 3 hours

Makes:
16 appetizer servings

Slow Cooker Size:
3 1/2- to 4-quart

1	pound lean ground beef
1/2	cup chopped onion (1 medium)
3	cloves garlic, minced
1	16-ounce jar salsa
1/2	cup raisins
1/4	cup chopped pimiento-stuffed green olives
2	tablespoons red wine vinegar
1/2	teaspoon ground cinnamon
1/2	teaspoon ground cumin
1/4	cup toasted slivered almonds
	Toasted Pita Wedges or bagel chips

1. In a large skillet cook ground beef until brown. Drain off fat. In a 3½- to 4-quart slow cooker stir together the beef, onion, garlic, salsa, raisins, olives, vinegar, cinnamon, and cumin.

2. Cover and cook on low-heat setting for 6 to 8 hours or on high-heat setting for 3 to 4 hours. Stir in almonds. Serve with Toasted Pita Wedges.

Toasted Pita Wedges: Split 4 pita bread rounds in half horizontally; cut each half into 6 wedges. Place wedges, cut sides up, in a single layer on ungreased baking sheets. Bake in a 375°F oven for 7 to 9 minutes or until light brown. Store pita wedges in an airtight container for up to 5 days.

Nutrition Facts per serving with 3 pita wedges: 127 cal., 4 g total fat (1 g sat. fat), 18 mg chol., 262 mg sodium, 15 g carbo., 1 g fiber, 8 g pro.
Daily Values: 4% vit. A, 8% vit. C, 4% calcium, 8% iron
Exchanges: ½ Starch, ½ Other Carbo., 1 Lean Meat

Bowl game parties are all about big food, and this big, bold, flavor-packed dish will definitely fit the bill!

VEGETABLE CHILI CON QUESO

1 15-ounce can pinto beans, rinsed and drained
1 15-ounce can black beans, rinsed and drained
1 15-ounce can chili beans with chili gravy
1 10-ounce can diced tomatoes and green chile peppers, undrained
1 medium zucchini, chopped
1 medium yellow summer squash, chopped
1 cup chopped onion (1 large)
¼ cup tomato paste
2 to 3 teaspoons chili powder
4 cloves garlic, minced
3 cups shredded Colby Jack cheese (12 ounces)
   Baked tortilla chips or corn chips

Prep:
20 minutes
Cook:
Low 6 hours, High 3 hours
Makes:
32 (¼-cup) servings
Slow Cooker Size:
3 ½- to 4-quart

1. In a 3½- to 4-quart slow cooker combine drained pinto beans, drained black beans, chili beans, undrained tomatoes, zucchini, yellow squash, onion, tomato paste, chili powder, and garlic.

2. Cover and cook on low-heat setting for 6 to 7 hours or on high-heat setting for 3 to 3½ hours. Stir in cheese until melted. Serve immediately or keep warm on low-heat setting for up to 1 hour. Serve dip with chips.

Nutrition Facts per serving (dip only): 82 cal., 4 g total fat (2 g sat. fat), 9 mg chol., 231 mg sodium, 8 g carbo., 2 g fiber, 5 g pro.
Daily Values: 4% vit. A, 5% vit. C, 9% calcium, 3% iron
Exchanges: ½ Starch, ½ High-Fat Meat

You'll love this dish warm, but it's great at room temperature too. If you like, make the dip ahead, then chill. Return dip to room temperature before serving.

WHITE BEAN SPREAD

Prep:
15 minutes

Cook:
Low 3 hours

Makes:
16 appetizer servings

Slow Cooker Size:
1½-quart

2 15-ounce cans Great Northern or white kidney beans (cannellini beans), rinsed and drained
½ cup chicken broth or vegetable broth
1 tablespoon olive oil
1 teaspoon snipped fresh marjoram or ¼ teaspoon dried marjoram, crushed
½ teaspoon snipped fresh rosemary or ⅛ teaspoon dried rosemary, crushed
⅛ teaspoon ground black pepper
3 cloves garlic, minced
Toasted Pita Wedges (see page 22) or baguette slices, toasted

1. In a 1½-quart slow cooker combine drained beans, broth, olive oil, marjoram, rosemary, pepper, and garlic. Cover and cook, on low-heat setting if available,* for 3 to 4 hours. Using a potato masher, mash bean mixture slightly.

2. Serve spread warm or at room temperature with pita wedges. (Mixture thickens as it cools.)

*Note: Not all 1½-quart slow cookers have heat setting options.

Nutrition Facts per serving (spread only): 70 cal., 1 g total fat (0 g sat. fat), 0 mg chol., 33 mg sodium, 11 g carbo., 3 g fiber, 4 g pro.
Daily Values: 1% vit. C, 3% calcium, 5% iron
Exchanges: ½ Starch, ½ Very Lean Meat, ½ Fat

The lively combination of cranberry, raspberry, and apple juices and a sprightly spark of lemon guarantee this recipe will be a spirited concoction—whether you choose to add brandy or rum!

CRANBERRY SIPPER

6 inches stick cinnamon, broken
12 whole cloves
8 cups water
1 12-ounce can frozen cranberry-raspberry juice concentrate, thawed (1½ cups)
1 6-ounce can frozen apple juice concentrate, thawed (¾ cup)
½ cup sugar
⅓ cup lemon juice
½ to ¾ cup brandy or rum or 6 regular tea bags (optional)
   Orange slices (optional)
10 4- to 6-inch cinnamon sticks (optional)

Prep:
15 minutes

Cook:
Low 5 hours,
High 2 ½ hours

Makes:
10 (8-ounce) servings

Slow Cooker Size:
3 ½- to 5-quart

1. For spice bag, cut a 6-inch square from a double thickness of 100-percent-cotton cheesecloth. Place broken stick cinnamon and cloves in center of cheesecloth square. Bring corners of cheesecloth together and tie with clean cotton kitchen string.

2. In a 3½- to 5-quart slow cooker combine water, cranberry-raspberry juice concentrate, apple juice concentrate, sugar, and lemon juice. Add spice bag to the juice mixture.

3. Cover and cook on low-heat setting for 5 to 6 hours or on high-heat setting for 2½ to 3 hours. Remove and discard the spice bag. If desired, about 5 minutes before serving, add brandy or tea bags to the slow cooker. Let stand for 5 minutes. Discard the tea bags, if using. Ladle beverage into mugs or cups. If desired, add an orange slice and cinnamon stick to each serving.

Nutrition Facts per serving: 141 cal., 0 g total fat (0 g sat. fat), 0 mg chol., 19 mg sodium, 35 g carbo., 0 g fiber, 0 g pro.
Daily Values: 75% vit. C, 2% iron
Exchanges: 1½ Fruit, 1 Other Carbo.

Once the punch has simmered, set the slow cooker on low to keep the beverage at perfect sipping temperature until the final serving.

SPICY CRANBERRY PUNCH

Prep:
10 minutes

Cook:
Low 4 hours, High 2 hours

Makes:
18 (4-ounce) servings

Slow Cooker Size:
3 1/2- to 5-quart

8 inches stick cinnamon, broken into 1-inch pieces
6 whole cloves
5 cups white grape juice
2⅔ cups water
1 12-ounce can frozen cranberry juice cocktail concentrate

1. For spice bag, cut a 6- to 8-inch square from a double thickness of 100-percent-cotton cheesecloth. Place broken stick cinnamon and cloves in center of cheesecloth square. Bring corners of cheesecloth together and tie with clean cotton kitchen string.

2. In a 3½- to 5-quart slow cooker combine grape juice, water, and frozen juice concentrate. Add spice bag to the juice mixture.

3. Cover and cook on low-heat setting for 4 to 6 hours or on high-heat setting for 2 to 2½ hours. Remove and discard the spice bag. Serve immediately or keep warm on low-heat setting for up to 2 hours. Ladle punch into cups.

Nutrition Facts per serving: 44 cal., 0 g total fat (0 g sat. fat), 0 mg chol., 12 mg sodium, 11 g carbo., 0 g fiber, 0 g pro.
Daily Values: 17% vit. C
Exchanges: 1 Fruit

To break cinnamon sticks, place the sticks in a heavy plastic bag and pound them with a meat mallet.

HOT MULLED CIDER

	Peel from ½ of an orange, cut into pieces
6	inches stick cinnamon, broken
1	1-inch piece fresh ginger, peeled and thinly sliced
1	teaspoon whole allspice
8	cups apple cider or apple juice
1	cup apple brandy (optional)
¼	cup honey or packed brown sugar

1. For spice bag, cut a 6- or 8-inch square from a double thickness of 100-percent-cotton cheesecloth. Place orange peel, broken stick cinnamon, ginger, and allspice in center of cheesecloth square. Bring corners of cheesecloth together and tie with clean cotton kitchen string.

2. In a 3½- to 5-quart slow cooker combine apple cider, apple brandy (if desired), and honey. Add spice bag to the cider mixture.

3. Cover and cook on low-heat setting for 4 to 6 hours or on high-heat setting for 2 to 3 hours. Remove and discard the spice bag. Ladle cider into cups.

Nutrition Facts per serving: 148 cal., 0 g total fat (0 g sat. fat), 0 mg chol., 8 mg sodium, 38 g carbo., 0 g fiber, 0 g pro.
Daily Values: 4% vit. C, 2% calcium, 5% iron
Exchanges: 2 Fruit, ½ Other Carbo.

Prep:
10 minutes

Cook:
Low 4 hours, High 2 hours

Makes:
8 or 9 (8-ounce) servings

Slow Cooker Size:
3 ½- to 5-quart

Fix this mellow beverage on fall and winter afternoons. It's a perfect drink to sip while cheering your favorite football or basketball team on to victory.

SPICED WINE TODDY

Prep:
10 minutes

Cook:
Low 4 hours, High 2 hours

Makes:
12 (6-ounce) servings

Slow Cooker Size:
3 ½- to 6-quart

16	whole cloves
8	inches stick cinnamon, broken
6	cups apple juice
2	cups water
1½	cups Burgundy
⅔	cup instant lemon-flavored tea powder
2	tablespoons packed brown sugar

1. For spice bag, cut a 6-inch square from a double thickness of 100-percent-cotton cheesecloth. Place cloves and broken stick cinnamon in center of cheesecloth square. Bring corners of cheesecloth together and tie with clean cotton kitchen string.

2. In a 3½- to 6-quart slow cooker combine apple juice, water, Burgundy, tea powder, and brown sugar. Add spice bag to the juice-tea mixture.

3. Cover and cook on low-heat setting for 4 to 6 hours or on high-heat setting for 2 to 3 hours. Remove and discard the spice bag. Ladle beverage into cups.

Nutrition Facts per serving: 90 cal., 0 g total fat (0 g sat. fat), 0 mg chol., 9 mg sodium, 18 g carbo., 0 g fiber, 0 g pro.
Daily Values: 2% vit. C, 1% calcium, 4% iron
Exchanges: 1 Fruit

Your choice of dried fruit and fruit juice flavor this spiced brew. It's a soothing beverage for a wintry day.

SPICED FRUIT TEA

6   inches stick cinnamon, broken
1   tablespoon crystallized ginger, chopped
4   cups brewed black tea
4   cups orange-peach-mango juice or orange juice
1   cup dried fruit, such as dried peaches, apricots, and/or pears
    Orange slices

Prep:
15 minutes
Cook:
Low 4 hours, High 2 hours
Makes:
8 (6-ounce) servings
Slow Cooker Size:
3 1/2- to 4 1/2-quart

1. For spice bag, cut a 6- or 8-inch square from a double thickness of 100-percent-cotton cheesecloth. Place broken stick cinnamon and ginger in center of cheesecloth square. Bring corners of cheesecloth together and tie with clean cotton kitchen string.

2. In a 3½- to 4½-quart slow cooker combine tea and juice. Add dried fruit and spice bag to the tea mixture.

3. Cover and cook on low-heat setting for 4 to 6 hours or on high-heat setting for 2 to 3 hours. Remove and discard the spice bag and dried fruit. Ladle tea into cups. Float an orange slice in each cup. If desired, sweeten to taste.

Nutrition Facts per serving: 56 cal., 0 g total fat (0 g sat. fat), 0 mg chol., 14 mg sodium, 14 g carbo., 0 g fiber, 0 g pro.
Daily Values: 50% vit. C, 1% calcium
Exchanges: 1 Fruit

For a spicier sipper, add several drops of bottled hot pepper sauce. It's a perfect starter for a brunch or tailgate party. Garnish with celery sticks, if you like.

TOMATO SIPPER

Prep:
10 minutes

Cook:
Low 4 hours, High 2 hours

Makes:
12 (4-ounce) servings

Slow Cooker Size:
3 1/2- to 4-quart

1 46-ounce can vegetable juice
1 stalk celery, halved crosswise
2 tablespoons packed brown sugar
2 tablespoons lemon juice
2 teaspoons Worcestershire sauce

1. In a 3½- to 4-quart slow cooker combine vegetable juice, celery, brown sugar, lemon juice, and Worcestershire sauce.

2. Cover and cook on low-heat setting for 4 to 5 hours or on high-heat setting for 2 to 2½ hours. Discard celery. Ladle beverage into heatproof cups.

Nutrition Facts per serving: 33 cal., 0 g total fat (0 g sat. fat), 0 mg chol., 295 mg sodium, 7 g carbo., 1 g fiber, 0 g pro.
Daily Values: 18% vit. A, 47% vit. C, 2% calcium, 3% iron
Exchanges: 1 Vegetable, ½ Other Carbo.

Chapter 2

BEEF & LAMB
Main Dishes

Pot roast heads for the untamed West when slow cooked with chili beans, corn, tomatoes, and spicy chile peppers in adobo sauce. Yellow corn bread is a quick and tasty side.

COWBOY BEEF

Prep:
10 minutes

Cook:
Low 10 hours, High 5 hours

Makes:
6 servings

Slow Cooker Size:
3 ½- to 4-quart

1 2- to 2½-pound boneless beef chuck pot roast
1 15-ounce can chili beans with chili gravy
1 11-ounce can whole kernel corn with sweet peppers, drained
1 10-ounce can chopped tomatoes and green chile peppers, undrained
1 to 2 teaspoons canned chipotle peppers in adobo sauce, finely chopped

1. Trim fat from meat. If necessary, cut meat to fit into a 3½- to 4-quart slow cooker. Place meat in the cooker. In a medium bowl combine undrained beans, drained corn, undrained tomatoes, and chipotle peppers. Pour bean mixture over meat in cooker.

2. Cover and cook on low-heat setting for 10 to 12 hours or on high-heat setting for 5 to 6 hours.

3. Remove meat from cooker and place on a cutting board. Slice meat and arrange in a shallow serving bowl. Using a slotted spoon, spoon bean mixture over meat. Drizzle some cooking liquid over all.

Nutrition Facts per serving: 307 cal., 7 g total fat (2 g sat. fat), 89 mg chol., 655 mg sodium, 23 g carbo., 5 g fiber, 37 g pro.
Daily Values: 6% vit. A, 14% vit. C, 4% calcium, 28% iron
Exchanges: 1 Vegetable, 1 Starch, 4½ Very Lean Meat, 1 Fat

Try a cooked fragrant rice, such as jasmine or basmati, with this fork-tender beef and rich, slightly sweet brown gravy.

JERK ROAST WITH RICE

1	2- to 2½-pound boneless beef chuck pot roast
¾	cup water
¼	cup raisins
¼	cup bottled steak sauce
3	tablespoons balsamic vinegar
2	tablespoons sugar
2	tablespoons quick-cooking tapioca
1	teaspoon cracked black pepper
1	teaspoon Jamaican jerk seasoning
2	cloves garlic, minced
3	cups hot cooked jasmine or basmati rice

Prep:
30 minutes

Cook:
Low 8 hours, High 4 hours

Makes:
6 servings

Slow Cooker Size:
3½- to 4-quart

1. Trim fat from meat. If necessary, cut meat to fit into a 3½- to 4-quart slow cooker. Place meat in the cooker. In a small bowl combine water, raisins, steak sauce, balsamic vinegar, sugar, tapioca, pepper, Jamaican jerk seasoning, and garlic. Pour mixture over meat.

2. Cover and cook on low-heat setting for 8 to 10 hours or on high-heat setting for 4 to 5 hours. Skim off fat from cooking liquid. Serve meat with rice and cooking liquid.

Nutrition Facts per serving: 359 cal., 7 g total fat (3 g sat. fat), 92 mg chol., 269 mg sodium, 39 g carbo., 1 g fiber, 33 g pro.
Daily Values: 2% vit. A, 4% vit. C, 3% calcium, 26% iron
Exchanges: 1½ Starch, 1 Other Carbo., 4 Very Lean Meat, ½ Fat

Luscious mushroom sauce turns a budget beef roast into a silver-spoon standout.

MUSHROOM–SAUCED POT ROAST

Prep:
20 minutes

Cook:
Low 10 hours, High 5 hours

Makes:
5 to 6 servings

Slow Cooker Size:
3 ½- to 4 ½-quart

1 1½-pound boneless beef chuck eye roast, eye of round roast, or round rump roast
4 medium potatoes, quartered (about 1½ pounds)
1 16-ounce package frozen tiny whole carrots
1 4-ounce can (drained weight) mushroom stems and pieces, drained
½ teaspoon dried tarragon or basil, crushed
¼ teaspoon salt
1 10¾-ounce can condensed golden mushroom soup

1. Trim fat from meat. If necessary, cut meat to fit into a 3½- to 4½-quart slow cooker. In the slow cooker combine potatoes, frozen carrots, drained mushrooms, tarragon, and salt. Place meat on top of vegetables. Pour soup over meat.

2. Cover and cook on low-heat setting for 10 to 12 hours or on high-heat setting for 5 to 6 hours.

Nutrition Facts per serving: 338 cal., 8 g total fat (3 g sat. fat), 62 mg chol., 817 mg sodium, 31 g carbo., 5 g fiber, 35 g pro. Daily Values: 355% vit. A, 26% vit. C, 4% calcium, 20% iron Exchanges: 1 Vegetable, 1½ Starch, 4 Very Lean Meat, 1 Fat

Different and delicious, this chuck roast with veggies and brown gravy gets its sweet kick from a can of cola. The meat is tender and the gravy is thick.

COLA POT ROAST

1   2½- to 3-pound boneless beef chuck pot roast
    Nonstick cooking spray
2   16-ounce packages frozen stew vegetables
1   12-ounce can cola
½   of a 2-ounce package onion soup mix (1 envelope)
2   tablespoons quick-cooking tapioca

1. Trim fat from meat. Lightly coat an unheated large skillet with nonstick cooking spray. Preheat over medium heat. Brown meat on all sides in hot skillet.

2. Place meat in a 4½- to 5-quart slow cooker. Top with frozen vegetables. In a small bowl stir together cola, soup mix, and tapioca. Pour over meat and vegetables in slow cooker.

3. Cover and cook on low-heat setting for 7 to 8 hours or on high-heat setting for 3½ to 4 hours.

Nutrition Facts per serving: 278 cal., 5 g total fat (2 g sat. fat), 75 mg chol., 582 mg sodium, 28 g carbo., 2 g fiber, 29 g pro.
Daily Values: 148% vit. A, 3% vit. C, 1% calcium, 17% iron
Exchanges: 1 Vegetable, 1½ Other Carbo., 4 Very Lean Meat, ½ Fat

Prep:
15 minutes

Cook:
Low 7 hours,
High 3½ hours

Makes:
6 servings

Slow Cooker Size:
4½- to 5-quart

Horseradish adds plenty of flavor to the gravy. Be sure to skim off fat from the cooking liquid.

SPICY BEEF ROAST

Prep:
15 minutes

Cook:
Low 10 hours, High 5 hours

Makes:
10 servings

Slow Cooker Size:
3 1/2- to 4 1/2-quart

1 3½- to 4-pound boneless beef chuck pot roast
   Salt
   Ground black pepper
2 tablespoons cooking oil (optional)
½ cup water
1 tablespoon Worcestershire sauce
1 tablespoon tomato paste
2 cloves garlic, minced
   Several dashes bottled hot pepper sauce
1 tablespoon cornstarch
1 tablespoon cold water
1 tablespoon prepared horseradish
½ teaspoon salt

1. Trim fat from meat. Sprinkle meat on both sides with salt and pepper. If necessary, cut meat to fit into a 3½- to 4½-quart slow cooker. (If desired, brown meat in a large skillet in hot oil over medium heat until brown on all sides. Drain off fat.) Place meat in cooker. In a small bowl stir together the ½ cup water, Worcestershire sauce, tomato paste, garlic, and hot pepper sauce. Pour over meat.

2. Cover and cook on low-heat setting for 10 to 12 hours or on high-heat setting for 5 to 6 hours. Transfer meat to a serving platter, reserving cooking liquid.

3. For gravy, strain cooking liquid and skim off fat. Transfer cooking liquid to a medium saucepan. In a small bowl stir together cornstarch and the 1 tablespoon water; stir into cooking liquid. Cook and stir over medium-high heat until thickened and bubbly. Cook and stir for 2 minutes more. Stir in horseradish and the ½ teaspoon salt. Serve gravy with meat.

Nutrition Facts per serving: 203 cal., 6 g total fat (2 g sat. fat), 94 mg chol., 278 mg sodium, 2 g carbo., 0 g fiber, 34 g pro.
Daily Values: 1% vit. C, 1% calcium, 23% iron
Exchanges: 4 Lean Meat

Using lettuce leaves as the wrapper makes this a very low-calorie main dish.

ASIAN LETTUCE WRAPS

1	3-pound boneless beef chuck pot roast
1½	cups diced jicama or chopped celery
½	cup chopped green onions (4)
¼	cup rice vinegar
¼	cup reduced-sodium soy sauce
2	tablespoons hoisin sauce
1	tablespoon finely chopped fresh ginger
½	teaspoon salt
½	teaspoon chili oil
¼	teaspoon ground black pepper
2	tablespoons cornstarch
2	tablespoons cold water
24	butterhead (Bibb or Boston) lettuce leaves or
	12 7- to 8-inch flour tortillas

Prep:
20 minutes

Cook:
Low 8 hours, High 4 hours;
plus 30 minutes on High

Makes:
12 servings

Slow Cooker Size:
3 ½- to 4-quart

1. Trim fat from meat. Place meat in a 3½- to 4-quart slow cooker. In a medium bowl combine jicama, green onions, rice vinegar, soy sauce, hoisin sauce, ginger, salt, chili oil, and pepper. Add mixture to the slow cooker.

2. Cover and cook on low-heat setting for 8 to 10 hours or on high-heat setting for 4 to 5 hours. In a small bowl stir together cornstarch and water. If using low-heat setting, turn to high-heat setting. Stir cornstarch mixture into liquid around the meat. Cover and cook about 30 minutes more or until thickened and bubbly.

3. Remove meat from cooker. Using 2 forks, pull meat apart into shreds. Stir meat into mixture in slow cooker. Spoon meat mixture onto lettuce leaves or tortillas and roll up.

Nutrition Facts per serving: 169 cal., 4 g total fat (1 g sat. fat), 67 mg chol., 401 mg sodium, 5 g carbo., 0 g fiber, 25 g pro.
Daily Values: 11% vit. A, 9% vit. C, 2% calcium, 18% iron
Exchanges: 1 Vegetable, 3 Very Lean Meat, 1 Fat

Serve the smoke-flavored beef on buns or rolls, if you like. Complete the hearty meal with coleslaw and fresh fruit for dessert.

SMOKY BARBECUED BEEF BRISKET

Prep:
15 minutes

Cook:
Low 10 hours, High 5 hours

Makes:
6 to 8 servings

Slow Cooker Size:
3 1/2- to 4-quart

1	2- to 3-pound fresh beef brisket
1	teaspoon chili powder
1/2	teaspoon garlic powder
1/4	teaspoon celery seeds
1/8	teaspoon ground black pepper
1/2	cup ketchup
1/2	cup chili sauce
1/4	cup packed brown sugar
2	tablespoons vinegar
2	tablespoons Worcestershire sauce
1 1/2	teaspoons liquid smoke
1/2	teaspoon dry mustard
1/3	cup cold water
3	tablespoons all-purpose flour

1. Trim fat from meat. Cut meat to fit into a 3½- to 4-quart slow cooker. In a small bowl combine chili powder, garlic powder, celery seeds, and pepper. Sprinkle mixture evenly over meat; rub in with your fingers. Place meat in the cooker.

2. In a medium bowl combine ketchup, chili sauce, brown sugar, vinegar, Worcestershire sauce, liquid smoke, and dry mustard. Pour over meat. Cover and cook on low-heat setting for 10 to 11 hours or on high-heat setting for 5 to 5½ hours.

3. Remove meat; keep warm. For sauce, skim off fat from cooking liquid. Measure 2½ cups of the cooking liquid; set aside. In a medium saucepan stir water into flour; add the reserved 2½ cups cooking liquid. Cook and stir until thickened and bubbly; cook and stir for 1 minute more. Thinly slice meat across the grain. Serve meat with sauce.

Nutrition Facts per serving: 305 cal., 8 g total fat (2 g sat. fat), 87 mg chol., 681 mg sodium, 24 g carbo., 2 g fiber, 34 g pro.
Daily Values: 10% vit. A, 12% vit. C, 3% calcium, 22% iron
Exchanges: 1½ Other Carbo., 5 Very Lean Meat, 1 Fat

For a real time-saver, freeze half of this plentiful main course. It'll be ready in minutes for dinner on a busy day.

SPICED BEEF BRISKET

1   3½- to 4-pound fresh beef brisket
2   cups water
¼   cup ketchup
½   of a 2-ounce package onion soup mix (1 envelope)
2   tablespoons Worcestershire sauce
½   teaspoon ground cinnamon
1   clove garlic, minced
¼   teaspoon ground black pepper
¼   cup cold water
3   tablespoons all-purpose flour

Prep:
15 minutes

Cook:
Low 10 hours, High 5 hours

Makes:
10 to 12 servings

Slow Cooker Size:
3 ½- to 4-quart

1. If necessary, cut meat to fit into a 3½- to 4-quart slow cooker. Place meat in cooker.

2. In a medium bowl combine the 2 cups water, ketchup, soup mix, Worcestershire sauce, cinnamon, garlic, and pepper. Pour over meat. Cover and cook on low-heat setting for 10 to 11 hours or on high-heat setting for 5 to 5½ hours.

3. Remove meat; keep warm. Skim off fat from cooking liquid. Measure 1½ cups of the cooking liquid; set aside. For gravy, in a small saucepan stir the ¼ cup water into flour. Stir in the reserved 1½ cups cooking liquid. Cook and stir until thickened and bubbly. Cook and stir for 1 minute more.

4. Thinly slice meat across the grain. Serve with gravy.

Nutrition Facts per serving: 247 cal., 9 g total fat (3 g sat. fat), 76 mg chol., 338 mg sodium, 5 g carbo., 0 g fiber, 33 g pro. Daily Values: 1% vit. A, 2% vit. C, 2% calcium, 19% iron Exchanges: 5 Very Lean Meat, 1½ Fat

Pack some tang, pack some heat. Your tools are beer and chili sauce, which do great things to beef brisket and sliced onions. Serve sliced meat with a side of vegetables or fork slices of meat onto kaiser rolls for a hearty sandwich.

BEER BRISKET

Prep:
15 minutes

Cook:
Low 10 hours, High 5 hours

Makes:
9 to 12 servings

Slow Cooker Size:
3 1/2- to 4-quart

1   3- to 4-pound fresh beef brisket
2   large onions, sliced
1   12-ounce bottle or can (1½ cups) beer
½   cup bottled chili sauce
2   teaspoons dried steak seasoning
9   to 12 kaiser rolls, split and toasted (optional)

1. Trim fat from meat. If necessary, cut meat to fit into a 3½- to 4-quart slow cooker. Place onions in the cooker. Top with meat. In a medium bowl stir together beer, chili sauce, and steak seasoning. Pour over onions and meat in cooker.

2. Cover and cook on low-heat setting for 10 to 12 hours or on high-heat setting for 5 to 6 hours.

3. To serve, remove meat from cooking liquid. Thinly slice meat across the grain. Using a slotted spoon, remove onions from cooking liquid and place on top of meat. Drizzle with some of the cooking liquid. If desired, serve sliced meat and onions on kaiser rolls.

Nutrition Facts per serving: 265 cal., 10 g total fat (4 g sat. fat), 94 mg chol., 378 mg sodium, 8 g carbo., 2 g fiber, 31 g pro.
Daily Values: 2% vit. A, 7% vit. C, 2% calcium, 17% iron
Exchanges: ½ Other Carbo., 4 Very Lean Meat, 2 Fat

Beef brisket needs long, slow cooking to become tender. Slice the brisket to serve in toasted hamburger buns.

SAVORY BRISKET SANDWICHES

1	2½- to 3-pound fresh beef brisket
1	10-ounce can chopped tomatoes with green chile peppers, undrained
1	8-ounce can applesauce
½	of a 6-ounce can (⅓ cup) tomato paste
¼	cup reduced-sodium soy sauce
¼	cup packed brown sugar
1	tablespoon Worcestershire sauce
10	to 12 hamburger buns, split and toasted

Prep:
30 minutes

Cook:
Low 10 hours;
plus 15 minutes in saucepan

Makes:
10 to 12 servings

Slow Cooker Size:
3½- to 5-quart

1. Trim fat from meat. If necessary, cut meat to fit into a 3½- to 5-quart slow cooker. Place meat in cooker. In a bowl stir together the undrained tomatoes, applesauce, tomato paste, soy sauce, brown sugar, and Worcestershire sauce; pour over meat.

2. Cover and cook on low-heat setting about 10 hours or until meat is tender. Remove meat; cover to keep warm.

3. Pour cooking liquid into a large saucepan. Bring to boiling; reduce heat. Boil gently, uncovered, for 15 to 20 minutes or until reduced to desired consistency, stirring frequently. Thinly slice meat across the grain. Divide meat among bottom bun halves. Drizzle with cooking liquid; add bun tops.

Nutrition Facts per serving: 339 cal., 9 g total fat (3 g sat. fat), 68 mg chol., 677 mg sodium, 35 g carbo., 2 g fiber, 29 g pro.
Daily Values: 4% vit. A, 9% vit. C, 8% calcium, 24% iron
Exchanges: 2 Starch, ½ Other Carbo., 3 Lean Meat

Depending on how much heat you like, use either sweet or hot Hungarian paprika to spice this goulash.

SLOW COOKER GOULASH

Prep:
25 minutes

Cook:
Low 8 hours,
High 3 1/2 hours;
plus 30 minutes on High

Makes:
6 servings

Slow Cooker Size:
3 1/2- to 4-quart

1 1/2   pounds beef stew meat
2   medium carrots, bias-sliced into 1/2-inch pieces
2   medium onions, thinly sliced
3   cloves garlic, minced
1 1/4   cups beef broth
1   6-ounce can tomato paste
1   tablespoon Hungarian paprika
1   teaspoon finely shredded lemon peel
1/2   teaspoon salt
1/2   teaspoon caraway seeds
1/4   teaspoon ground black pepper
1   bay leaf
1   red or green sweet pepper, cut into bite-size strips
3   cups hot cooked noodles
    Light dairy sour cream or yogurt

1. In a 3 1/2- to 4-quart slow cooker combine meat, carrots, onions, and garlic. In a small bowl combine broth, tomato paste, paprika, lemon peel, salt, caraway seeds, black pepper, and bay leaf. Stir into vegetable and meat mixture.

2. Cover and cook on low-heat setting for 8 to 9 hours or on high-heat setting for 3 1/2 to 4 1/2 hours.

3. If using low-heat setting, turn to high-heat setting. Stir in sweet pepper strips. Cover and cook for 30 minutes more. Remove and discard bay leaf. Serve with hot cooked noodles. Top with a dollop of sour cream.

Nutrition Facts per serving: 356 cal., 11 g total fat (4 g sat. fat), 85 mg chol., 678 mg sodium, 33 g carbo., 4 g fiber, 32 g pro.
Daily Values: 153% vit. A, 81% vit. C, 6% calcium, 26% iron
Exchanges: 1/2 Vegetable, 1 Starch, 1 Other Carbo., 3 1/2 Very Lean Meat

This stew has a rich wine taste, mellowed with mushrooms and stew vegetables. Hot cooked noodles or mashed potatoes are tasty on the side.

BEEF BURGUNDY

2 pounds beef stew meat
  Nonstick cooking spray
1 16-ounce package frozen stew vegetables
1 10¾-ounce can condensed golden mushroom soup
⅔ cup Burgundy
⅓ cup water
1 tablespoon quick-cooking tapioca

1. If necessary, cut up large pieces of meat. Lightly coat an unheated large skillet with nonstick cooking spray. Preheat over medium heat. Brown meat, half at a time, in hot skillet; drain off fat. Set aside.

2. Place frozen vegetables in a 3½- to 4-quart slow cooker. Top with meat. In a medium bowl stir together soup, Burgundy, water, and tapioca. Pour over meat and vegetables in cooker.

3. Cover and cook on low-heat setting for 7 to 9 hours or on high-heat setting for 3½ to 4½ hours.

Nutrition Facts per serving: 291 cal., 8 g total fat (3 g sat. fat), 91 mg chol., 535 mg sodium, 14 g carbo., 1 g fiber, 34 g pro.
Daily Values: 80% vit. A, 2% vit. C, 1% calcium, 23% iron
Exchanges: ½ Vegetable, 1 Other Carbo., 4½ Very Lean Meat, 1 Fat

Prep:
20 minutes

Cook:
Low 7 hours,
High 3½ hours

Makes:
6 servings

Slow Cooker Size:
3½- to 4-quart

Only five ingredients plus a little seasoning turn stew meat into a company-special main dish.

BEEF IN RED WINE GRAVY

Prep:
15 minutes

Cook:
Low 10 hours, High 5 hours

Makes:
6 servings

Slow Cooker Size:
3 1/2- to 4-quart

1 1/2   pounds beef stew meat, cut into 1-inch cubes
2   medium onions, cut up
2   beef bouillon cubes or 1/2 of 2-ounce package onion soup mix (1 envelope)
3   tablespoons cornstarch
   Salt
   Ground black pepper
1 1/2   cups dry red wine
   Hot cooked noodles (optional)

1. In a 3 1/2- to 4-quart slow cooker combine stew meat and onions. Add bouillon cubes. Sprinkle with cornstarch, salt, and pepper. Pour wine over all.

2. Cover and cook on low-heat setting for 10 to 12 hours or on high-heat setting for 5 to 6 hours. If desired, serve over noodles.

Nutrition Facts per serving: 211 cal., 4 g total fat (1 g sat. fat), 67 mg chol., 430 mg sodium, 8 g carbo., 0 g fiber, 24 g pro.
Daily Values: 2% vit. C, 2% calcium, 18% iron
Exchanges: 1/2 Other Carbo., 3 Lean Meat

The slightly spicy ginger-flavored sauce goes equally well over pork or lamb. Serve with hot cooked rice.

GINGERED BEEF AND VEGETABLES

1½	pounds boneless beef round steak, cut into 1-inch cubes
4	medium carrots, bias-sliced into ½-inch pieces
1½	cups water
½	cup bias-sliced green onions (4)
2	cloves garlic, minced
2	tablespoons soy sauce
2	teaspoons grated fresh ginger
1½	teaspoons instant beef bouillon granules
¼	teaspoon crushed red pepper
3	tablespoons cornstarch
3	tablespoons cold water
½	cup chopped red sweet pepper
2	cups frozen sugar snap peas, thawed
3	cups hot cooked rice

Prep:
20 minutes

Cook:
Low 9 hours,
High 4½ hours;
plus 20 minutes on High

Makes:
6 servings

Slow Cooker Size:
3½- to 4-quart

1. In a 3½- to 4-quart slow cooker combine beef, carrots, the 1½ cups water, green onions, garlic, soy sauce, ginger, bouillon granules, and crushed red pepper.

2. Cover and cook on low-heat setting for 9 to 10 hours or on high-heat setting for 4½ to 5 hours.

3. If using low-heat setting, turn to high-heat setting. In a small bowl stir together cornstarch and the 3 tablespoons water; stir into meat mixture along with sweet pepper. Cover and cook for 20 to 30 minutes more or until thickened, stirring once. Stir in sugar snap peas. Serve over rice.

Nutrition Facts per serving: 350 cal., 10 g total fat (4 g sat. fat), 68 mg chol., 400 mg sodium, 35 g carbo., 3 g fiber, 29 g pro.
Daily Values: 232% vit. A, 52% vit. C, 6% calcium, 21% iron
Exchanges: 1 Vegetable, 2 Starch, 3 Very Lean Meat, 1 Fat

Bottom round steak, less expensive than top round steak, is a good choice for the slow cooker because the moist-heat cooking tenderizes the meat.

HERBED STEAK AND MUSHROOMS

Prep:
15 minutes

Cook:
Low 8 hours, High 4 hours

Makes:
6 servings

Slow Cooker Size:
3 1/2- to 4-quart

2 pounds beef round steak, cut ¾ inch thick
1 medium onion, sliced
2 cups sliced fresh mushrooms or two 4½-ounce jars (drained weight) sliced mushrooms, drained
1 10¾-ounce can condensed cream of mushroom soup
¼ cup dry white wine or beef broth
½ teaspoon dried basil, crushed
¼ teaspoon dried marjoram, crushed
¼ teaspoon ground black pepper
3 cups hot cooked noodles

1. Trim fat from meat. Cut meat into serving-size portions. In a 3½- to 4-quart slow cooker combine onion and mushrooms. Place meat on top of vegetables.

2. In a small bowl combine soup, wine, basil, marjoram, and pepper; pour over meat. Cover and cook on low-heat setting for 8 to 10 hours or on high-heat setting for 4 to 5 hours. Serve meat and sauce over noodles.

Nutrition Facts per serving: 332 cal., 7 g total fat (2 g sat. fat), 87 mg chol., 442 mg sodium, 26 g carbo., 2 g fiber, 38 g pro.
Daily Values: 1% vit. A, 1% vit. C, 3% calcium, 25% iron
Exchanges: ½ Vegetable, 1 Starch, ½ Other Carbo., 4½ Very Lean Meat, 1 Fat

What a treat to come home after a busy day to the wonderful aroma of this meat dish that's served over noodles.

ITALIAN ROUND STEAK

1½ pounds boneless beef bottom round steak
2 medium carrots, cut into ½-inch pieces
2 stalks celery, cut into ½-inch pieces
1 cup quartered fresh mushrooms
½ cup sliced green onions (4)
1 14½-ounce can Italian-style stewed tomatoes, undrained
1 cup beef broth
½ cup dry red wine, dry white wine, or beef broth
3 tablespoons quick-cooking tapioca
1 teaspoon dried Italian seasoning, crushed
½ teaspoon salt
¼ teaspoon ground black pepper
1 bay leaf
3 cups hot cooked noodles

Prep:
20 minutes

Cook:
Low 9 hours,
High 4½ hours

Makes:
6 servings

Slow Cooker Size:
3½- to 4-quart

1. Trim fat from meat; cut meat into 1-inch cubes.

2. Place meat in a 3½- to 4-quart slow cooker. Add carrots, celery, mushrooms, green onions, undrained tomatoes, the 1 cup beef broth, wine, tapioca, Italian seasoning, salt, pepper, and bay leaf.

3. Cover and cook on low-heat setting for 9 to 10 hours or on high-heat setting for 4½ to 5 hours. Remove and discard bay leaf. Serve over noodles.

Nutrition Facts per serving: 324 cal., 7 g total fat (2 g sat. fat), 83 mg chol., 552 mg sodium, 33 g carbo., 3 g fiber, 27 g pro. Daily Values: 104% vit. A, 7% vit. C, 5% calcium, 25% iron Exchanges: 1 Vegetable, 1 Starch, 1 Other Carbo., 3 Very Lean Meat, 1 Fat

Heat a package of refrigerated mashed potatoes to serve with this saucy round steak. For extra flavor, stir snipped fresh basil or grated Parmesan cheese into the cooked potatoes.

STEAK WITH MUSHROOMS

Prep:
10 minutes

Cook:
Low 8 hours, High 4 hours

Makes:
4 servings

Slow Cooker Size:
3 ½- to 4-quart

1 pound boneless beef round steak, cut 1 inch thick
2 medium onions, sliced
2 4½-ounce jars (drained weight) whole mushrooms, drained
1 12-ounce jar beef gravy
¼ cup dry red wine or apple juice

1. Trim fat from meat. Cut meat into 4 serving-size pieces. Place onions in a 3½- to 4-quart slow cooker. Arrange drained mushrooms over onions; add meat. In a medium bowl stir together gravy and wine. Pour over meat.

2. Cover and cook on low-heat setting for 8 to 10 hours or on high-heat setting for 4 to 5 hours.

Nutrition Facts per serving: 220 cal., 4 g total fat (2 g sat. fat), 51 mg chol., 814 mg sodium, 11 g carbo., 3 g fiber, 31 g pro.
Daily Values: 3% vit. A, 3% calcium, 20% iron
Exchanges: ½ Vegetable, ½ Other Carbo., 4 Very Lean Meat, ½ Fat

In the mood for Mexican, Cajun, or Italian? Just vary the seasoned tomatoes for robust flavor that usually comes only from a long list of seasonings.

SO–EASY PEPPER STEAK

2 pounds boneless beef round steak,
  cut ¾ to 1 inch thick
  Salt
  Ground black pepper
1 14½-ounce can Cajun-, Mexican-, or Italian-style
  stewed tomatoes, undrained
⅓ cup tomato paste with Italian seasoning
½ teaspoon bottled hot pepper sauce
1 16-ounce package frozen (yellow, green, and red)
  peppers and onion stir-fry vegetables
4 cups hot cooked noodles or mashed potatoes

Prep:
15 minutes

Cook:
Low 10 hours, High 5 hours

Makes:
8 servings

Slow Cooker Size:
3 ½- to 4-quart

1. Trim fat from meat. Cut meat into 8 serving-size pieces. Lightly sprinkle meat with salt and black pepper. Place meat in a 3½- to 4-quart slow cooker. In a medium bowl combine undrained tomatoes, tomato paste, and hot pepper sauce. Pour over meat. Top with frozen vegetables.

2. Cover and cook on low-heat setting for 10 to 12 hours or on high-heat setting for 5 to 6 hours. Serve over noodles.

Nutrition Facts per serving: 308 cal., 7 g total fat (2 g sat. fat), 89 mg chol., 372 mg sodium, 29 g carbo., 2 g fiber, 31 g pro.
Daily Values: 7% vit. A, 49% vit. C, 3% calcium, 24% iron
Exchanges: 1 Vegetable, 1½ Starch, 3½ Very Lean Meat, 1 Fat

These delicious steak rolls have an Italian flair from the addition of Parmesan cheese and spaghetti sauce. Serve them with spaghetti or your favorite pasta.

VEGETABLE–STUFFED STEAK ROLLS

Prep:
30 minutes

Cook:
Low 8 hours, High 4 hours

Makes:
6 servings

Slow Cooker Size:
3 ½- to 4-quart

½ cup shredded carrot (1 medium)
⅓ cup chopped zucchini
⅓ cup chopped red or green sweet pepper
¼ cup sliced green onions (2)
2 tablespoons grated Parmesan cheese
1 tablespoon snipped fresh parsley
1 clove garlic, minced
¼ teaspoon ground black pepper
6 tenderized beef round steaks (about 2 pounds total)*
2 cups meatless spaghetti sauce
3 cups hot cooked spaghetti

1. In a small bowl combine carrot, zucchini, sweet pepper, green onions, Parmesan cheese, parsley, garlic, and black pepper. Spoon ¼ cup of the vegetable filling on each piece of meat. Roll up meat around the filling and tie each roll with clean cotton kitchen string or secure with wooden toothpicks.

2. Transfer meat rolls to a 3½- to 4-quart slow cooker. Pour spaghetti sauce over meat rolls.

3. Cover and cook on low-heat setting for 8 to 10 hours or on high-heat setting for to 4 to 5 hours. Discard string or toothpicks. Serve meat rolls with hot cooked spaghetti.

*Note: If you can't find tenderized round steak, ask a butcher to tenderize 2 pounds boneless beef round steak and cut it into 6 pieces. Or cut 2 pounds boneless beef round steak into 6 serving-size pieces; place the meat between 2 pieces of plastic wrap and, with a meat mallet, pound the steak to ¼- to ½-inch thickness.

Nutrition Facts per serving: 372 cal., 10 g total fat (3 g sat. fat), 89 mg chol., 537 mg sodium, 31 g carbo., 4 g fiber, 39 g pro.
Daily Values: 54% vit. A, 34% vit. C, 6% calcium, 30% iron
Exchanges: 1 Starch, 1 Other Carbo., 4½ Very Lean Meat, 1 Fat

Put these on the menu for a fun family meal. Set the table with tortillas, a platter of seasoned shredded meat, and bowls of sour cream and diced tomatoes. Then let family members roll their own meals.

SLOW-COOKED BEEF FAJITAS

1½   pounds beef flank steak
1   16-ounce package frozen (yellow, green, and red) peppers and onion stir-fry vegetables
1   16-ounce jar green salsa (about 1¾ cups)
8   9- to 10-inch flour tortillas, warmed*
½   cup dairy sour cream

Prep:
15 minutes

Cook:
Low 8 hours, High 4 hours

Makes:
8 servings

Slow Cooker Size:
3 ½- to 4-quart

1. Trim fat from meat. If necessary, cut meat to fit into a 3½- to 4-quart slow cooker.

2. Place frozen vegetables in the slow cooker. Top with meat. Pour salsa over all.

3. Cover and cook on low-heat setting for 8 to 10 hours or on high-heat setting for 4 to 5 hours. Remove meat; slice across the grain. Strain vegetables, reserving ⅓ cup of the cooking liquid. Stir meat and the reserved ⅓ cup cooking liquid into vegetables. Serve meat-vegetable mixture in tortillas. Top with sour cream.

*Note: To warm tortillas, wrap them in white microwave-safe paper towels; microwave on high for 15 to 30 seconds or until tortillas are softened. (Or preheat oven to 350°F. Wrap tortillas in foil. Heat in the oven for 10 to 15 minutes or until warmed.)

Nutrition Facts per serving: 325 cal., 12 g total fat (5 g sat. fat), 39 mg chol., 463 mg sodium, 30 g carbo., 3 g fiber, 23 g pro.
Daily Values: 2% vit. A, 8% vit. C, 10% calcium, 16% iron
Exchanges: 1 Vegetable, 2 Starch, 2 Lean Meat, 1 Fat

Flank steak, peppers, onions, and tomatoes spiked with chili powder simmer into a stew that tastes great wrapped in a warmed tortilla.

SOUTHWESTERN STEAK ROLL–UPS

Prep:
15 minutes

Cook:
Low 7 hours,
High 3 ½ hours

Makes:
4 servings

Slow Cooker Size:
3 ½- to 4-quart

1   pound beef flank steak
1   16-ounce package frozen (yellow, green, and red) peppers and onion stir-fry vegetables
1   14½-ounce can Mexican-style stewed tomatoes, undrained
1   small fresh jalapeño chile pepper, seeded and finely chopped* (optional)
2   teaspoons chili powder
4   9- to 10-inch flour tortillas, warmed**

1. Trim fat from meat. If necessary, cut meat to fit into a 3½- to 4-quart slow cooker. Place frozen vegetables in the slow cooker. Top with meat. In a medium bowl stir together undrained tomatoes, jalapeño pepper (if desired), and chili powder. Pour over meat.

2. Cover and cook on low-heat setting for 7 to 8 hours or on high-heat setting for 3½ to 4 hours. Remove meat from cooker; slice across the grain. Using a slotted spoon, remove vegetables from cooker. Divide meat and vegetables among warm tortillas; roll up.

*Note: Because chile peppers contain volatile oils that can burn your skin and eyes, avoid direct contact with them as much as possible. When working with chile peppers, wear plastic or rubber gloves. If your bare hands do touch the peppers, wash your hands and nails well with soap and warm water.

**Note: To warm tortillas, wrap them in white microwave-safe paper towels; microwave on high for 15 to 30 seconds or until tortillas are softened. (Or preheat oven to 350°F. Wrap tortillas in foil. Heat in the oven for 10 to 15 minutes or until warmed.)

Nutrition Facts per serving: 389 cal., 12 g total fat (5 g sat. fat), 46 mg chol., 647 mg sodium, 36 g carbo., 4 g fiber, 32 g pro.
Daily Values: 29% vit. A, 54% vit. C, 10% calcium, 24% iron
Exchanges: 1½ Vegetable, 2 Starch, 3 Lean Meat, ½ Fat

Lemon peel brightens the flavors of this succulent, savory dish. Try it when you have a house full of guests and want to spend time away from the kitchen.

SHORT RIBS WITH LEEKS

8	ounces fresh mushrooms, halved
4	medium carrots, cut into 1-inch pieces
4	medium leeks, cut into 1-inch slices
2	pounds boneless beef short ribs
2	teaspoons finely shredded lemon peel
½	teaspoon ground black pepper
½	teaspoon dried rosemary, crushed
½	teaspoon dried thyme, crushed
¼	teaspoon salt
¾	cup beef broth
⅓	cup dairy sour cream
1	tablespoon all-purpose flour

Prep:
30 minutes

Cook:
Low 7 hours,
High 3½ hours

Makes:
6 servings

Slow Cooker Size:
3½- to 4-quart

1. In a 3½- to 4-quart slow cooker combine mushrooms, carrots, and leeks. Place meat over vegetables. Sprinkle with lemon peel, pepper, rosemary, thyme, and salt. Add broth. Cover and cook on low-heat setting for 7 to 8 hours or on high-heat setting for 3½ to 4 hours.

2. Using a slotted spoon, transfer meat and vegetables to a serving dish. Cover to keep warm.

3. For sauce, skim off fat from remaining cooking liquid. Measure 1 cup of the cooking liquid; place in a small saucepan. In a small bowl stir together sour cream and flour. Stir into cooking liquid using a whisk. Cook and stir over medium heat until slightly thickened and bubbly; cook and stir for 1 minute more. Ladle sauce over meat and vegetables.

Nutrition Facts per serving: 173 cal., 8 g total fat (4 g sat. fat), 33 mg chol., 252 mg sodium, 10 g carbo., 2 g fiber, 15 g pro.
Daily Values: 208% vit. A, 10% vit. C, 5% calcium, 12% iron
Exchanges: 1 Vegetable, 2 Medium-Fat Meat

A rarebit burger is a hamburger on a bun draped with a cheesy rarebit sauce. With this version, everyone can enjoy the irresistible beefy, cheesy, and saucy hallmarks of the sandwich, easily dished up from the slow cooker.

RAREBIT BURGERS

Prep:
20 minutes

Cook:
Low 6 hours, High 3 hours

Makes:
16 to 20 servings

Slow Cooker Size:
4- to 5-quart

2½ pounds lean ground beef
1½ cups chopped onions (3 medium)
4 cloves garlic, minced
1 15- to 16-ounce can nacho cheese sauce
8 plum tomatoes, seeded and chopped
2 teaspoons Worcestershire sauce
1 teaspoon dry mustard
   Salt
   Ground black pepper
16 to 20 kaiser rolls or hamburger buns, split and toasted

1. In a 12-inch skillet cook ground beef, onions, and garlic until meat is brown and onions are tender. Drain off fat.

2. Transfer meat mixture to a 4- to 5-quart slow cooker. Stir in cheese sauce, tomatoes, Worcestershire sauce, and dry mustard.

3. Cover and cook on low-heat setting for 6 to 8 hours or on high-heat setting for 3 to 4 hours. Season to taste with salt and pepper. Spoon meat mixture into kaiser rolls.

Nutrition Facts per serving: 336 cal., 12 g total fat (4 g sat. fat), 49 mg chol., 584 mg sodium, 36 g carbo., 2 g fiber, 20 g pro.
Daily Values: 4% vit. A, 11% vit. C, 10% calcium, 20% iron
Exchanges: 2 Starch, ½ Other Carbo., 2 Lean Meat, ½ Fat

These kid-pleasing saucy sandwiches are perfect fare for birthday parties and family-style potlucks. The recipe makes a large batch and requires little attention.

SLOPPY JOES

2½	pounds lean ground beef
½	cup chopped onion (1 medium)
3	cloves garlic, minced
1¼	cups ketchup
¾	cup chopped green sweet pepper (1 medium)
1	cup chopped celery (2 stalks)
⅓	cup water
3	tablespoons packed brown sugar
3	tablespoons yellow mustard
3	tablespoons vinegar
3	tablespoons Worcestershire sauce
1	tablespoon chili powder
16	to 20 hamburger buns, split and toasted

1. In a large skillet cook ground beef, onion, and garlic until meat is brown. Drain off fat.

2. In a 3½- to 4-quart slow cooker combine ketchup, sweet pepper, celery, water, brown sugar, mustard, vinegar, Worcestershire sauce, and chili powder. Stir in meat mixture.

3. Cover and cook on low-heat setting for 6 to 8 hours or on high-heat setting for 3 to 4 hours. Spoon meat mixture into buns.

Nutrition Facts per serving: 298 cal., 12 g total fat (4 g sat. fat), 44 mg chol., 579 mg sodium, 31 g carbo., 2 g fiber, 17 g pro.
Daily Values: 17% vit. C, 8% calcium, 17% iron
Exchanges: 2 Starch, 1½ Medium-Fat Meat, 1 Fat

Prep:
25 minutes

Cook:
Low 6 hours, High 3 hours

Makes:
16 to 20 servings

Slow Cooker Size:
3½- to 4-quart

Canned tomato soup, mustard, Worcestershire sauce, and chili powder make this a family-pleasing sandwich.

SOUPER SLOPPY JOES

Prep:
20 minutes

Cook:
Low 6 hours, High 3 hours

Makes:
12 servings

Slow Cooker Size:
3 1/2- to 4-quart

2 pounds lean ground beef
2 cups chopped onions (2 large)
1 10¾-ounce can reduced-sodium and reduced-fat condensed tomato soup
3 tablespoons yellow mustard
3 tablespoons Worcestershire sauce
1 tablespoon chili powder
¼ teaspoon salt
¼ teaspoon ground black pepper
12 hamburger buns, split and toasted

1. In a large skillet cook meat and onions, half at a time, until meat is brown. Drain off fat.

2. In a 3½- to 4-quart slow cooker combine soup, mustard, Worcestershire sauce, chili powder, salt, and pepper. Stir in meat-onion mixture.

3. Cover and cook on low-heat setting for 6 to 7 hours or on high-heat setting for 3 to 3½ hours. Stir; spoon mixture into buns.

Nutrition Facts per serving: 282 cal., 10 g total fat (3 g sat. fat), 48 mg chol., 476 mg sodium, 29 g carbo., 2 g fiber, 18 g pro.
Daily Values: 4% vit. A, 8% vit. C, 7% calcium, 18% iron
Exchanges: 2 Starch, 1½ Medium-Fat Meat, ½ Fat

In Cincinnati chili parlors, chili is often served over spaghetti. This totable version has the consistency of a casserole, and with ziti (thick tube shapes) or gemelli (short twists), it's easily spooned up from the potluck table.

CINCINNATI-STYLE CHILI CASSEROLE

2 pounds lean ground beef
2 cups chopped onions (2 large)
1 26-ounce jar garlic pasta sauce
1 15-ounce can red kidney beans, rinsed and drained
½ cup water
2 tablespoons chili powder
2 tablespoons semisweet chocolate pieces
1 tablespoon vinegar
1 teaspoon ground cinnamon
1 teaspoon instant beef bouillon granules
¼ teaspoon cayenne pepper
¼ teaspoon ground allspice
1 pound dried cut ziti or gemelli
Shredded cheddar cheese (optional)

Prep:
25 minutes

Cook:
Low 8 hours, High 4 hours

Makes:
16 servings

Slow Cooker Size:
4- to 5-quart

1. In a 12-inch skillet cook ground beef and onions until meat is brown. Drain off fat. Transfer meat mixture to a 4- to 5-quart slow cooker. Stir in pasta sauce, drained kidney beans, water, chili powder, chocolate pieces, vinegar, cinnamon, bouillon granules, cayenne pepper, and allspice.

2. Cover and cook on low-heat setting for 8 to 10 hours or on high-heat setting for 4 to 5 hours.

3. Before serving, cook pasta according to package directions; drain well. Add pasta to meat mixture in slow cooker; toss gently to combine. If desired, sprinkle with cheese.

Nutrition Facts per serving: 257 cal., 7 g total fat (2 g sat. fat), 36 mg chol., 277 mg sodium, 33 g carbo., 4 g fiber, 17 g pro.
Daily Values: 10% vit. A, 7% vit. C, 5% calcium, 16% iron
Exchanges: ½ Vegetable, 2 Starch, 1½ Lean Meat

This Mediterranean classic features the bold flavors of the region. Top with feta cheese for additional tang.

GREEK CABBAGE ROLLS

Prep:
30 minutes

Cook:
Low 6 hours, High 3 hours

Makes:
5 servings
(2 rolls per serving)

Slow Cooker Size:
3 1/2- to 4-quart

1 large head green cabbage
1 pound lean ground beef or ground lamb
2 teaspoons Greek seasoning
1 26-ounce jar mushroom and ripe olive tomato pasta sauce
1 cup cold cooked rice
   Crumbled feta cheese (optional)

1. Remove 10 large outer leaves from the cabbage.* In a Dutch oven cook cabbage leaves in boiling water for 3 to 4 minutes or just until leaves are limp. Drain cabbage leaves. Trim the thick rib from the center of each leaf. Set leaves aside. Shred 2 cups of the remaining cabbage; set aside. (Wrap and chill remaining cabbage for another use.)

2. In a large skillet cook meat with Greek seasoning until meat is brown; drain off fat. Add the shredded cabbage, 1/2 cup of the pasta sauce, and the rice; stir to combine. Evenly divide the meat mixture among the 10 cabbage leaves. Fold sides of leaves over filling and roll up. Place cabbage rolls in a 3 1/2- to 4-quart slow cooker. Top with remaining pasta sauce.

3. Cover and cook on low-heat setting for 6 to 7 hours or on high-heat setting for 3 to 3 1/2 hours. If desired, top with feta cheese.

*Note: To easily remove the cabbage leaves, place the cabbage head in boiling water for 2 to 3 minutes to loosen the outer leaves.

Nutrition Facts per serving: 303 cal., 11 g total fat (3 g sat. fat), 57 mg chol., 600 mg sodium, 30 g carbo., 6 g fiber, 21 g pro.
Daily Values: 17% vit. A, 85% vit. C, 14% calcium, 20% iron
Exchanges: 3 Vegetable, 1 Starch, 2 Medium-Fat Meat

The combination of spices and flavors adds exotic richness to this roast. For convenience and extra vitamins, leave the skin on the potatoes.

SAUCY LAMB AND VEGETABLES

1½ pounds tiny new potatoes or 5 medium potatoes
2 cups packaged, peeled baby carrots
2 small onions, cut into wedges
1 tablespoon honey
1 tablespoon grated fresh ginger or ¾ teaspoon ground ginger
½ teaspoon salt
½ teaspoon anise seeds or ¼ teaspoon ground allspice
½ teaspoon ground cinnamon
⅛ to ¼ teaspoon cayenne pepper
1 2½- to 3-pound boneless lamb shoulder roast
1¼ cups reduced-sodium beef broth
½ cup cold water
¼ cup all-purpose flour
1 teaspoon finely shredded orange peel
Salt
Ground black pepper

Prep:
15 minutes

Cook:
Low 10 hours, High 5 hours; plus 10 minutes in saucepan

Makes:
8 servings

Slow Cooker Size:
3 ½- to 5-quart

1. Remove a narrow strip of peel from the center of each new potato or peel (if desired) and quarter each medium potato. In a 3½- to 5-quart slow cooker combine potatoes, carrots, and onions. Drizzle with honey and sprinkle with ginger, the ½ teaspoon salt, anise seeds, cinnamon, and cayenne pepper.

2. Trim fat from meat. If necessary, cut meat to fit into the slow cooker. Place meat over vegetables. Pour broth over meat and vegetables. Cover and cook on low-heat setting for 10 to 12 hours or on high-heat setting for 5 to 6 hours.

3. Using a slotted spoon, remove meat and vegetables; keep warm. For gravy, skim off fat from cooking liquid. Measure 1½ cups of the cooking liquid; set aside. In a small saucepan combine water, flour, and orange peel. Stir in the reserved 1½ cups cooking liquid. Cook and stir until thickened and bubbly. Cook and stir for 1 minute more. Season to taste with salt and black pepper. Pass gravy with the meat and vegetables.

Nutrition Facts per serving: 279 cal., 6 g total fat (2 g sat. fat), 90 mg chol., 334 mg sodium, 24 g carbo., 3 g fiber, 32 g pro.
Daily Values: 66% vit. A, 25% vit. C, 4% calcium, 22% iron
Exchanges: 1 Vegetable, 1 Starch, 3½ Lean Meat

Curry adds intrigue to this colorful main dish. Round out the meal with a fresh spinach, cucumber, and tomato salad.

BROWN RICE RISOTTO WITH LAMB

Prep:
15 minutes

Cook:
Low 8 hours, High 4 hours

Stand:
5 minutes

Makes:
6 servings

Slow Cooker Size:
3 1/2- to 4-quart

1	2- to 2½-pound boneless lamb shoulder roast
1	tablespoon cooking oil
2½	cups hot-style vegetable juice
1	cup regular brown rice
1	teaspoon curry powder
¼	teaspoon salt
1	cup diced carrots (2 medium)
¾	cup diced green sweet pepper (1 medium)

1. Trim fat from meat. In a large skillet brown meat on all sides in hot oil.

2. Meanwhile, in a 3½- to 4-quart slow cooker combine vegetable juice, uncooked rice, curry powder, and salt. Add carrots. Place meat over carrots. Cover and cook on low-heat setting for 8 to 9 hours or on high-heat setting for 4 to 4½ hours.

3. Add sweet pepper to the cooker. Cover and let stand for 5 to 10 minutes before serving.

Nutrition Facts per serving: 299 cal., 12 g total fat (3 g sat. fat), 99 mg chol., 537 mg sodium, 15 g carbo., 2 g fiber, 32 g pro.
Daily Values: 122% vit. A, 53% vit. C, 4% calcium, 18% iron
Exchanges: 1 Vegetable, 1 Starch, 3½ Very Lean Meat

The exotic aromas of a North African spice market fill the kitchen as this dish cooks. For even more flavor, add ¼ to ½ teaspoon ground turmeric to the slow cooker along with the couscous.

MOROCCAN-STYLE LAMB

2	pounds lean boneless lamb
2	large carrots, cut into 1-inch pieces
2	large onions, cut into wedges
2	cups chicken broth
3	medium tomatoes, chopped
1½	teaspoons ground cumin
½	teaspoon ground turmeric
¼	teaspoon crushed red pepper (optional)
1	10-ounce package quick-cooking couscous (1½ cups)
¼	cup dried currants, raisins, or golden raisins

Prep:
15 minutes

Cook:
Low 9 hours,
High 4 ½ hours;
plus 5 minutes on High

Makes:
8 servings

Slow Cooker Size:
3 ½- to 4-quart

1. Trim fat from meat. Cut meat into ¾-inch cubes. In a 3½- to 4-quart slow cooker combine meat, carrots, onions, broth, tomatoes, cumin, turmeric, and, if desired, crushed red pepper.

2. Cover and cook on low-heat setting for 9 to 10 hours or on high-heat setting for 4½ to 5½ hours.

3. If using low-heat setting, turn to high-heat setting. Using a slotted spoon, transfer meat mixture to a serving bowl; keep warm. Skim off fat from cooking liquid; reserve cooking liquid in cooker. Stir the couscous and currants into cooking liquid. Cover and cook for 5 to 7 minutes.

4. With a fork, fluff couscous just before serving. Divide couscous among 8 shallow bowls or pasta dishes. Spoon meat over couscous.

Nutrition Facts per serving: 328 cal., 6 g total fat (2 g sat. fat), 71 mg chol., 354 mg sodium, 38 g carbo., 3 g fiber, 29 g pro.
Daily Values: 44% vit. A, 16% vit. C, 4% calcium, 21% iron
Exchanges: ½ Vegetable, 2 Starch, 3 Lean Meat

An exotic mix of garlic, wine, allspice, mint, and yogurt flavors the lamb. Serve in pitas topped with lettuce, tomato, and cumin-spiked yogurt.

MEDITERRANEAN LAMB PITAS

Prep:
25 minutes

Cook:
Low 8 hours, High 4 hours;
plus 15 minutes

Makes:
12 servings

Slow Cooker Size:
3 1/2- to 4-quart

1 2-pound portion boneless lamb leg roast
1 tablespoon olive oil
1 15-ounce can garbanzo beans (chickpeas), rinsed and drained
¾ cup dry red wine
½ of a 6-ounce can (⅓ cup) tomato paste
¼ cup water
1 cup chopped onion (1 large)
4 cloves garlic, minced
½ teaspoon ground allspice
½ teaspoon dried mint, crushed
¼ teaspoon salt
¼ teaspoon ground black pepper
6 large pita bread rounds, halved crosswise
   Lettuce leaves and/or thinly sliced cucumber
1 8-ounce carton plain yogurt
¼ teaspoon ground cumin
1 medium tomato, chopped

1. Trim fat from meat. If necessary, cut meat to fit into a 3½- to 4-quart slow cooker. In a large skillet brown meat on all sides in hot oil.

2. Meanwhile, in the slow cooker combine drained garbanzo beans, wine, tomato paste, water, onion, garlic, allspice, mint, salt, and pepper. Place meat over bean mixture. Cover and cook on low-heat setting for 8 to 10 hours or on high-heat setting for 4 to 5 hours.

3. Remove meat from cooker; shred the meat and return it to the cooker. Cover and cook for 15 minutes more. Using a slotted spoon, remove meat and beans.

4. To serve, open each pita bread half to form a large pocket. Line pitas with lettuce and/or cucumber. In a small bowl combine yogurt and cumin. Spoon meat mixture, then yogurt mixture into pitas. Sprinkle with chopped tomato.

Nutrition Facts per serving: 255 cal., 6 g total fat (2 g sat. fat), 51 mg chol., 434 mg sodium, 27 g carbo., 3 g fiber, 21 g pro.
Daily Values: 6% vit. A, 11% vit. C, 8% calcium, 16% iron
Exchanges: 1 Starch, 1 Other Carbo., 2 Lean Meat

Perfect for a simple Sunday supper, the lamb shanks cook while you hike in the woods, play a game of tag football, or snuggle in to watch a favorite movie.

BARLEY LAMB SHANKS

3   to 3½ pounds lamb shanks or beef shank crosscuts
1   tablespoon cooking oil
1   cup regular barley
½   cup chopped onion (1 medium)
2   cups carrots cut into ½-inch slices (4 medium)
1½ cups celery cut into ½-inch slices (3 stalks)
1   14½-ounce can diced tomatoes, undrained
1   14-ounce can chicken broth
⅓   cup water
½   teaspoon ground black pepper
2   tablespoons balsamic vinegar (optional)

Prep:
20 minutes

Cook:
Low 7 hours

Makes:
6 to 8 servings

Slow Cooker Size:
5- to 6-quart

1. In a large skillet brown lamb shanks in hot oil over medium heat. Drain off fat.

2. In a 5- to 6-quart slow cooker combine barley, onion, carrots, celery, undrained tomatoes, broth, water, and pepper. Add lamb.

3. Cover and cook on low-heat setting for 7 to 9 hours or until lamb pulls easily from bones and barley is tender. Transfer meat to a serving platter. Skim off fat from vegetable-barley mixture. If desired, stir vinegar into vegetable-barley mixture. Serve with lamb.

Nutrition Facts per serving: 370 cal., 8 g total fat (2 g sat. fat), 99 mg chol., 529 mg sodium, 36 g carbo., 7 g fiber, 37 g pro.
Daily Values: 24% vit. C, 7% calcium, 24% iron
Exchanges: 1 Vegetable, 2 Starch, 4½ Very Lean Meat, 1 Fat

Curry powder imparts a sunny color and a spicy taste to lamb and veggies. Sprinkle each serving with coconut, raisins, and sunflower seeds for an Indian classic.

LAMB CURRY

Prep:
10 minutes

Cook:
Low 7 hours,
High 3 ½ hours

Makes:
10 servings

Slow Cooker Size:
3 ½- to 4-quart

2 pounds lamb stew meat
1 16-ounce package frozen loose-pack broccoli, cauliflower, and carrots
2 10¾-ounce cans condensed cream of onion soup
½ cup water
2 to 3 teaspoons curry powder
5 cups hot cooked rice

1. In a 3½- to 4-quart slow cooker combine lamb, frozen vegetables, soup, water, and curry powder.

2. Cover and cook on low-heat setting for 7 to 8 hours or on high-heat setting for 3½ to 4 hours. Serve over hot cooked rice.

Nutrition Facts per serving: 295 cal., 7 g total fat (2 g sat. fat), 68 mg chol., 727 mg sodium, 33 g carbo., 2 g fiber, 23 g pro.
Daily Values: 22% vit. A, 9% vit. C, 5% calcium, 18% iron
Exchanges: ½ Vegetable, 1½ Starch, ½ Other Carbo., 2 Lean Meat

Chapter 3

PORK
Main Dishes

You'll have plenty of mustard-spiked apricot sauce to pass with succulent slices of pork roast. Cook some rice to serve on the side.

APRICOT–GLAZED PORK ROAST

Prep:
15 minutes

Cook:
Low 10 hours, High 5 hours

Makes:
8 servings

Slow Cooker Size:
3 1/2- to 6-quart

1   3- to 3½-pound boneless pork shoulder roast
1   18-ounce jar apricot preserves
1   cup chopped onion (1 large)
¼   cup chicken broth
2   tablespoons Dijon-style mustard
    Hot cooked rice (optional)

1. Trim fat from roast. If necessary, cut roast to fit into a 3½- to 6-quart slow cooker. Place meat in cooker. In a bowl combine preserves, onion, broth, and mustard; pour over meat.

2. Cover and cook on low-heat setting for 10 to 12 hours or on high-heat setting for 5 to 6 hours. Transfer meat to a serving platter. Skim off fat from sauce. Spoon some of the sauce over meat. If desired, serve remaining sauce with rice.

Nutrition Facts per serving: 424 cal., 10 g total fat (3 g sat. fat), 110 mg chol., 281 mg sodium, 47 g carbo., 1 g fiber, 35 g pro.
Daily Values: 13% vit. C, 3% calcium, 14% iron
Exchanges: 3 Other Carbo., 4½ Lean Meat

Serve noodles or brown rice with the fragrant apple-spice sauce and super tender meat. Complete your menu with coleslaw and fresh fruit for dessert.

PORK ROAST AND HARVEST VEGETABLES

1	1½- to 2-pound boneless pork shoulder roast
1	tablespoon cooking oil
2	cups parsnips cut into ½-inch pieces (3 medium)
1½	cups carrots cut into ½-inch pieces (3 medium)
1	large green sweet pepper, cut into wedges
1	cup celery cut into ½-inch pieces (2 stalks)
3	tablespoons quick-cooking tapioca
1	6-ounce can frozen apple juice concentrate, thawed
¼	cup water
1	teaspoon instant beef bouillon granules
¼	teaspoon ground cinnamon
¼	teaspoon ground black pepper

Prep:
30 minutes

Cook:
Low 10 hours, High 5 hours

Makes:
6 servings

Slow Cooker Size:
3 ½- to 5-quart

1. Trim fat from roast. If necessary, cut roast to fit into a 3½- to 5-quart slow cooker. In a large skillet brown meat on all sides in hot oil. In cooker combine parsnips, carrots, sweet pepper, and celery. Sprinkle with tapioca.

2. In a small bowl combine apple juice concentrate, water, bouillon granules, cinnamon, and black pepper. Pour over vegetables. Place meat on top of vegetables.

3. Cover and cook on low-heat setting for 10 to 12 hours or on high-heat setting for 5 to 6 hours. Transfer meat and vegetables to a serving platter. Strain cooking juices; skim off fat. Drizzle some of the cooking juices over meat; pass remaining juices.

Nutrition Facts per serving: 309 cal., 9 g total fat (3 g sat. fat), 73 mg chol., 272 mg sodium, 32 g carbo., 4 g fiber, 24 g pro. Daily Values: 157% vit. A, 50% vit. C, 5% calcium, 13% iron Exchanges: 1 Vegetable, 2 Other Carbo., 3 Lean Meat

The three types of seeds—caraway, dill, and celery—add a unique flavor to a slowly cooked pork roast.

SEEDED PORK ROAST

Prep:
20 minutes

Cook:
Low 7 hours,
High 3 1/2 hours

Makes:
8 servings

Slow Cooker Size:
3 1/2- to 4-quart

1 2½- to 3-pound boneless pork shoulder roast
1 tablespoon soy sauce
1 teaspoon caraway seeds, crushed
1 teaspoon dillseeds, crushed
1 teaspoon celery seeds, crushed
1¼ cups beef broth

1. Remove netting from roast, if present. If necessary, cut roast to fit into a 3½- to 4-quart slow cooker. Brush soy sauce over surface of meat. On a large piece of foil combine caraway seeds, dillseeds, and celery seeds. Roll roast in seeds to coat evenly. Place meat in cooker. Pour broth around meat.

2. Cover and cook on low-heat setting for 7 to 9 hours or on high-heat setting for 3½ to 4½ hours. Transfer meat to a serving platter. Skim off fat from cooking juices. Serve juices with meat.

Nutrition Facts per serving: 201 cal., 8 g total fat (3 g sat. fat), 92 mg chol., 371 mg sodium, 0 g carbo., 0 g fiber, 29 g pro.
Daily Values: 2% vit. C, 2% calcium, 11% iron
Exchanges: 4 Lean Meat

On busy days, this savory one-dish meal makes a perfect dinner. Just put everything in your slow cooker, and several hours later dinner is ready and waiting.

CRANBERRY PORK ROAST

4 medium potatoes, peeled and cubed
1 3-pound boneless pork top loin roast (single loin)
1 16-ounce can whole cranberry sauce
1 15-ounce can apricot halves in light syrup, drained
½ cup chopped onion (1 medium)
½ cup snipped dried apricots
2 tablespoons sugar
1 teaspoon dry mustard
¼ teaspoon cayenne pepper
1 tablespoon cornstarch
1 tablespoon cold water

Prep:
20 minutes
Cook:
Low 5 ½ hours
Makes:
12 servings
Slow Cooker Size:
5- to 6-quart

1. Place potatoes in a 5- to 6-quart slow cooker. Place meat on top of potatoes; set aside. In a blender or food processor combine cranberry sauce, drained apricots, onion, dried apricots, sugar, mustard, and cayenne pepper. Cover and blend or process until nearly smooth. Pour fruit mixture over pork.

2. Cover and cook on low-heat setting for 5½ to 6½ hours. Remove meat and potatoes from cooker to serving platter. Cover; keep warm.

3. For sauce, transfer cooking juices from cooker to a 4-cup glass measure. Skim off fat. Measure 2 cups juices; discard remaining juices. Pour juices into a medium saucepan. Stir together cornstarch and water. Add to saucepan, stirring to combine. Cook and stir over medium heat until thickened and bubbly; cook and stir for 2 minutes more. Slice roast. Serve sauce with potatoes and roast.

Nutrition Facts per serving: 291 cal., 6 g total fat (2 g sat. fat), 62 mg chol., 64 mg sodium, 33 g carbo., 2 g fiber, 26 g pro.
Daily Values: 14% vit. A, 12% vit. C, 4% calcium, 8% iron
Exchanges: ½ Fruit, ½ Starch, 1 Other Carbo., 3 Lean Meat

Make their mouths water with fruit-studded stuffing topped with a peach-glazed roast. A salad and your favorite vegetables round out this sweet home-style dinner.

PORK ROAST WITH CORN BREAD STUFFING

Prep:
25 minutes

Cook:
Low 5 hours,
High 2 ½ hours

Makes:
8 servings

Slow Cooker Size:
3 ½- to 4-quart

Nonstick cooking spray
1 2- to 2½ pound boneless pork top loin roast (single loin)
Ground black pepper
1 tablespoon cooking oil
4 cups corn bread stuffing mix
¾ cup reduced-sodium chicken broth
½ cup mixed dried fruit bits
¼ cup chopped onion
½ cup peach spreadable fruit
1 teaspoon finely shredded lemon peel
¼ teaspoon ground cinnamon

1. Lightly coat a 3½- to 4-quart slow cooker with cooking spray. Trim fat from roast. If necessary, cut roast to fit into cooker. Sprinkle meat with pepper. In a large skillet brown meat on all sides in hot oil. Drain off fat. Set aside.

2. In a large bowl toss together stuffing mix, broth, dried fruit, and onion. In prepared cooker place stuffing mixture. Add meat. In a small bowl stir together spreadable fruit, lemon peel, and cinnamon. Spread over meat in cooker.

3. Cover and cook on low-heat setting for 5 to 6 hours or on high-heat setting for 2½ to 3 hours. Remove meat from cooker. Cut meat into slices. Stir stuffing; serve with meat.

Nutrition Facts per serving: 406 cal., 9 g total fat (2 g sat. fat), 62 mg chol., 590 mg sodium, 52 g carbo., 0 g fiber, 30 g pro.
Daily Values: 2% vit. C, 4% calcium, 13% iron
Exchanges: 1 Fruit, 2½ Starch, 3 Lean Meat

Simpler than stir-fry, this Asian-inspired meal may become a regular for weeknights.

PINEAPPLE–GINGER PORK

2 pounds boneless pork shoulder, trimmed of fat and cut into 1-inch pieces
2 tablespoons cooking oil
¾ cup chicken broth
3 tablespoons quick-cooking tapioca
3 tablespoons reduced-sodium soy sauce
3 tablespoons oyster sauce (optional)
1 teaspoon grated fresh ginger
1 15¼-ounce can pineapple chunks (juice pack)
2 cups carrots cut into ½-inch slices (4 medium)
1 large onion, cut into 1-inch pieces
1 8-ounce can sliced water chestnuts, drained
1½ cups fresh snow pea pods or one 6-ounce package frozen pea pods
3 cups hot cooked rice

Prep:
30 minutes

Cook:
Low 6 hours, High 3 hours; plus 10 minutes on High

Makes:
6 to 8 servings

Slow Cooker Size:
3½- to 4-quart

1. In a large skillet brown half of the pork at a time in hot oil. Drain off fat.

2. In a 3½- to 4-quart slow cooker combine broth, tapioca, soy sauce, oyster sauce (if desired), and ginger. Drain pineapple, reserving juice. Stir juice into broth mixture; cover and chill pineapple chunks. Add carrots, onion, and drained water chestnuts to cooker. Add pork.

3. Cover and cook on low-heat setting for 6 to 8 hours or on high-heat setting for 3 to 4 hours.

4. If using low-heat setting, turn to high-heat setting. Stir pineapple chunks and peas into cooker. Cover and cook for 10 to 15 minutes more or until peas are crisp-tender. Serve over rice.

Nutrition Facts per serving: 402 cal., 11 g total fat (3 g sat. fat), 62 mg chol., 477 mg sodium, 51 g carbo., 5 g fiber, 23 g pro.
Daily Values: 33% vit. C, 7% calcium, 17% iron
Exchanges: 2½ Vegetable, ½ Fruit, 2 Starch, 2 Lean Meat, 1 Fat

The deep South is known for hot weather and even hotter food. This pork stew bears only mild Cajun seasoning—a good introduction for those new to the flavor.

CAJUN PORK

Prep:
20 minutes

Cook:
Low 6 hours, High 3 hours; plus 30 minutes on High

Makes:
6 to 8 servings

Slow Cooker Size:
3 ½- to 4-quart

Nonstick cooking spray

2½ to 3 pounds boneless pork shoulder, trimmed of fat and cut into 1-inch cubes

2 medium yellow sweet peppers, cut into 1-inch pieces

1 tablespoon Cajun seasoning

1 14½-ounce can diced tomatoes with green pepper and onion, undrained

1 16-ounce package frozen cut okra

Bottled hot pepper sauce (optional)

1. Lightly coat a large skillet with cooking spray. Heat over medium heat. In hot skillet cook meat, half at a time, until brown; drain fat.

2. In a 3½- to 4-quart slow cooker place meat and sweet peppers. Sprinkle with Cajun seasoning. Top with undrained tomatoes.

3. Cover and cook on low-heat setting for 6 to 7 hours or on high-heat setting for 3 to 3½ hours.

4. If using low-heat setting, turn to high-heat setting. Stir in frozen okra. Cover and cook for 30 minutes more. If desired, pass hot pepper sauce.

Nutrition Facts per serving: 233 cal., 8 g total fat (3 g sat. fat), 77 mg chol., 444 mg sodium, 15 g carbo., 4 g fiber, 25 g pro.
Daily Values: 10% vit. A, 187% vit. C, 10% calcium, 14% iron
Exchanges: 2 Vegetable, 3 Lean Meat

This delicious entrée, made even easier by not browning the chops, is terrific for family and guests. Round out the meal with steamed broccoli.

CRANBERRY–ORANGE PORK CHOPS

1 16-ounce package peeled baby carrots
8 boneless pork chops, cut about ¾ inch thick (about 1¾ pounds)
1 10-ounce carton frozen cranberry-orange sauce, thawed
2 tablespoons quick-cooking tapioca
1 teaspoon finely shredded lemon peel
¼ teaspoon ground cardamom
3 fresh plums and/or apricots, pitted and sliced (about 8 ounces)
4 cups hot cooked couscous or rice

1. Place carrots in a 3½- to 4-quart slow cooker. Top with pork.

2. Combine cranberry-orange sauce, tapioca, lemon peel, and cardamom; pour over meat.

3. Cover and cook on low-heat setting for 7 to 8 hours or on high-heat setting for 3½ to 4 hours. Stir in fruit. Cover; let stand with cooker turned off for 5 minutes. Serve with hot couscous.

Nutrition Facts per serving: 344 cal., 6 g total fat (2 g sat. fat), 54 mg chol., 100 mg sodium, 45 g carbo., 5 g fiber, 26 g pro.
Daily Values: 125% vit. A, 19% vit. C, 5% calcium, 7% iron
Exchanges: 1 Vegetable, 1½ Starch, 1 Other Carbo., 3 Very Lean Meat, 1 Fat

Prep:
15 minutes

Cook:
Low 7 hours,
High 3½ hours

Stand:
5 minutes

Makes:
8 servings

Slow Cooker Size:
3½- to 4-quart

If using fresh corn, two medium ears will yield the 1 cup whole kernel corn needed for the recipe.

SOUTHWEST PORK CHOPS

Prep:
15 minutes

Cook:
Low 5 hours,
High 2 ½ hours;
plus 30 minutes on High

Makes:
6 servings

Slow Cooker Size:
3 ½- to 4-quart

 6   pork rib chops, cut ¾ inch thick (about 2½ pounds)
 1   15½-ounce can Mexican-style or Tex-Mex-style chili beans
1¼   cups bottled salsa
 1   cup fresh or frozen whole kernel corn
 2   cups hot cooked rice
     Snipped fresh cilantro (optional)

1. Trim fat from chops. Place chops in a 3½- to 4-quart slow cooker. Add chili beans and salsa.

2. Cover and cook on low-heat setting for 5 hours or on high-heat setting for 2½ hours. If using low-heat setting, turn to high-heat setting. Stir in corn. Cover and cook for 30 minutes more. Serve over rice. If desired, sprinkle with cilantro.

Nutrition Facts per serving: 334 cal., 7 g total fat (2 g sat. fat), 77 mg chol., 716 mg sodium, 34 g carbo., 4 g fiber, 33 g pro.
Daily Values: 5% vit. A, 13% vit. C, 6% calcium, 19% iron
Exchanges: ½ Vegetable, 2 Starch, 4 Very Lean Meat, 1 Fat

When the meat counter doesn't have ¾-inch-thick chops, ask the butcher to cut a bone-in top loin roast into ¾-inch-thick slices.

DIJON PORK CHOPS

1   10¾-ounce can condensed cream of mushroom soup
¼   cup dry white wine or reduced-sodium chicken broth
¼   cup Dijon-style mustard
1   teaspoon dried thyme, crushed
1   clove garlic, minced
¼   teaspoon ground black pepper
5   medium potatoes, cut into ¼-inch slices (1⅓ pounds)
1   medium onion, sliced
4   pork loin chops, cut ¾ inch thick

1. In a large bowl combine soup, wine, mustard, thyme, garlic, and pepper. Add potatoes and onion, stirring to coat. Transfer to a 4- to 5-quart slow cooker. Place chops on potato-onion mixture.

2. Cover and cook on low-heat setting for 7 to 8 hours or on high-heat setting for 3½ hours.

Nutrition Facts per serving: 385 cal., 12 g total fat (3 g sat. fat), 48 mg chol., 658 mg sodium, 39 g carbo., 4 g fiber, 26 g pro.
Daily Values: 2% vit. A, 47% vit. C, 9% calcium, 18% iron
Exchanges: 2½ Starch, 2½ Very Lean Meat, 2 Fat

Prep:
20 minutes
Cook:
Low 7 hours,
High 3 ½ hours
Makes:
4 servings
Slow Cooker Size:
4- to 5-quart

Orange marmalade and mustard team up in a piquant, glistening sauce to top chops and winter squash slices. Steam green beans to serve on the side, if you like.

ORANGE–MUSTARD PORK CHOPS

Prep:
20 minutes

Cook:
Low 5 hours,
High 2 ½ hours

Makes:
6 servings

Slow Cooker Size:
5- to 6-quart

2   small or medium acorn squash (1½ to 2 pounds total)
1   large onion, halved and sliced
6   pork chops (with bone), cut ¾ inch thick
      (about 2½ pounds)
½   cup chicken broth
⅓   cup orange marmalade
1   tablespoon honey mustard or Dijon-style mustard
1   teaspoon dried marjoram or thyme, crushed
¼   teaspoon ground black pepper
2   tablespoons cornstarch
2   tablespoons cold water

1. Cut squash in half lengthwise. Discard seeds and membranes. Cut each half into 3 wedges. In a 5- to 6-quart slow cooker place squash and onion. Trim fat from chops. Place chops on top of squash and onion in cooker.

2. In a bowl stir together broth, marmalade, mustard, marjoram, and pepper. Pour broth mixture over chops and vegetables.

3. Cover and cook on low-heat setting for 5 to 6 hours or on high-heat setting for 2½ to 3 hours. Lift chops and vegetables from cooker to a serving platter, reserving juices; cover and keep warm.

4. For sauce, strain cooking juices into a 2-cup glass measure; skim off fat. Measure 1¾ cups juices, adding water, if necessary. Pour juices into a medium saucepan. Stir together cornstarch and water. Add to saucepan, stirring to combine. Cook and stir over medium heat until thickened and bubbly; cook and stir for 2 minutes more. Serve sauce with chops and vegetables.

Nutrition Facts per serving: 265 cal., 8 g total fat (3 g sat. fat), 65 mg chol., 168 mg sodium, 27 g carbo., 3 g fiber, 21 g pro.
Daily Values: 6% vit. A, 20% vit. C, 7% calcium, 10% iron
Exchanges: 1 Starch, 1 Other Carbo., 2½ Very Lean Meat, 1 Fat

Chile peppers in adobo sauce add plenty of spicy flavor to these tender chops.

SASSY PORK CHOPS

2   medium red, green, and/or yellow sweet peppers, cut into strips
1   cup thinly sliced celery (2 stalks)
½   cup chopped onion (1 medium)
8   pork loin chops (with bone), cut ¾ inch thick
½   teaspoon garlic salt
¼   teaspoon ground black pepper
2   tablespoons cooking oil
¼   cup reduced-sodium chicken broth
¼   cup orange juice
1   tablespoon chopped canned chipotle peppers in adobo sauce
½   teaspoon dried oregano, crushed

Prep:
25 minutes

Cook:
Low 6 hours, High 3 hours

Makes:
8 servings

Slow Cooker Size:
4- to 5-quart

1. In a 4- to 5-quart slow cooker place sweet peppers, celery, and onion; set aside. Trim fat from chops. Season chops with garlic salt and black pepper. In a 12-inch skillet cook chops, half at a time, in hot oil over medium heat until brown on both sides. Place chops on top of vegetables in cooker.

2. In a small bowl stir together broth, orange juice, chipotle peppers, and oregano. Pour over chops in cooker.

3. Cover and cook on low-heat setting for 6 to 7 hours or on high-heat setting for 3 to 3½ hours. Transfer chops and vegetables to a serving platter. Discard cooking liquid.

Nutrition Facts per serving: 215 cal., 7 g total fat (1 g sat. fat), 78 mg chol., 363 mg sodium, 4 g carbo., 1 g fiber, 33 g pro.
Daily Values: 21% vit. A, 103% vit. C, 2% calcium, 6% iron
Exchanges: 1 Vegetable, 4 Lean Meat

There's very little work needed to get these meaty ribs ready for the slow cooker.

CHIPOTLE COUNTRY–STYLE RIBS

Prep:
15 minutes

Cook:
Low 10 hours, High 5 hours;
plus 15 minutes on High

Makes:
6 to 8 servings

Slow Cooker Size:
4- to 5-quart

3 to 3½ pounds boneless pork country-style ribs
1 12- to 13-ounce bottle barbecue sauce
2 canned chipotle peppers in adobo sauce, finely chopped
2 tablespoons cornstarch
2 tablespoons cold water

1. Place ribs in a 4- to 5-quart slow cooker. In a medium bowl stir together barbecue sauce and peppers. Pour over ribs in cooker.

2. Cover and cook on low-heat setting for 10 to 12 hours or on high-heat setting for 5 to 6 hours.

3. Transfer ribs to a serving platter; cover with foil to keep warm. If using low-heat setting, turn to high-heat setting. In a small bowl stir together cornstarch and water; stir into cooking juices. Cover and cook about 15 minutes more or until thickened. Serve ribs with sauce.

Nutrition Facts per serving: 251 cal., 11 g total fat (4 g sat. fat), 81 mg chol., 571 mg sodium, 10 g carbo., 1 g fiber, 26 g pro.
Daily Values: 1% vit. A, 8% vit. C, 4% calcium, 10% iron
Exchanges: ½ Other Carbo., 3½ Lean Meat, ½ Fat

The simple pleasure of eating ribs that fall right off the bone starts with a simple blend of seasonings, barbecue sauce, and a jar of honey mustard.

HONEY–MUSTARD BARBECUE PORK RIBS

3½ pounds boneless pork country-style ribs
1 cup bottled barbecue sauce
1 8-ounce jar honey mustard
2 teaspoons zesty herb grill seasoning blend

1. Place ribs in a 3½- to 4-quart slow cooker. In a small bowl combine barbecue sauce, honey mustard, and seasoning blend. Pour over ribs. Stir to coat.

2. Cover and cook on low-heat setting for 8 to 10 hours or on high-heat setting for 4 to 5 hours. Transfer ribs to a serving platter. Strain sauce; skim off fat from sauce. Drizzle some of the sauce over the ribs and pass remaining sauce.

Nutrition Facts per serving: 322 cal., 12 g total fat (4 g sat. fat), 94 mg chol., 497 mg sodium, 18 g carbo., 1 g fiber, 29 g pro.
Daily Values: 7% vit. A, 6% vit. C, 4% calcium, 10% iron
Exchanges: 1 Other Carbo., 4 Lean Meat

Prep:
15 minutes

Cook:
Low 8 hours, High 4 hours

Makes:
6 to 8 servings

Slow Cooker Size:
3 ½- to 4-quart

Sauerkraut and onions join the classic apple and pork combo for a luscious sweet-salty sensation. Pair this with slices of rye bread.

RIBS AND SAUERKRAUT

Prep:
20 minutes

Cook:
Low 6 hours, High 3 hours

Makes:
6 to 8 servings

Slow Cooker Size:
4- to 4 1/2-quart

1　14-ounce can sauerkraut, drained
1　large sweet onion, sliced (2 cups)
2　medium tart cooking apples, peeled, cored, and sliced (about 2 cups)
2　pounds boneless pork country-style ribs
1　cup apple juice

1. In a 4- to 4½-quart slow cooker place drained sauerkraut, onion, and apples. Top with pork. Pour apple juice over all.

2. Cover and cook on low-heat setting for 6 to 7 hours or on high-heat setting for 3 to 3½ hours. Serve with a slotted spoon.

Nutrition Facts per serving: 312 cal., 12 g total fat (4 g sat. fat), 96 mg chol., 541 mg sodium, 19 g carbo., 4 g fiber, 30 g pro.
Daily Values: 1% vit. A, 28% vit. C, 7% calcium, 16% iron
Exchanges: 1 Vegetable, ½ Fruit, ½ Other Carbo., 4 Lean Meat

Have the robust sandwich filling ready in your slow cooker for a quick meal after leaf raking or ice-skating.

PULLED PORK SANDWICHES

1   2½- to 3-pound pork shoulder roast
½   cup water
3   tablespoons vinegar
2   tablespoons Worcestershire sauce
1   teaspoon ground cumin or chili powder
1   recipe Homemade BBQ Sauce
12   to 16 kaiser rolls or hamburger buns, split

Prep:
15 minutes

Cook:
Low 10 hours, High 5 hours; plus 30 minutes on High

Makes:
12 to 16 sandwiches

Slow Cooker Size:
3 ½- to 4-quart

1. Trim fat from roast. If necessary, cut roast to fit into a 3½- to 4-quart slow cooker. Place roast in cooker. Add water, vinegar, Worcestershire sauce, and cumin.

2. Cover and cook on low-heat setting for 10 to 12 hours or on high-heat setting for 5 to 6 hours. Prepare Homemade BBQ Sauce.

3. Remove meat from cooker; discard cooking liquid. Using 2 forks, pull meat apart and return it to the cooker. Stir in 2 cups of the Homemade BBQ Sauce. If using low-heat setting, turn to high-heat setting. Cover and cook for 30 to 45 minutes more or until heated through. Serve on rolls. Pass remaining sauce.

Homemade BBQ Sauce: In a medium saucepan combine 2½ cups reduced-sodium ketchup; 1 cup finely chopped onion; ¼ cup packed brown sugar; 3 tablespoons vinegar; 3 tablespoons bottled Pickapeppa or Worcestershire sauce; 3 cloves garlic, minced; and ¼ teaspoon bottled hot pepper sauce. Bring mixture to boiling; reduce heat. Cover and simmer for 15 minutes, stirring occasionally. Use the sauce immediately or let it cool; cover and chill up to 3 days. Makes about 3 cups.

Nutrition Facts per sandwich: 404 cal., 12 g total fat (4 g sat. fat), 57 mg chol., 727 mg sodium, 44 g carbo., 0 g fiber, 29 g pro.
Daily Values: 31% vit. C, 34% iron
Exchanges: 1½ Starch, 1½ Other Carbo., 3½ Lean Meat

For variety, try mesquite- or hickory-flavored barbecue sauce.

BBQ PORK SANDWICHES

Prep:
20 minutes

Cook:
Low 11 hours,
High 5 ½ hours;
plus 15 minutes on High

Makes:
10 to 12 sandwiches

Slow Cooker Size:
3 ½- to 5-quart

2 large green sweet peppers, cut into strips
1 medium onion, thinly sliced and separated into rings
2 tablespoons quick-cooking tapioca
1 2½- to 3-pound pork shoulder roast
1 cup bottled barbecue sauce
3 to 4 teaspoons chili powder
10 to 12 kaiser rolls, split and toasted
    Coleslaw, drained (optional)

1. In a 3½- to 5-quart slow cooker combine sweet peppers and onion. Sprinkle tapioca over vegetables. Trim fat from roast. If necessary, cut roast to fit into cooker. Place roast over vegetables.

2. In a medium bowl combine barbecue sauce and chili powder. Pour the sauce over the meat.

3. Cover and cook on low-heat setting for 11 to 12 hours or on high-heat setting for 5½ to 6 hours. Remove roast from cooker, reserving sauce in cooker; thinly slice or shred the meat. Skim fat from sauce. Return meat to cooker; cover. If using low-heat setting, turn to high-heat setting. Cook for 15 to 30 minutes more to heat through. Serve on rolls. If desired, top meat with coleslaw.

Nutrition Facts per sandwich: 362 cal., 10 g total fat (3 g sat. fat), 73 mg chol., 616 mg sodium, 38 g carbo., 2 g fiber, 29 g pro.
Daily Values: 7% vit. A, 46% vit. C, 7% calcium, 20% iron
Exchanges: 2 Starch, ½ Other Carbo., 3 Lean Meat

This feeds a crowd of hungry tailgaters. A foolproof trick is to toast the buns to keep them from getting soggy when the barbecue is added.

DOWN-SOUTH BARBECUE

1½	pounds boneless pork shoulder roast
1½	pounds boneless beef chuck roast
1	6-ounce can tomato paste
½	cup packed brown sugar
¼	cup cider vinegar
¼	cup water
2	tablespoons chili powder
2	teaspoons Worcestershire sauce
1	teaspoon salt
1	teaspoon dry mustard
16	hamburger buns, split and toasted

1. If necessary, cut meat to fit into a 3½- to 4-quart slow cooker. Place meat in cooker. In a small bowl combine tomato paste, brown sugar, vinegar, water, chili powder, Worcestershire sauce, salt, and mustard. Pour over meat in cooker.

2. Cover and cook on low-heat setting for 10 to 12 hours or on high-heat setting for 5 to 6 hours.

3. Remove meat from cooker, reserving sauce. Using 2 forks, shred meat. Stir together shredded meat and reserved sauce in cooker. Serve meat on buns.

Nutrition Facts per sandwich: 273 cal., 6 g total fat (2 g sat. fat), 53 mg chol., 442 mg sodium, 31 g carbo., 2 g fiber, 22 g pro.
Daily Values: 6% vit. A, 5% vit. C, 7% calcium, 20% iron
Exchanges: 1½ Starch, ½ Other Carbo., 2½ Lean Meat

Prep:
25 minutes

Cook:
Low 10 hours, High 5 hours

Makes:
16 sandwiches

Slow Cooker Size:
3½- to 4-quart

For a variation on these barbecue sandwiches, spoon some of the pork onto flour tortillas instead of the hamburger buns and roll up.

HONEY BBQ SHREDDED PORK

Prep:
25 minutes

Cook:
Low 13 hours,
High 6 ½ hours

Makes:
10 to 12 sandwiches

Slow Cooker Size:
4- to 5-quart

1   3- to 4-pound boneless pork shoulder roast
1 ¼   cups ketchup
1   cup chopped celery (2 stalks)
1   cup chopped onion (1 large)
½   cup water
½   cup honey
¼   cup lemon juice
3   tablespoons white vinegar
2   tablespoons dry mustard
2   tablespoons Worcestershire sauce
½   teaspoon ground black pepper
10   to 12 hamburger buns, split and toasted

1. Remove string or netting from pork, if present. Trim fat from pork. If necessary, cut roast to fit into a 4- to 5-quart slow cooker. Place meat in cooker. In a medium bowl stir together ketchup, celery, onion, water, honey, lemon juice, vinegar, mustard, Worcestershire sauce, and pepper. Pour over meat in cooker.

2. Cover and cook on low-heat setting for 13 to 14 hours or on high-heat setting for 6½ to 7 hours. Remove meat from cooker, reserving sauce. Using 2 forks, shred meat and place in a large bowl.

3. Skim fat from sauce. Add enough of the reserved sauce to moisten pork (about 1 cup). Serve pork on rolls.

Nutrition Facts per sandwich: 357 cal., 10 g total fat (3 g sat. fat), 88 mg chol., 510 mg sodium, 33 g carbo., 1 g fiber, 32 g pro.
Daily Values: 4% vit. A, 9% vit. C, 8% calcium, 19% iron
Exchanges: 1½ Starch, ½ Other Carbo., 4 Lean Meat

In eastern North Carolina, home of vinegar-sauced barbecued pork, coleslaw is a must-have accompaniment. Spoon some coleslaw onto the bun with the meat, if you like, or serve it alongside.

PORK AND SLAW BARBECUE ROLLS

1	4- to 5-pound pork shoulder roast or pork shoulder blade Boston roast (Boston butt)
¾	cup cider vinegar
2	tablespoons packed brown sugar
½	teaspoon salt
½	teaspoon crushed red pepper
¼	teaspoon ground black pepper
16	kaiser rolls, split and toasted
8	cups coleslaw

Prep:
10 minutes

Cook:
Low 10 hours, High 5 hours

Makes:
16 sandwiches

Slow Cooker Size:
4- to 6-quart

1. If necessary, cut roast to fit into a 4- to 6-quart slow cooker. Place meat in cooker. In a small bowl combine vinegar, brown sugar, salt, crushed red pepper, and black pepper. Pour over meat.

2. Cover and cook on low-heat setting for 10 to 12 hours or on high-heat setting for 5 to 6 hours.

3. Transfer meat to a cutting board; reserve cooking juices. When cool enough to handle, cut meat off bones and coarsely chop. In a medium bowl combine meat and as much of the juices as desired to moisten. Serve meat on rolls and add coleslaw.

Nutrition Facts per sandwich: 305 cal., 8 g total fat (2 g sat. fat), 46 mg chol., 449 mg sodium, 40 g carbo., 2 g fiber, 19 g pro.
Daily Values: 5% vit. A, 33% vit. C, 9% calcium, 17% iron
Exchanges: ½ Vegetable, 2 Starch, ½ Other Carbo., 2 Lean Meat

These Southern-style barbecue sandwiches carry just the right amount of heat. Serve with corn on the cob for a picnic-style meal.

SHREDDED PORK SANDWICHES

Prep:
15 minutes

Cook:
Low 8 hours, High 4 hours

Makes:
8 to 10 sandwiches

Slow Cooker Size:
3 1/2- to 4-quart

1   2½- to 3-pound pork sirloin roast
½   teaspoon garlic powder
½   teaspoon ground ginger
½   teaspoon dried thyme, crushed
1   cup chicken broth
½   cup vinegar
½   teaspoon cayenne pepper
8   to 10 hamburger buns, split and toasted

1. Remove string from pork, if present. Trim fat from pork. If necessary, cut roast to fit into a 3½- to 4-quart slow cooker. In a small bowl combine garlic powder, ginger, and thyme. Sprinkle mixture over meat and rub in with fingers. Place meat in cooker. Pour broth over roast.

2. Cover and cook on low-heat setting for 8 to 10 hours or on high-heat setting for 4 to 5 hours.

3. Remove meat from cooker, reserving cooking liquid. Skim off fat from liquid. Using 2 forks, shred meat and place in a large bowl. Add 1 cup of the cooking liquid, the vinegar, and cayenne pepper to meat in bowl; toss to combine. Serve on buns.

Nutrition Facts per sandwich: 292 cal., 7 g total fat (2 g sat. fat), 79 mg chol., 402 mg sodium, 23 g carbo., 1 g fiber, 31 g pro.
Daily Values: 1% vit. A, 2% vit. C, 8% calcium, 15% iron
Exchanges: 1½ Starch, 4 Very Lean Meat, 1 Fat

Chapter 4

POULTRY
Main Dishes

As easy as carry-out, this savory dish is a fun way to celebrate the Chinese New Year—or any red-letter day.

CASHEW CHICKEN

Prep:
15 minutes

Cook:
Low 6 hours, High 3 hours

Makes:
6 servings

Slow Cooker Size:
3 1/2- to 4-quart

1 10¾-ounce can condensed golden mushroom soup
2 tablespoons reduced-sodium soy sauce
½ teaspoon ground ginger
1½ pounds chicken breast tenderloins
1 cup sliced fresh mushrooms or one 4-ounce can (drained weight) sliced mushrooms, drained
1 cup sliced celery (2 stalks)
1 cup shredded carrots (2 medium)
1 8-ounce can sliced water chestnuts, drained
½ cup cashews
3 cups hot cooked rice

1. In a 3½- to 4-quart slow cooker combine soup, soy sauce, and ginger. Stir in chicken, mushrooms, celery, carrots, and drained water chestnuts.

2. Cover and cook on low-heat setting for 6 to 8 hours or on high-heat setting for 3 to 4 hours.

3. Stir cashews into chicken mixture. Serve over hot cooked rice.

Nutrition Facts per serving: 397 cal., 11 g total fat (2 g sat. fat), 67 mg chol., 704 mg sodium, 44 g carbo., 2 g fiber, 33 g pro.
Daily Values: 52% vit. A, 7% vit. C, 16% calcium, 15% iron
Exchanges: 1 Vegetable, 2½ Starch, 3½ Very Lean Meat, 1 Fat

You'll get a different burrito each time you try a new blend of salsa. Experiment!

CHICKEN AND BEAN BURRITOS

2   pounds skinless, boneless chicken breast halves
1   15-ounce can pinto beans in chili sauce
1   16-ounce bottle (1⅔ cups) salsa with chipotle chile peppers
8   10-inch flour tortillas, warmed*
1½ cups shredded Monterey Jack cheese (6 ounces)
    Shredded lettuce, chopped tomato, and/or light dairy sour cream (optional)

1. In a 3½-quart slow cooker combine chicken and undrained beans. Pour salsa over all.

2. Cover and cook on low-heat setting for 5 to 6 hours or on high-heat setting for 2½ to 3 hours.

3. Transfer chicken from cooker to a cutting board; use two forks to shred chicken into bite-size pieces. Using a potato masher, mash beans slightly in cooker. Return chicken to cooker, stirring to mix.

4. Divide chicken mixture evenly among the warmed tortillas. Top with cheese. Fold bottom edge of each tortilla up and over filling; fold in opposite sides just until they meet. Roll up from the bottom. If necessary, secure with toothpicks. If desired, serve with lettuce, tomato, and/or sour cream.

*Note: To warm tortillas, wrap them in white microwave-safe paper towels; microwave on high for 15 to 30 seconds or until tortillas are softened. (Or preheat oven to 350°F. Wrap tortillas in foil. Heat in the oven for 10 to 15 minutes or until warmed.)

Nutrition Facts per serving: 400 cal., 12 g total fat (5 g sat. fat), 84 mg chol., 662 mg sodium, 34 g carbo., 5 g fiber, 38 g pro.
Daily Values: 11% vit. A, 16% vit. C, 25% calcium, 18% iron
Exchanges: 1 Vegetable, 2 Starch, 3 Very Lean Meat,1 High-Fat Meat

Prep:
5 minutes

Cook:
Low 5 hours,
High 2 ½ hours

Makes:
8 servings

Slow Cooker Size:
3 ½-quart

Your tortilla options are no longer limited to flour and corn. Look for green spinach and orange chile flour tortillas in your grocery store. Wrap this zippy chicken and rice filling in an assortment of flour tortillas.

CHICKEN AND RICE BURRITOS

Prep:
25 minutes

Cook:
Low 6 hours, High 3 hours

Stand:
5 minutes

Makes:
6 to 8 servings

Slow Cooker Size:
3 ½- to 4-quart

1   medium zucchini
1   large green sweet pepper, cubed
½   cup coarsely chopped onion (1 medium)
½   cup coarsely chopped celery (1 stalk)
1½   pounds skinless, boneless chicken breast halves,
      cut into ½-inch strips
1   8-ounce bottle green taco sauce
1   teaspoon instant chicken bouillon granules
½   teaspoon ground cumin
1   cup uncooked instant rice
6   to 8 9- to 10-inch spinach, chile, or plain flour
      tortillas, warmed*
¾   cup shredded Monterey Jack cheese with jalapeño chile
      peppers (3 ounces)
2   small tomatoes, chopped
¼   cup sliced green onions (2)

1. Cut zucchini in half lengthwise; cut into ¾-inch slices. In a 3½- to 4-quart slow cooker combine zucchini, sweet pepper, onion, and celery. Top with chicken strips. In a small bowl combine taco sauce, bouillon granules, and cumin. Pour over chicken.

2. Cover and cook on low-heat setting for 6 to 7 hours or on high-heat setting for 3 to 3½ hours. Stir in rice. Cover and let stand for 5 minutes.

3. Divide chicken mixture evenly among warmed tortillas. Top with cheese, tomatoes, and green onions. Fold bottom edge of each tortilla up and over filling; fold in opposite sides just until they meet. Roll up from the bottom. If necessary, secure with toothpicks.

*Note: To warm tortillas, wrap them in white microwave-safe paper towels; microwave on high for 15 to 30 seconds or until tortillas are softened. (Or preheat oven to 350°F. Wrap tortillas in foil. Heat in the oven for 10 to 15 minutes or until warmed.)

Nutrition Facts per serving: 408 cal., 10 g total fat (4 g sat. fat), 81 mg chol., 735 mg sodium, 43 g carbo., 3 g fiber, 35 g pro.
Daily Values: 25% vit. A, 58% vit. C, 18% calcium, 19% iron
Exchanges: 1 Vegetable, 2½ Starch, 3½ Very Lean Meat, 1½ Fat

If you want to cut the cook time, brown the chicken slices in hot oil in a large skillet—you'll need to do two batches. If you brown the chicken, plan on the shorter side of the cooking time range.

EASY CHICKEN RAREBIT

1¾ pounds skinless, boneless chicken breast halves
1 14- to 16-ounce jar cheddar cheese pasta sauce
1 tablespoon Worcestershire sauce
1 large onion, halved crosswise and thinly sliced
6 pumpernickel or rye buns, split and toasted, or 6 slices pumpernickel or rye bread, toasted and halved diagonally
4 slices bacon, crisp-cooked, drained, and crumbled (optional)
1 tomato, chopped (optional)

Prep:
25 minutes

Cook:
Low 4 hours, High 2 hours

Makes:
6 servings

Slow Cooker Size:
3 ½- to 4-quart

1. Cut chicken diagonally into ½-inch-thick slices; set aside. In a 3½- to 4-quart slow cooker stir together pasta sauce and Worcestershire sauce. Add onion and chicken slices.

2. Cover and cook on low-heat setting for 4 to 5 hours or on high-heat setting for 2 to 2½ hours.

3. To serve, spoon chicken and sauce mixture over bun halves. If desired, sprinkle with bacon and tomato.

Nutrition Facts per serving: 340 cal., 12 g total fat (4 g sat. fat), 102 mg chol., 823 mg sodium, 21 g carbo., 3 g fiber, 36 g pro.
Daily Values: 5% vit. A, 5% vit. C, 12% calcium, 11% iron
Exchanges: 1½ Starch, 4½ Very Lean Meat, 1½ Fat

Prepare a dinner that may be less hassle than ordering take-out. Along with this tasty one-dish chicken dinner, bake frozen egg roll appetizers and serve fortune cookies for dessert.

SWEET AND SOUR CHICKEN

Prep:
15 minutes

Cook:
Low 5 hours,
High 2 ½ hours

Makes:
4 servings

Slow Cooker Size:
3 ½- to 4-quart

1   pound skinless, boneless chicken breast halves, cut into 1-inch pieces
2   9-ounce jars sweet-and-sour sauce
1   16-ounce package frozen loose-pack broccoli, carrots, and water chestnuts
2½ cups hot cooked rice
¼   cup chopped almonds, toasted (optional)

1. In a 3½- to 4-quart slow cooker combine chicken, sweet-and-sour sauce, and frozen vegetables.

2. Cover and cook on low-heat setting for 5 to 5½ hours or on high-heat setting for 2½ to 2¾ hours. Serve with hot cooked rice. If desired, sprinkle with almonds.

Nutrition Facts per serving: 430 cal., 2 g total fat (0 g sat. fat), 66 mg chol., 418 mg sodium, 70 g carbo., 3 g fiber, 31 g pro.
Daily Values: 56% vit. A, 36% vit. C, 3% calcium, 17% iron
Exchanges: 1 Vegetable, 2 Starch, 2½ Other Carbo., 3 Very Lean Meat

Here's a sauce that's sweet and full of flavor. For variety and to pack in extra nutrition, serve with hot cooked brown rice.

TERIYAKI CHICKEN WITH ORANGE SAUCE

1   16-ounce package frozen loose-pack broccoli, baby carrots, and water chestnuts
2   tablespoons quick-cooking tapioca
1   pound skinless, boneless chicken breast halves or thighs, cut into 1-inch pieces
¾   cup chicken broth
3   tablespoons orange marmalade
2   tablespoons bottled reduced-sodium teriyaki sauce
1   teaspoon dry mustard
½   teaspoon ground ginger
2   cups hot cooked rice

Prep:
15 minutes

Cook:
Low 4 hours, High 2 hours

Makes:
4 servings

Slow Cooker Size:
3 ½- to 4-quart

1. Place vegetables in a 3½- to 4-quart slow cooker. Sprinkle tapioca over vegetables. Stir to combine. Place chicken on vegetables.

2. For sauce, in a small bowl combine broth, marmalade, teriyaki sauce, mustard, and ginger. Pour sauce over chicken.

3. Cover and cook on low-heat setting for 4 to 5 hours or on high-heat setting for 2 to 2½ hours. Serve with hot cooked rice.

Nutrition Facts per serving: 334 cal., 2 g total fat (1 g sat. fat), 66 mg chol., 420 mg sodium, 45 g carbo., 3 g fiber, 31 g pro. Daily Values: 56% vit. A, 36% vit. C, 3% calcium, 10% iron Exchanges: 1½ Vegetable, 1½ Starch, 1 Other Carbo., 3½ Very Lean Meat

An intriguing blend of spices makes this slow-simmered chicken and potato dish sizzle with flavors that are typical of Indian cuisine.

INDIAN CURRY WITH CHICKEN

Prep:
30 minutes

Cook:
Low 8 hours, High 4 hours;
plus 15 minutes on High

Makes:
5 servings

Slow Cooker Size:
3 1/2- to 6-quart

5 medium white potatoes, peeled (1 1/2 pounds)
1 medium green sweet pepper, cut into 1-inch pieces
1 medium onion, sliced
1 pound skinless, boneless chicken breast halves or thighs, cut into 1-inch pieces
1 1/2 cups chopped tomato
1 tablespoon ground coriander
1 1/2 teaspoons paprika
1 teaspoon grated fresh ginger or 1/4 teaspoon ground ginger
3/4 teaspoon salt
1/2 teaspoon ground turmeric
1/4 to 1/2 teaspoon crushed red pepper
1/4 teaspoon ground cinnamon
1/8 teaspoon ground cloves
1 cup chicken broth
2 tablespoons cold water
4 teaspoons cornstarch

1. In a 3 1/2- to 6-quart slow cooker combine potatoes, sweet pepper, and onion. Place chicken on top of vegetables.

2. In a medium bowl combine tomato, coriander, paprika, ginger, salt, turmeric, crushed red pepper, cinnamon, and cloves; stir in broth. Pour over chicken.

3. Cover and cook on low-heat setting for 8 to 10 hours or on high-heat setting for 4 to 5 hours.

4. If using low-heat setting, turn to high-heat setting. In a small bowl combine water and cornstarch; stir into mixture in cooker. Cover and cook for 15 to 20 minutes more or until slightly thickened and bubbly.

Nutrition Facts per serving: 246 cal., 2 g total fat (0 g sat. fat), 53 mg chol., 609 mg sodium, 31 g carbo., 5 g fiber, 26 g pro.
Daily Values: 90% vit. C, 3% calcium, 14% iron
Exchanges: 1 1/2 Vegetable, 1 1/2 Starch, 2 1/2 Very Lean Meat

Twelve cloves of garlic may sound like a lot, but the garlic mellows as it slowly cooks, enveloping the chicken in a delightful flavor.

GARLIC CHICKEN WITH ARTICHOKES

12 cloves garlic, minced
½ cup chopped onion (1 medium)
1 tablespoon olive oil or cooking oil
1 8- or 9-ounce package frozen artichoke hearts
1 red sweet pepper, cut into strips
½ cup chicken broth
1 tablespoon quick-cooking tapioca
2 teaspoons dried rosemary, crushed
1 teaspoon finely shredded lemon peel
½ teaspoon ground black pepper
1½ pounds skinless, boneless chicken breast halves or thighs
4 cups hot cooked brown rice

1. In a small skillet cook garlic and onion in hot oil over medium heat about 5 minutes or until tender, stirring occasionally. In a 3½- to 4-quart slow cooker combine garlic mixture, frozen artichoke hearts, sweet pepper, broth, tapioca, rosemary, lemon peel, and black pepper. Add chicken; spoon some of the artichoke mixture over chicken.

2. Cover and cook on low-heat setting for 6 to 7 hours or on high-heat setting for 3 to 3½ hours. Serve with brown rice.

Nutrition Facts per serving: 340 cal., 6 g total fat (1 g sat. fat), 66 mg chol., 176 mg sodium, 40 g carbo., 6 g fiber, 32 g pro.
Daily Values: 14% vit. A, 63% vit. C, 7% calcium, 10% iron
Exchanges: 2 Vegetable, 2 Starch, 3 Very Lean Meat, ½ Fat

Prep:
20 minutes
Cook:
Low 6 hours, High 3 hours
Makes:
6 servings
Slow Cooker Size:
3½- to 4-quart

You may want to serve this chicken and vegetable dish in bowls since there's plenty of flavorful sauce.

CHICKEN WITH ARTICHOKES AND OLIVES

Prep:
15 minutes

Cook:
Low 7 hours,
High 3 1/2 hours;
plus 15 minutes on High

Makes:
8 servings

Slow Cooker Size:
4- to 5-quart

2 cups sliced fresh mushrooms
1 14½-ounce can diced tomatoes, undrained
1 cup chicken broth
½ cup chopped onion (1 medium)
¼ cup dry white wine or chicken broth
1 2¼-ounce can sliced, pitted ripe olives or ¼ cup capers, drained
2 to 3 teaspoons curry powder
1 teaspoon dried thyme, crushed
¼ teaspoon salt
¼ teaspoon ground black pepper
1 8- or 9-ounce package frozen artichoke hearts
2½ pounds skinless, boneless chicken breast halves and/or thighs
3 tablespoons cornstarch
3 tablespoons cold water

1. In a 4- to 5-quart slow cooker combine mushrooms, undrained tomatoes, the 1 cup broth, onion, wine, drained olives, curry powder, thyme, salt, and pepper. Add artichoke hearts. Place chicken on top; spoon some of the tomato mixture over chicken.

2. Cover and cook on low-heat setting for 7 to 8 hours or on high-heat setting for 3½ to 4 hours. Using a slotted spoon, transfer chicken and artichoke hearts to a serving bowl, reserving tomato mixture in cooker. Cover chicken with foil to keep warm.

3. If using low-heat setting, turn to high-heat setting. In a small bowl stir together cornstarch and water; stir into tomato mixture in cooker. Cover and cook about 15 minutes more or until slightly thickened. Serve tomato mixture over chicken and artichokes.

Nutrition Facts per serving: 229 cal., 4 g total fat (1 g sat. fat), 82 mg chol., 447 mg sodium, 10 g carbo., 3 g fiber, 35 g pro.
Daily Values: 3% vit. A, 15% vit. C, 7% calcium, 11% iron
Exchanges: 1 Vegetable, 4½ Very Lean Meat, 1 Fat

Substitutions are encouraged for this recipe: Try spinach or red pepper fettuccine. Regular frozen green beans work equally well.

ITALIAN CHICKEN AND PASTA

1   9-ounce package frozen Italian-style green beans
1   cup fresh mushrooms, quartered
1   small onion, cut into ¼-inch-thick slices
12 ounces skinless, boneless chicken thighs, cut into
    1-inch pieces
1   14½-ounce can Italian-style stewed tomatoes,
    undrained
1   6-ounce can Italian-style tomato paste
1   teaspoon dried Italian seasoning, crushed
2   cloves garlic, minced
6   ounces dried fettuccine, cooked and drained
3   tablespoons finely shredded or grated Parmesan cheese

Prep:
15 minutes

Cook:
Low 5 hours,
High 2 ½ hours

Makes:
4 servings

Slow Cooker Size:
3 ½- to 4-quart

1. In a 3½- to 4-quart slow cooker combine green beans, mushrooms, and onion. Place chicken on vegetables.

2. In a small bowl combine undrained tomatoes, tomato paste, Italian seasoning, and garlic. Pour over chicken.

3. Cover and cook on low-heat setting for 5 to 6 hours or on high-heat setting for 2½ to 3 hours. Serve over fettuccine. Sprinkle with Parmesan cheese.

Nutrition Facts per serving: 405 cal., 7 g total fat (2 g sat. fat), 75 mg chol., 728 mg sodium, 55 g carbo., 4 g fiber, 28 g pro.
Daily Values: 7% vit. A, 46% vit. C, 15% calcium, 26% iron
Exchanges: 3½ Vegetable, 2½ Starch, 2 Lean Meat

There's no need to cook the rice separately. Simply stir it into the chicken mixture and cook in the sauce for a convenient one-dish dinner.

EASY CHICKEN AND RICE

Prep:
15 minutes

Cook:
Low 5 hours,
High 2 1/2 hours;
plus 10 minutes on High

Makes:
4 servings

Slow Cooker Size:
3 1/2- to 4-quart

2 cups sliced fresh mushrooms
1 cup sliced celery (2 stalks)
1/2 cup chopped onion (1 medium)
1 1/2 teaspoons dried dill
1/4 teaspoon ground black pepper
2 pounds chicken thighs, skinned and fat removed
1 10 3/4-ounce can reduced-fat and reduced-sodium condensed cream of mushroom or cream of chicken soup
3/4 cup reduced-sodium chicken broth
1 1/2 cups uncooked instant rice

1. In a 3 1/2- to 4-quart slow cooker combine mushrooms, celery, onion, dill, and pepper. Top with chicken. In a small bowl combine soup and broth. Pour over chicken.

2. Cover and cook on low-heat setting for 5 to 6 hours or on high-heat setting for 2 1/2 to 3 hours.

3. If using low-heat setting, turn to high-heat setting. Stir rice into the mushroom mixture. Cover and cook for 10 minutes more.

Nutrition Facts per serving: 357 cal., 7 g total fat (1 g sat. fat), 110 mg chol., 534 mg sodium, 41 g carbo., 2 g fiber, 31 g pro.
Daily Values: 4% vit. A, 4% vit. C, 4% calcium, 19% iron
Exchanges: 2 Vegetable, 2 Starch, 3 Lean Meat

Adding the sweet pepper strips near the end of cooking lends plenty of color to the chicken and mushrooms.

CHICKEN WITH PEPPERS AND MUSHROOMS

8	ounces fresh mushrooms, quartered
2	shallots, sliced
2½	pounds chicken thighs, skinned
¼	cup chicken broth
¼	cup dry white wine
1	teaspoon dried basil, crushed
½	teaspoon salt
¼	teaspoon ground black pepper
2	tablespoons cornstarch
2	tablespoons cold water
1	medium yellow sweet pepper, cut into 1-inch-wide strips
1	medium red sweet pepper, cut into 1-inch-wide strips
2	plum tomatoes, chopped
	Finely shredded Parmesan cheese

Prep:
25 minutes

Cook:
Low 4 hours, High 2 hours; plus 15 minutes on High

Makes:
6 servings

Slow Cooker Size:
3 1/2- to 4-quart

1. In a 3½- to 4-quart slow cooker combine mushrooms and shallots. Top with chicken. In a small bowl stir together broth, wine, basil, salt, and black pepper. Pour over chicken.

2. Cover and cook on low-heat setting for 4 to 5 hours or on high-heat setting for 2 to 2½ hours. Transfer chicken and vegetables to a serving dish, reserving cooking liquid in cooker. Cover chicken and vegetables with foil to keep warm.

3. If using low-heat setting, turn to high-heat setting. In a small bowl stir together cornstarch and water; stir into cooking liquid. Stir in sweet pepper strips. Cover and cook for 15 minutes more. Spoon mixture over chicken and vegetables. Top with tomatoes and Parmesan cheese.

Nutrition Facts per serving: 175 cal., 6 g total fat (2 g sat. fat), 70 mg chol., 377 mg sodium, 9 g carbo., 1 g fiber, 21 g pro.
Daily Values: 22% vit. A, 168% vit. C, 8% calcium, 9% iron
Exchanges: 1 Vegetable, 2½ Lean Meat

You'll need to use a wire whisk to incorporate the sour cream-cornstarch mixture into the sauce to make it smooth.

SMOKY PAPRIKA CHICKEN THIGHS

Prep:
20 minutes

Cook:
Low 6 hours, High 3 hours; plus 15 minutes on High

Makes:
8 servings

Slow Cooker Size:
4 1/2- to 5 1/2-quart

1 tablespoon smoked paprika or paprika
1 teaspoon salt
1/4 teaspoon garlic powder
1/4 teaspoon ground black pepper
3 pounds chicken thighs, skinned
1/2 cup chicken broth
1 tablespoon tomato paste
1 8-ounce carton light dairy sour cream
2 tablespoons cornstarch

1. In a small bowl stir together paprika, salt, garlic powder, and pepper. Sprinkle evenly over chicken; rub in with your fingers. Place chicken in a 4 1/2- to 5 1/2-quart slow cooker. In another small bowl whisk together broth and tomato paste. Pour over chicken.

2. Cover and cook on low-heat setting for 6 to 7 hours or on high-heat setting for 3 to 3 1/2 hours. Transfer chicken to a serving platter, reserving cooking liquid in cooker. Cover chicken with foil to keep warm.

3. If using low-heat setting, turn to high-heat setting. In a small bowl stir together sour cream and cornstarch; whisk into cooking liquid in cooker until smooth. Cover and cook about 15 minutes more or until slightly thickened. Spoon sauce over chicken.

Nutrition Facts per serving: 164 cal., 6 g total fat (2 g sat. fat), 90 mg chol., 439 mg sodium, 5 g carbo., 0 g fiber, 21 g pro.
Daily Values: 12% vit. A, 1% vit. C, 7% calcium, 6% iron
Exchanges: 3 Lean Meat

Nutty cumin, citrus, and jalapeño pepper jelly provide the zing in this piquant dish.

SAVORY BARBECUE CHICKEN

½ cup tomato sauce
2 tablespoons jalapeño pepper jelly
2 tablespoons lime juice or lemon juice
2 tablespoons quick-cooking tapioca
1 teaspoon packed brown sugar
1 teaspoon ground cumin
¼ to ½ teaspoon crushed red pepper
8 to 10 chicken thighs and/or drumsticks, skinned
   (2 to 2½ pounds)
5 8-inch flour tortillas

1. In a 3½- to 4-quart slow cooker combine tomato sauce, jelly, lime juice, tapioca, brown sugar, cumin, and crushed red pepper. Place chicken pieces, meaty sides down, on tomato sauce mixture.

2. Cover and cook on low-heat setting for 6 to 7 hours or on high-heat setting for 3 to 3½ hours. Serve with tortillas.

Nutrition Facts per serving: 268 cal., 7 g total fat (2 g sat. fat), 91 mg chol., 312 mg sodium, 27 g carbo., 1 g fiber, 24 g pro.
Daily Values: 1% vit. A, 3% vit. C, 5% calcium, 13% iron
Exchanges: 1½ Starch, ½ Other Carbo., 2½ Lean Meat

Prep:
15 minutes

Cook:
Low 6 hours, High 3 hours

Makes:
5 servings

Slow Cooker Size:
3½- to 4-quart

Chicken drumsticks or thighs are great for the slow cooker because they stay moist and tender during the long cooking.

GINGER–TOMATO CHICKEN

Prep:
20 minutes

Cook:
Low 6 hours, High 3 hours

Makes:
6 servings

Slow Cooker Size:
3 ½- to 4-quart

12	chicken drumsticks and/or thighs, skinned (2½ to 3 pounds)
2	14½-ounce cans tomatoes, undrained
2	tablespoons quick-cooking tapioca
1	tablespoon grated fresh ginger
1	tablespoon snipped fresh cilantro or parsley
4	cloves garlic, minced
2	teaspoons brown sugar (optional)
½	teaspoon crushed red pepper
½	teaspoon salt
	Hot cooked brown rice (optional)

1. Place chicken in a 3½- to 4-quart slow cooker.

2. Drain 1 can of the tomatoes; chop tomatoes from both cans. For sauce, in a medium bowl combine chopped tomatoes and the juice from 1 can, the tapioca, ginger, cilantro, garlic, brown sugar (if desired), crushed red pepper, and salt. Pour over chicken.

3. Cover and cook on low-heat setting for 6 to 7 hours or on high-heat setting for 3 to 3½ hours. Skim off fat from sauce. Serve chicken with sauce in shallow bowls. If desired, serve with rice.

Nutrition Facts per serving: 192 cal., 5 g total fat (1 g sat. fat), 82 mg chol., 454 mg sodium, 9 g carbo., 1 g fiber, 26 g pro.
Daily Values: 6% vit. A, 22% vit. C, 6% calcium, 14% iron
Exchanges: 1½ Vegetable, 3 Lean Meat

Serve this Italian classic with plenty of pasta to sop up all the sauce. Like the traditional dish, this one is brimming with onions, mushrooms, and tomatoes perfectly seasoned with herbs.

CHICKEN CACCIATORE

2   cups sliced fresh mushrooms
1   cup sliced celery (2 stalks)
1   cup chopped carrots (2 medium)
2   medium onions, cut into wedges
1   green, yellow, or red sweet pepper, cut into strips
4   cloves garlic, minced
12 chicken drumsticks, skinned (about 3½ pounds)
½   cup chicken broth
¼   cup dry white wine
2   tablespoons quick-cooking tapioca
2   bay leaves
1   teaspoon dried oregano, crushed
1   teaspoon sugar
½   teaspoon salt
¼   teaspoon ground black pepper
1   14½-ounce can diced tomatoes, undrained
⅓   cup tomato paste
3   cups hot cooked pasta

Prep:
25 minutes

Cook:
Low 6 hours, High 3 hours; plus 15 minutes on High

Makes:
6 servings

Slow Cooker Size:
5- to 6-quart

1. In a 5- to 6-quart slow cooker combine mushrooms, celery, carrots, onions, sweet pepper, and garlic. Place chicken on top of vegetables. Combine broth, wine, tapioca, bay leaves, oregano, sugar, salt, and black pepper; pour over chicken.

2. Cover and cook on low-heat setting for 6 to 7 hours or on high-heat setting for 3 to 3½ hours.

3. Remove chicken and keep warm. Remove and discard bay leaves. If using low-heat setting, turn to high-heat setting. Stir in undrained tomatoes and tomato paste. Cover and cook for 15 minutes more. Serve vegetable mixture over chicken and pasta.

Nutrition Facts per serving: 338 cal., 6 g total fat (1 g sat. fat), 82 mg chol., 620 mg sodium, 37 g carbo., 4 g fiber, 31 g pro.
Daily Values: 53% vit. A, 48% vit. C, 8% calcium, 19% iron
Exchanges: 3 Vegetable, 1½ Starch, 3 Lean Meat

Thyme, garlic, a little orange juice, and a splash of balsamic vinegar flavor these moist, fork-tender chicken breasts.

CHICKEN WITH THYME AND GARLIC SAUCE

Prep:
30 minutes

Cook:
Low 5 hours,
High 2 ½ hours

Makes:
6 to 8 servings

Slow Cooker Size:
3 ½- to 4-quart

3 to 4 pounds whole chicken breasts (with bone), halved and skinned
6 cloves garlic, minced
1½ teaspoons dried thyme, crushed
¼ cup orange juice
1 tablespoon balsamic vinegar

1. Sprinkle chicken with garlic and thyme. Place chicken in a 3½- to 4-quart slow cooker. Pour orange juice and balsamic vinegar over chicken.

2. Cover and cook on low-heat setting for 5 to 6 hours or on high-heat setting for 2½ to 3 hours.

3. Remove chicken from cooker; cover chicken with foil to keep warm. Skim off fat from cooking liquid. Strain cooking liquid into a saucepan. Bring to boiling; reduce heat. Boil gently, uncovered, about 10 minutes or until reduced to 1 cup. Serve cooking liquid to spoon over chicken.

Nutrition Facts per serving: 178 cal., 2 g total fat (0 g sat. fat), 85 mg chol., 78 mg sodium, 3 g carbo., 0 g fiber, 34 g pro.
Daily Values: 13% vit. C, 3% calcium, 7% iron
Exchanges: 5 Very Lean Meat

The bok choy gets a quick cooking in the slow cooker after the chicken is removed.

TERIYAKI CHICKEN

3 to 3½ pounds meaty chicken pieces (breast halves, thighs, and drumsticks), skinned
¼ cup reduced-sodium soy sauce
¼ cup dry sherry
¼ cup water
1 tablespoon toasted sesame oil
1 tablespoon grated fresh ginger
1 tablespoon rice vinegar
2 cloves garlic, minced
6 cups sliced bok choy or shredded Chinese cabbage
2 teaspoons toasted sesame seeds

Prep:
20 minutes
Cook:
Low 5 hours,
High 2 ½ hours
Stand:
5 minutes
Makes:
6 to 8 servings
Slow Cooker Size:
3 ½- to 4-quart

1. Place chicken in a 3½- to 4-quart slow cooker. In a small bowl stir together soy sauce, sherry, water, sesame oil, ginger, vinegar, and garlic. Pour over chicken.

2. Cover and cook on low-heat setting for 5 to 6 hours or on high-heat setting for 2½ to 3 hours. Transfer chicken to a serving platter, reserving cooking liquid in cooker. Cover chicken with foil to keep warm.

3. Stir bok choy into liquid in cooker. Cover and let stand for 5 minutes. Transfer bok choy to serving platter with chicken. Sprinkle chicken and bok choy with sesame seeds. If desired, spoon a little of the cooking liquid over chicken and cabbage. Discard remaining cooking liquid.

Nutrition Facts per serving: 253 cal., 10 g total fat (2 g sat. fat), 92 mg chol., 513 mg sodium, 4 g carbo., 1 g fiber, 32 g pro.
Daily Values: 63% vit. A, 54% vit. C, 10% calcium, 11% iron
Exchanges: 1 Vegetable, 4 Lean Meat

What to do with the extra chipotle chile peppers? Pack them in their sauce in a freezer container. Seal, label, and freeze for up to two months; thaw when needed in the refrigerator.

SWEET AND SMOKY CHICKEN

Prep:
15 minutes

Cook:
Low 6 hours, High 3 hours

Makes:
6 servings

Slow Cooker Size:
3 1/2- to 4-quart

2 1/2   to 3 pounds meaty chicken pieces (breast halves, thighs, and drumsticks), skinned
1/4   teaspoon salt
1/8   teaspoon ground black pepper
1   cup chicken broth
1/2   cup seedless raspberry jam
1/2   cup snipped dried apricots
1   to 2 canned chipotle peppers in adobo sauce, chopped, plus 1 tablespoon adobo sauce
1   tablespoon quick-cooking tapioca, finely ground

1. Place chicken in a 3 1/2- to 4-quart slow cooker. Sprinkle with salt and black pepper. For sauce, in a small bowl stir together broth, raspberry jam, dried apricots, chipotle peppers and adobo sauce, and tapioca. Pour over chicken.

2. Cover and cook on low-heat setting for 6 to 7 hours or on high-heat setting for 3 to 3 1/2 hours. Transfer chicken to a serving platter. Serve sauce over chicken.

Nutrition Facts per serving: 272 cal., 6 g total fat (2 g sat. fat), 77 mg chol., 362 mg sodium, 27 g carbo., 1 g fiber, 25 g pro.
Daily Values: 9% vit. A, 4% vit. C, 2% calcium, 8% iron
Exchanges: 2 Other Carbo., 3 Lean Meat

Spicy red pepper sauce is the choice for this recipe. If you can't find it, use your favorite variety of pasta sauce.

SPICY CHICKEN WITH PEPPERS AND OLIVES

2½ to 3 pounds meaty chicken pieces (breast halves, thighs, and drumsticks), skinned
Salt
Ground black pepper
1 small yellow sweet pepper, coarsely chopped
½ cup sliced, pitted ripe olives and/or pimiento-stuffed green olives
1 26-ounce jar spicy red pepper pasta sauce
Hot cooked whole wheat pasta (optional)

Prep:
20 minutes

Cook:
Low 6 hours, High 3 hours

Makes:
6 servings

Slow Cooker Size:
3 ½- to 4-quart

1. Place chicken in a 3½- to 4-quart slow cooker. Sprinkle lightly with salt and black pepper. Add sweet pepper and olives to cooker. Pour pasta sauce over all.

2. Cover and cook on low-heat setting for 6 to 7 hours or on high-heat setting for 3 to 3½ hours. If desired, serve chicken and sauce over hot cooked pasta.

Nutrition Facts per serving: 239 cal., 10 g total fat (2 g sat. fat), 77 mg chol., 592 mg sodium, 10 g carbo., 3 g fiber, 27 g pro.
Daily Values: 10% vit. A, 79% vit. C, 8% calcium, 12% iron
Exchanges: 2 Vegetable, 3½ Lean Meat

Capers and olives give this sauce its spirited, southern Italian angle. If you prefer, substitute your favorite pasta for the rice-shape orzo.

PUTTANESCA CHICKEN

Prep:
20 minutes

Cook:
Low 6 hours, High 3 hours

Makes:
6 servings

Slow Cooker Size:
3 ½- to 4-quart

2½ to 3 pounds meaty chicken pieces (breast halves, thighs, and drumsticks), skinned
¼ teaspoon salt
⅛ teaspoon ground black pepper
1 26-ounce jar pasta sauce with olives
2 tablespoons drained capers
1 teaspoon finely shredded lemon peel
3 cups hot cooked orzo (rosamarina)

1. Place chicken in a 3½- to 4-quart slow cooker. Sprinkle with the salt and pepper. For sauce, in a medium bowl stir together pasta sauce, capers, and lemon peel. Pour over chicken.

2. Cover and cook on low-heat setting for 6 to 7 hours or on high-heat setting for 3 to 3½ hours. Serve chicken and sauce over hot cooked orzo.

Nutrition Facts per serving: 315 cal., 8 g total fat (2 g sat. fat), 77 mg chol., 678 mg sodium, 30 g carbo., 3 g fiber, 30 g pro.
Daily Values: 10% vit. A, 11% vit. C, 8% calcium, 16% iron
Exchanges: 1½ Vegetable, 1½ Starch, 3 Lean Meat

Serve the flavorful cooking juices with a side of hot cooked rice or couscous.

MOROCCAN-SPICED CHICKEN

1½ teaspoons ground cumin
1 teaspoon salt
½ teaspoon ground cinnamon
½ teaspoon ground coriander
¼ teaspoon ground turmeric
¼ teaspoon ground black pepper
3½ to 4 pounds meaty chicken pieces (breast halves, thighs, and drumsticks), skinned
½ cup chicken broth

1. In a small bowl stir together cumin, salt, cinnamon, coriander, turmeric, and pepper. Sprinkle evenly over chicken; rub in with your fingers. Place chicken in a 3½- to 4-quart slow cooker. Pour broth over chicken.

2. Cover and cook on low-heat setting for 6 to 8 hours or on high-heat setting for 3 to 4 hours.

Nutrition Facts per serving: 230 cal., 9 g total fat (2 g sat. fat), 108 mg chol., 567 mg sodium, 1 g carbo., 0 g fiber, 35 g pro.
Daily Values: 3% calcium, 9% iron
Exchanges: 4½ Lean Meat

Prep:
10 minutes

Cook:
Low 6 hours, High 3 hours

Makes:
6 servings

Slow Cooker Size:
3½- to 4-quart

Enjoy the full citrus flavor of this chicken dish. Chili powder adds plenty of spicy flavor as well.

LEMON–LIME CHILI CHICKEN

Prep:
15 minutes

Cook:
Low 5 hours,
High 2 ½ hours

Makes:
6 to 8 servings

Slow Cooker Size:
4- to 5-quart

2 tablespoons chili powder
1 teaspoon salt
½ teaspoon ground black pepper
3 to 3 ½ pounds meaty chicken pieces (breast halves, thighs, and drumsticks), skinned
1 medium zucchini or yellow summer squash, halved lengthwise and cut into 1-inch pieces
1 medium onion, cut into wedges
¼ cup reduced-sodium chicken broth
¼ cup lime juice
¼ cup lemon juice
2 cloves garlic, minced

1. In a small bowl stir together chili powder, salt, and pepper. Sprinkle evenly over chicken; rub in with your fingers. Place chicken in a 4- to 5-quart slow cooker. Arrange zucchini and onion over chicken. In a small bowl stir together broth, lime juice, lemon juice, and garlic. Pour over chicken and vegetables.

2. Cover and cook on low-heat setting for 5 to 6 hours or on high-heat setting for 2 ½ to 3 hours. Transfer chicken and vegetables to a serving platter or serving plates; discard cooking liquid.

Nutrition Facts per serving: 156 cal., 4 g total fat (1 g sat. fat), 76 mg chol., 525 mg sodium, 6 g carbo., 1 g fiber, 24 g pro.
Daily Values: 20% vit. A, 31% vit. C, 3% calcium, 9% iron
Exchanges: ½ Other Carbo., 3 Very Lean Meat, ½ Fat

The herb-lemon rub adds some color to the chicken pieces, and the cheese and parsley finish off the color and flavor.

FETA-TOPPED CHICKEN

1	teaspoon finely shredded lemon peel
1	teaspoon dried basil, crushed
1	teaspoon dried rosemary, crushed
2	cloves garlic, minced
½	teaspoon salt
¼	teaspoon ground black pepper
3½	to 4 pounds meaty chicken pieces (breast halves, thighs, and drumsticks), skinned
½	cup reduced-sodium chicken broth
½	cup crumbled feta cheese (2 ounces)
2	tablespoons snipped fresh Italian (flat-leaf) parsley

Prep:
15 minutes

Cook:
Low 5 hours,
High 2 ½ hours

Makes:
6 servings

Slow Cooker Size:
4- to 5-quart

1. In a small bowl stir together lemon peel, basil, rosemary, garlic, salt, and pepper. Sprinkle lemon peel mixture evenly over chicken; rub in with your fingers. Place chicken in a 4- to 5-quart slow cooker. Pour broth over chicken.

2. Cover and cook on low-heat setting for 5 to 6 hours or on high-heat setting for 2½ to 3 hours. Transfer chicken to a serving platter or serving plates; discard cooking liquid. Sprinkle chicken with feta cheese and parsley.

Nutrition Facts per serving: 179 cal., 6 g total fat (2 g sat. fat), 97 mg chol., 425 mg sodium, 1 g carbo., 0 g fiber, 29 g pro.
Daily Values: 4% vit. A, 8% vit. C, 7% calcium, 7% iron
Exchanges: 3½ Lean Meat

An easy-to-make family dinner, this chicken dish goes together quickly. Pair with a green salad and crisp rolls. Finish with fresh fruit for dessert.

EASY ITALIAN CHICKEN

Prep:
10 minutes

Cook:
Low 6 hours, High 3 hours

Makes:
4 to 6 servings

Slow Cooker Size:
3 1/2- to 6-quart

½ of a medium head cabbage, cut into wedges (about 12 ounces)
1 medium onion, sliced and separated into rings
1 4½-ounce jar (drained weight) sliced mushrooms, drained
2 tablespoons quick-cooking tapioca
2 to 2½ pounds meaty chicken pieces (breast halves, thighs, and drumsticks), skinned
2 cups meatless spaghetti sauce
Grated Parmesan cheese

1. In a 3½- to 6-quart slow cooker combine cabbage, onion, and drained mushrooms. Sprinkle tapioca over vegetables. Place chicken on vegetables. Pour spaghetti sauce over chicken.

2. Cover and cook on low-heat setting for 6 to 7 hours or on high-heat setting for 3 to 3½ hours. Transfer to a serving platter. Sprinkle with a little Parmesan cheese.

Nutrition Facts per serving: 300 cal., 9 g total fat (3 g sat. fat), 94 mg chol., 662 mg sodium, 24 g carbo., 4 g fiber, 35 g pro.
Daily Values: 7% vit. A, 62% vit. C, 11% calcium, 18% iron
Exchanges: 1½ Vegetable, 1 Other Carbo., 4 Lean Meat

If you like, serve the chicken with hot cooked rice. A half-cup serving of cooked brown rice adds 108 calories to the day's calorie tally.

CAESAR-STYLE CHICKEN

4	slices turkey bacon
3½	to 4 pounds meaty chicken pieces (breast halves, thighs, and drumsticks), skinned
1	teaspoon paprika
½	teaspoon salt
¼	teaspoon ground black pepper
½	cup chicken broth
⅓	cup dry white wine
4	anchovy fillets, finely chopped
¼	cup sliced green onions (2)
2	cloves garlic, minced
1	teaspoon finely shredded lemon peel
2	tablespoons cornstarch
2	tablespoons cold water
	Finely shredded Parmesan cheese (optional)

Prep:
30 minutes

Cook:
Low 5 hours,
High 2 ½ hours

Makes:
8 servings

Slow Cooker Size:
4- to 6-quart

1. In a large skillet cook bacon over medium heat until crisp. Drain bacon on paper towels, reserving drippings in skillet. When cool enough to handle, crumble bacon. Place bacon in a small bowl; cover and chill until serving time.

2. Sprinkle chicken with paprika, salt, and pepper. In the same skillet cook chicken, half at a time, in reserved drippings over medium heat until brown on all sides. Place chicken in a 4- to 6-quart slow cooker. In a small bowl stir together broth, wine, anchovies, green onions, garlic, and lemon peel. Pour over chicken.

3. Cover and cook on low-heat setting for 5 to 6 hours or on high-heat setting for 2½ to 3 hours. Transfer chicken to a serving platter, reserving cooking liquid. Cover chicken with foil to keep warm. Skim off fat from cooking liquid.

4. For sauce, transfer cooking liquid to a small saucepan. In a small bowl stir together cornstarch and water; add to saucepan. Cook and stir over medium heat until thickened and bubbly; cook and stir 2 minutes more. Spoon sauce over chicken. Sprinkle chicken with bacon and, if desired, Parmesan cheese.

Nutrition Facts per serving: 206 cal., 8 g total fat (2 g sat. fat), 87 mg chol., 449 mg sodium, 3 g carbo., 0 g fiber, 28 g pro.
Daily Values: 3% vit. A, 2% vit. C, 2% calcium, 7% iron
Exchanges: 4 Very Lean Meat, 1½ Fat

This he-man spaghetti sauce is lower in calories and fat than most sauces made with ground beef. If 8 cups of sauce is more than your family will eat at one meal, freeze the leftover sauce for another time.

CHICKEN SPAGHETTI SAUCE

Prep:
25 minutes

Cook:
Low 8 hours, High 4 hours

Makes:
8 to 10 servings

Slow Cooker Size:
3 ½- to 4-quart

1	pound uncooked ground chicken or turkey
6	cloves garlic, minced
3	14½-ounce cans stewed tomatoes, undrained
2	6-ounce cans tomato paste
½	cup chopped green sweet pepper
1½	teaspoons dried Italian seasoning, crushed
½	teaspoon salt
1	bay leaf
⅛	teaspoon bottled hot pepper sauce (optional)
8	cups hot cooked pasta
	Grated Parmesan cheese (optional)

1. For sauce, in a large skillet cook chicken and garlic until chicken is no longer pink. Drain off fat.

2. In a 3½- to 4-quart slow cooker combine chicken mixture, undrained tomatoes, tomato paste, sweet pepper, Italian seasoning, salt, bay leaf, and, if desired, hot pepper sauce.

3. Cover and cook on low-heat setting for 8 to 9 hours or on high-heat setting for 4 to 4½ hours.

4. Remove and discard bay leaf. Serve sauce over hot cooked pasta. If desired, sprinkle with Parmesan cheese.

Nutrition Facts per serving: 369 cal., 6 g total fat (0 g sat. fat), 0 mg chol., 479 mg sodium, 60 g carbo., 5 g fiber, 21 g pro.
Daily Values: 39% vit. A, 44% vit. C, 8% calcium, 25% iron
Exchanges: 3 Vegetable, 3 Starch, 1 Lean Meat

A can of cola moistens and slightly sweetens this sandwich filling. Slather on the mustard and serve sandwiches with forks in case some of the filling escapes the buns.

CHICKEN SLOPPY JOES

2 pounds uncooked ground chicken or turkey
1½ cups finely chopped celery (3 stalks)
1 cup finely chopped onion (1 large)
1 12-ounce can cola
2 teaspoons dry mustard
½ teaspoon salt
½ teaspoon ground black pepper
¼ teaspoon cayenne pepper (optional)
  Yellow mustard
10 to 12 hamburger buns, split and toasted
  Dill pickle slices
  Chopped onion

Prep:
20 minutes
Cook:
Low 6 hours, High 3 hours
Makes:
10 to 12 servings
Slow Cooker Size:
3½- to 4-quart

1. In a large skillet cook chicken, celery, and 1 cup onion until chicken is no longer pink, stirring often to break into small pieces. Drain off fat. Transfer chicken mixture to a 3½- to 4-quart slow cooker. In a small bowl combine cola, dry mustard, salt, black pepper, and, if desired, cayenne pepper. Pour over chicken mixture; stir to combine.

2. Cover and cook on low-heat setting for 6 to 7 hours or on high-heat setting for 3 to 3½ hours.

3. Spread yellow mustard on bottom halves of buns. Using a slotted spoon, divide chicken mixture among bun bottoms. Top with pickle slices and additional chopped onion. Add bun tops.

Nutrition Facts per serving: 284 cal., 10 g total fat (1 g sat. fat), 0 mg chol., 415 mg sodium, 28 g carbo., 2 g fiber, 20 g pro.
Daily Values: 3% vit. C, 9% calcium, 13% iron
Exchanges: 1 Vegetable, 1½ Starch, 2 Medium-Fat Meat

Traditionally made with lamb or mutton, shepherd's pie works equally well slow cooked with turkey and frozen vegetables. Dried thyme infuses an herbal note.

TURKEY SHEPHERD'S PIE

Prep:
20 minutes

Cook:
Low 6 hours, High 3 hours;
plus 10 minutes on High

Makes:
4 servings

Slow Cooker Size:
3 1/2- to 4-quart

 1 10-ounce package frozen loose-pack mixed vegetables
12 ounces turkey breast tenderloin or skinless, boneless chicken breast halves, cut into 1/2-inch-wide strips
 1 12-ounce jar turkey or chicken gravy
 1 teaspoon dried thyme, crushed
 1 20-ounce package refrigerated mashed potatoes

1. Place frozen vegetables in a 3 1/2- to 4-quart slow cooker. Top with turkey. In a small bowl stir together gravy and thyme; pour over turkey.

2. Cover and cook on low-heat setting for 6 to 7 hours or on high-heat setting for 3 to 3 1/2 hours.

3. If cooking on low-heat setting, turn to high-heat setting. Using a spoon, drop mashed potatoes into 8 small mounds on top of turkey mixture. Cover and cook for 10 minutes more. To serve, in each of 4 shallow bowls spoon some of the turkey mixture and 2 of the potato mounds.

Nutrition Facts per serving: 297 cal., 5 g total fat (1 g sat. fat), 51 mg chol., 781 mg sodium, 33 g carbo., 4 g fiber, 27 g pro. Daily Values: 74% vit. A, 54% vit. C, 5% calcium, 15% iron Exchanges: 2 Starch, 3 Very Lean Meat, 1/2 Fat

Great for the family, this recipe serves many and doesn't take long to prepare for the slow cooker. A sprinkling of Parmesan lends a sharp note to the creamy blend.

TURKEY AND PASTA PRIMAVERA

2 pounds turkey breast tenderloins or skinless, boneless chicken breast halves, cut into 1-inch pieces

1 16-ounce package frozen loose-pack sugar snap stir-fry vegetables (sugar snap peas, carrots, onions, and mushrooms)

2 teaspoons dried basil, oregano, or Italian seasoning, crushed

1 16-ounce jar Alfredo pasta sauce

12 ounces dried spaghetti or linguine, broken
Shredded Parmesan cheese (optional)

Prep:
15 minutes

Cook:
Low 4 hours, High 2 hours

Makes:
8 servings

Slow Cooker Size:
4 ½- to 6-quart

1. In a 4½- to 6-quart slow cooker combine turkey and frozen vegetables. Sprinkle with basil. Stir in Alfredo sauce.

2. Cover and cook on low-heat setting for 4 to 5 hours or on high-heat setting for 2 to 2½ hours.

3. Cook pasta according to package directions. Drain. Stir pasta into mixture in cooker. To serve, spoon pasta mixture into shallow bowls. If desired, sprinkle with Parmesan cheese.

Nutrition Facts per serving: 407 cal., 11 g total fat (5 g sat. fat), 103 mg chol., 447 mg sodium, 39 g carbo., 2 g fiber, 36 g pro.
Daily Values: 77% vit. A, 10% vit. C, 9% calcium, 19% iron
Exchanges: ½ Vegetable, 2½ Starch, 4 Very Lean Meat, 1 Fat

Texans love their meaty black-eyed peas. What better way to discover this Southwestern specialty than in this tasty dish?

TEXAS TURKEY BONANZA

Prep:
20 minutes

Cook:
Low 8 hours, High 4 hours; plus 30 minutes on High

Makes:
6 servings

Slow Cooker Size:
4- to 4 1/2-quart

2 cups dry black-eyed peas
1 to 3 fresh jalapeño chile peppers, seeded and quartered lengthwise*
1 1/2 teaspoons dried sage, crushed
1 teaspoon salt
1 pound turkey tenderloin, cut into 1 1/2-inch pieces
2 medium yellow summer squash, cut into wedges
1/2 cup finely chopped red onion
  Snipped fresh cilantro
1 recipe Lime Sour Cream (optional)
  Finely chopped fresh jalapeño chile pepper* (optional)

1. Sort through peas to remove any pebbles or other foreign matter. Rinse peas. In a large saucepan combine peas and 5 cups water. Bring to boiling; reduce heat. Cook, uncovered, for 10 minutes. Remove from heat. (Standing time is not needed.) Drain; rinse peas.

2. In a 4- to 4½-quart slow cooker combine peas, 3 cups water, quartered jalapeño peppers, sage, and salt. Top with turkey.

3. Cover and cook on low-heat setting for 8 to 10 hours or on high-heat setting for 4 to 5 hours.

4. If using low-heat setting, turn to high-heat setting. Stir squash into stew. Cover and cook for 30 minutes more. Sprinkle servings with onion and cilantro. If desired, top with Lime Sour Cream and chopped jalapeño pepper.

Lime Sour Cream: In a small bowl combine ½ cup light dairy sour cream, ½ teaspoon finely shredded lime peel, and 1 tablespoon lime juice. Cover and chill until serving time.

*Note: Because chile peppers contain volatile oils that can burn your skin and eyes, avoid direct contact with them as much as possible. When working with chile peppers, wear plastic or rubber gloves. If your bare hands do touch the peppers, wash your hands and nails well with soap and warm water.

Nutrition Facts per serving: 144 cal., 1 g total fat (0 g sat. fat), 47 mg chol., 423 mg sodium, 13 g carbo., 4 g fiber, 21 g pro.
Daily Values: 11% vit. A, 14% vit. C, 8% calcium, 8% iron
Exchanges: 1 Vegetable, ½ Starch, 2½ Very Lean Meat

Turkey is good year-round nutrition. Complement this easy-to-prepare meal with steamed green beans.

MAPLE–MUSTARD–SAUCED TURKEY THIGHS

1   pound new potatoes, quartered
2   to 2½ pounds turkey thighs (about 2 thighs), skinned
⅓   cup coarse-grain brown mustard
¼   cup maple syrup or maple-flavored syrup
1   tablespoon quick-cooking tapioca

1. Place potatoes in a 3½- to 4-quart slow cooker. Place turkey on potatoes. In a small bowl stir together mustard, syrup, and tapioca. Pour over turkey.

2. Cover and cook on low-heat setting for 6 to 7 hours or on high-heat setting for 3 to 3½ hours.

Nutrition Facts per serving: 377 cal., 10 g total fat (3 g sat. fat), 93 mg chol., 369 mg sodium, 36 g carbo., 2 g fiber, 36 g pro.
Daily Values: 24% vit. C, 9% calcium, 26% iron
Exchanges: 1 Starch, 1½ Other Carbo., 4 Lean Meat

Prep:
20 minutes

Cook:
Low 6 hours, High 3 hours

Makes:
4 servings

Slow Cooker Size:
3 ½- to 4-quart

Look for the dried peppercorn mixture in the spice section of your supermarket.

PEPPERCORN–TOPPED TURKEY

Prep:
15 minutes

Cook:
Low 5 hours,
High 2 ½ hours

Makes:
8 servings

Slow Cooker Size:
3 ½- to 4-quart

2 tablespoons dried whole mixed peppercorns, coarsely crushed
1 teaspoon coarse salt
1 teaspoon dried thyme, crushed
3 pounds turkey thighs, skinned
¼ cup reduced-sodium chicken broth
¼ cup dry white wine

1. In a small bowl stir together peppercorns, salt, and thyme. Sprinkle evenly over turkey; rub in with your fingers. Place turkey in a 3½- to 4-quart slow cooker. Add broth and wine.

2. Cover and cook on low-heat setting for 5 to 6 hours or on high-heat setting for 2½ to 3 hours. Transfer turkey to a serving platter or serving plates. Spoon some of the cooking liquid over the turkey. Discard any remaining cooking liquid.

Nutrition Facts per serving: 132 cal., 3 g total fat (1 g sat. fat), 73 mg chol., 344 mg sodium, 1 g carbo., 0 g fiber, 22 g pro.
Daily Values: 1% vit. A, 1% vit. C, 3% calcium, 14% iron
Exchanges: 3 Very Lean Meat, ½ Fat

This recipe makes enough for a crowd. Refrigerate leftover filling for another meal, and the next time, serve it on buns.

SESAME–GINGER TURKEY WRAPS

Nonstick cooking spray
3 turkey thighs, skinned (3½ to 4 pounds)
1 cup bottled sesame-ginger stir-fry sauce
¼ cup water
1 16-ounce package shredded broccoli (broccoli slaw mix)
12 8-inch flour tortillas, warmed*
¾ cup sliced green onions (6)

1. Lightly coat a 3½- to 4-quart slow cooker with nonstick cooking spray. Place turkey in prepared cooker. In a small bowl stir together stir-fry sauce and water. Pour over turkey.

2. Cover and cook on low-heat setting for 6 to 7 hours or on high-heat setting for 3 to 3½ hours.

3. Remove turkey from slow cooker; cool slightly. Remove turkey from bones; discard bones. Using 2 forks, shred turkey into bite-size pieces. Place broccoli in sauce mixture in slow cooker. Stir to coat; cover and let stand for 5 minutes. Remove from cooker with a slotted spoon.

4. To assemble, place some of the turkey on each tortilla. Top with some of the broccoli mixture and green onions. Spoon some of the sauce from cooker on top of onions. Roll up and serve immediately.

*Note: To warm tortillas, wrap them in white microwave-safe paper towels; microwave on high for 15 to 30 seconds or until tortillas are softened. (Or preheat oven to 350°F. Wrap tortillas in foil. Heat in the oven for 10 to 15 minutes or until warmed.)

Nutrition Facts per serving: 207 cal., 5 g total fat (1 g sat. fat), 67 mg chol., 422 mg sodium, 20 g carbo., 2 g fiber, 20 g pro.
Daily Values: 25% vit. A, 57% vit. C, 6% calcium, 15% iron
Exchanges: 1 Vegetable, 1 Starch, 2 Lean Meat

Prep:
20 minutes

Cook:
Low 6 hours, High 3 hours

Stand:
5 minutes

Makes:
12 servings

Slow Cooker Size:
3 1/2- to 4-quart

Who needs a grill for barbecue? And who says slow cooking means mush? These shapely, saucy thighs hold their form nicely in slow heat.

TURKEY THIGHS IN BARBECUE SAUCE

Prep:
15 minutes

Cook:
Low 10 hours, High 5 hours

Makes:
4 to 6 servings

Slow Cooker Size:
3 ½- to 4-quart

½   cup ketchup
2   tablespoons packed brown sugar
1   tablespoon quick-cooking tapioca
1   tablespoon vinegar
1   teaspoon Worcestershire sauce
¼   teaspoon ground cinnamon
¼   teaspoon crushed red pepper
2   to 2½ pounds turkey thighs (about 2 thighs) or meaty chicken pieces (breast halves, thighs, and drumsticks), skinned
    Hot cooked rice or noodles (optional)

1. In a 3½- to 4-quart slow cooker combine ketchup, brown sugar, tapioca, vinegar, Worcestershire sauce, cinnamon, and crushed red pepper. Place turkey, meaty sides down, on ketchup mixture.

2. Cover and cook on low-heat setting for 10 to 12 hours or on high-heat setting for 5 to 6 hours. Transfer turkey to a serving dish. Spoon cooking liquid into a small bowl or glass measure; skim off fat. Serve turkey with cooking liquid. If desired, serve with rice.

Nutrition Facts per serving: 239 cal., 6 g total fat (2 g sat. fat), 100 mg chol., 449 mg sodium, 16 g carbo., 1 g fiber, 30 g pro.
Daily Values: 6% vit. A, 8% vit. C, 3% calcium, 16% iron
Exchanges: 1 Other Carbo., 4 Very Lean Meat, 1 Fat

Chapter 5

MEATLESS
Main Dishes

Tender red beans go from tame to sassy when mixed with cumin. Slice lime wedges to serve on the side: A spritz of citrus is a nice twist.

RED BEANS OVER SPANISH RICE

Prep:
25 minutes

Stand:
1 hour

Cook:
Low 10 hours, High 5 hours

Makes:
6 to 8 servings

Slow Cooker Size:
3 1/2- to 4-quart

2   cups dry red beans or dry red kidney beans
     Nonstick cooking spray
2½   cups chopped onion (2 large)
1   tablespoon bottled minced garlic (6 cloves)
1   tablespoon ground cumin
1   6¾-ounce package Spanish rice mix
     Lime wedges (optional)

1. Rinse beans. In a large saucepan combine dry beans and 5 cups water. Bring to boiling; reduce heat. Simmer, uncovered, for 10 minutes. Remove from heat. Cover and let stand for 1 hour. (Or place beans in 5 cups water in saucepan. Cover and let soak in a cool place for 6 to 8 hours or overnight.) Drain and rinse beans.

2. Lightly coat a 3½- to 4-quart slow cooker with nonstick cooking spray. In the prepared cooker place drained beans, 4 cups water, onions, garlic, and cumin.

3. Cover and cook on low-heat setting for 10 to 11 hours or on high-heat setting for 5 to 5½ hours.

4. Prepare rice mix according to package directions. Remove beans from cooker using a slotted spoon. Serve beans over cooked rice. If desired, spoon some of the cooking liquid from the cooker and a squeeze of lime juice over beans and rice.

Nutrition Facts per serving: 344 cal., 1 g total fat (0 g sat. fat), 0 mg chol., 450 mg sodium, 68 g carbo., 17 g fiber, 19 g pro.
Daily Values: 6% vit. A, 14% vit. C, 17% calcium, 34% iron
Exchanges: 1 Vegetable, 4 Starch, ½ Very Lean Meat

Brown rice is the least-processed form of rice. Layers of bran are left on the kernels, giving a tan color and chewy texture. Spoon beans over a bed of the rice.

SAVORY BEANS AND RICE

1¼ cups dry red beans or dry red kidney beans
1 cup chopped onion (1 large)
¾ cup sliced celery (1½ stalks)
2 cloves garlic, minced
½ of a vegetable bouillon cube
1 teaspoon dried basil, crushed
1 bay leaf
1¼ cups water
1¼ cups uncooked regular brown rice
1 14½-ounce can stewed tomatoes, undrained
1 4-ounce can diced green chile peppers, drained
   Few dashes bottled hot pepper sauce

Prep:
20 minutes

Stand:
1 hour

Cook:
Low 9 hours, High 4 hours; plus 30 minutes on High

Makes:
5 servings

Slow Cooker Size:
3 ½- to 4-quart

1. Rinse beans. In a large saucepan add enough water to cover beans by 2 inches. Bring to boiling; reduce heat. Simmer, uncovered, for 10 minutes. Remove from heat. Cover and let stand for 1 hour. (Or place beans in cold water in saucepan. Cover and let soak in a cool place overnight.) Drain and rinse beans.

2. In a 3½- to 4-quart slow cooker combine drained beans, onion, celery, garlic, bouillon cube, basil, and bay leaf. Pour the 1¼ cups water over all.

3. Cover and cook on low-heat setting for 9 to 10 hours or on high-heat setting for 4 to 5 hours.

4. Cook brown rice according to package directions; keep warm. Remove and discard bay leaf. If using low-heat setting, turn to high-heat setting. Stir undrained tomatoes, drained chile peppers, and hot pepper sauce into cooked beans. Cover and cook for 30 minutes more. Serve bean mixture over rice.

Nutrition Facts per serving: 383 cal., 3 g total fat (0 g sat. fat), 0 mg chol., 406 mg sodium, 74 g carbo., 10 g fiber, 16 g pro.
Daily Values: 4% vit. A, 22% vit. C, 11% calcium, 21% iron
Exchanges: 1 Vegetable, 4½ Starch

As an option to the jalapeños, try such pepper varieties as serranos, Anaheims, or small poblanos.

SPICY BLACK BEANS AND RICE

Prep:
30 minutes

Stand:
1 hour

Cook:
Low 10 hours, High 5 hours;
plus 30 minutes on High

Makes:
8 servings

Slow Cooker Size:
3 ½- to 4-quart

2 cups dry black beans
1 cup chopped onion (1 large)
1 cup chopped celery (2 stalks)
1 cup chopped carrots (2 medium)
¾ cup chopped yellow or green sweet pepper (1 medium)
2 fresh jalapeño chile peppers, chopped*
4 cloves garlic, minced
1½ teaspoons ground cumin
1½ teaspoons ground coriander
1 teaspoon dried thyme, crushed
1 teaspoon salt
½ teaspoon ground black pepper
2 bay leaves
2 14-ounce cans reduced-sodium chicken broth
2 tablespoons butter, softened
2 tablespoons all-purpose flour
4 cups hot cooked rice

1. Rinse beans. In a large saucepan add enough water to cover beans by 2 inches. Bring to boiling; reduce heat. Simmer, uncovered, for 10 minutes. Remove from heat. Cover and let stand for 1 hour. (Or place beans in cold water in saucepan. Cover and let soak in a cool place overnight.) Drain and rinse beans. In a 3½- to 4-quart slow cooker combine drained beans, onion, celery, carrots, sweet pepper, jalapeño peppers, garlic, cumin, coriander, thyme, salt, black pepper, and bay leaves. Pour broth over all.

2. Cover and cook on low-heat setting for 10 to 11 hours or on high-heat setting for 5 to 5½ hours. If using low-heat setting, turn to high-heat setting. Stir together butter and flour to make a paste. Whisk into bean mixture. Cover and cook for 30 minutes more. Remove and discard bay leaves. Serve with rice.

*Note: Because chile peppers contain volatile oils that can burn your skin and eyes, avoid direct contact with them as much as possible. When working with chile peppers, wear plastic or rubber gloves. If your bare hands do touch the peppers, wash your hands and nails well with soap and warm water.

Nutrition Facts per serving: 333 cal., 4 g total fat (2 g sat. fat), 8 mg chol., 576 mg sodium, 60 g carbo., 9 g fiber, 14 g pro. Daily Values: 38% vit. A, 67% vit. C, 10% calcium, 22% iron Exchanges: 1½ Vegetable, 3½ Starch, ½ Fat

Kidney and black beans elevate scalloped potatoes from a supporting role to the main attraction. To cut down on prep time, leave the peels on the potatoes.

SCALLOPED POTATOES AND BEANS

1   15-ounce can red kidney beans, rinsed and drained
1   15-ounce can black beans, rinsed and drained
1   cup chopped onion (1 large)
1   cup celery sliced ¼ inch thick (2 stalks)
1   cup frozen peas
1   large green sweet pepper, seeded and chopped
1   10¾-ounce can reduced-fat and reduced-sodium condensed cream of mushroom soup
4   cloves garlic, minced
1   teaspoon dried thyme, crushed
¼   teaspoon ground black pepper
1   pound potatoes, sliced ¼ inch thick
1   cup shredded cheddar cheese (4 ounces) (optional)

1. In a large bowl combine drained kidney beans, drained black beans, onion, celery, peas, sweet pepper, soup, garlic, thyme, and black pepper.

2. Spoon half of the bean mixture into a 3½- to 4-quart slow cooker. Top with potatoes and the remaining bean mixture.

3. Cover and cook on low-heat setting for 8 to 10 hours or on high-heat setting for 4 to 5 hours. If desired, top servings with cheddar cheese.

Nutrition Facts per serving: 272 cal., 2 g total fat (0 g sat. fat), 2 mg chol., 656 mg sodium, 55 g carbo., 13 g fiber, 16 g pro.
Daily Values: 17% vit. A, 70% vit. C, 9% calcium, 23% iron
Exchanges: 2 Vegetable, 3 Starch

Prep:
15 minutes

Cook:
Low 8 hours, High 4 hours

Makes:
5 servings

Slow Cooker Size:
3 ½- to 4-quart

For variety, use a tube of polenta with wild mushrooms or even Italian-style polenta. Look for the tubes of polenta in the produce section of your supermarket.

SWEET BEANS AND LENTILS OVER POLENTA

Prep:
20 minutes

Cook:
Low 7 hours,
High 3 1/2 hours

Makes:
6 servings

Slow Cooker Size:
3 1/2- to 4-quart

1 14-ounce can vegetable broth
1/2 cup water
1 cup dry brown lentils
1 12-ounce package frozen sweet soybeans (edamame)
1 medium red sweet pepper, chopped
1 teaspoon dried oregano, crushed
2 cloves garlic, minced
1/2 teaspoon salt
2 medium tomatoes, chopped
1 16-ounce tube refrigerated polenta

1. In a 3½- to 4-quart slow cooker combine broth, water, lentils, soybeans, sweet pepper, oregano, garlic, and salt.

2. Cover and cook on low-heat setting for 7 to 8 hours or on high-heat setting for 3½ to 4 hours. Stir in tomatoes.

3. Meanwhile, prepare polenta according to package directions. Serve lentil mixture over polenta.

Nutrition Facts per serving: 280 cal., 5 g total fat (1 g sat. fat), 0 mg chol., 794 mg sodium, 43 g carbo., 15 g fiber, 19 g pro.
Daily Values: 30% vit. A, 85% vit. C, 12% calcium, 26% iron
Exchanges: 1 Vegetable, 2½ Starch, 1½ Very Lean Meat

Tofu is the main protein source for this meatless main dish. It's a good recipe to introduce your family to this healthful ingredient.

NOODLE CASSEROLE

2½ cups water
1 10¾-ounce can reduced-fat and reduced-sodium condensed cream of mushroom soup
1 cup sliced celery (2 stalks)
1 cup sliced carrots (2 medium)
1 cup chopped onion (1 large)
2 cloves garlic, minced
1 14½-ounce can no-salt-added diced tomatoes, undrained
1½ teaspoons dried Italian seasoning, crushed
¼ teaspoon salt
¼ teaspoon ground black pepper
8 ounces dried extra-wide noodles
1 16-ounce package extra-firm tofu (fresh bean curd), drained, if necessary, and cubed
½ cup shredded reduced-fat cheddar cheese (2 ounces)

Prep:
25 minutes

Cook:
Low 7 hours,
High 3 ½ hours;
plus 20 minutes on High

Makes:
6 servings

Slow Cooker Size:
3 ½- to 4-quart

1. In a 3½- to 4-quart slow cooker whisk together water and soup until combined. Add celery, carrots, onion, garlic, undrained tomatoes, Italian seasoning, salt, and pepper; stir to combine.

2. Cover and cook on low-heat setting for 7 to 8 hours or high-heat setting for 3½ to 4 hours.

3. If using low-heat setting, turn to high-heat setting. Stir in noodles; cover and cook for 20 to 30 minutes more or until tender, stirring once halfway through cooking. Gently stir in tofu cubes. Sprinkle with cheese; cover and let stand until cheese is melted.

Nutrition Facts per serving: 316 cal., 8 g total fat (2 g sat. fat), 44 mg chol., 447 mg sodium, 42 g carbo., 4 g fiber, 17 g pro. Daily Values: 53% vit. A, 14% vit. C, 18% calcium, 17% iron Exchanges: 1 Vegetable, 2 Starch, ½ Other Carbo., 1 Medium-Fat Meat, ½ Fat

Goulash is typically a meaty dish flavored with paprika and served with noodles. This version does not include the meat.

MUSHROOM GOULASH

Prep:
25 minutes

Cook:
Low 8 hours, High 4 hours

Makes:
6 servings

Slow Cooker Size:
3 1/2- to 4-quart

16 ounces fresh baby portobello mushrooms, sliced
1 tablespoon dried minced onion
3 cloves garlic, minced
1 14-ounce can vegetable broth
1 14½-ounce can no-salt-added diced tomatoes, undrained
1 6-ounce can no-salt-added tomato paste
2 tablespoons paprika
1 teaspoon dried oregano, crushed
1 teaspoon caraway seeds
¼ teaspoon salt
¼ teaspoon ground black pepper
½ cup light dairy sour cream
8 ounces dried egg noodles, cooked and drained

1. In a 3½- to 4-quart slow cooker combine mushrooms, onion, and garlic. Stir in broth, undrained tomatoes, tomato paste, paprika, oregano, caraway seeds, salt, and pepper.

2. Cover and cook on low-heat setting for 8 to 9 hours or on high-heat setting for 4 to 4½ hours.

3. Stir sour cream into mushroom mixture before serving. Serve with noodles.

Nutrition Facts per serving: 251 cal., 5 g total fat (2 g sat. fat), 43 mg chol., 443 mg sodium, 43 g carbo., 5 g fiber, 12 g pro.
Daily Values: 37% vit. A, 21% vit. C, 9% calcium, 19% iron
Exchanges: 2 Vegetable, 2 Starch, 1 Fat

With the earthy mushrooms, crunchy fennel, and beans in the full-flavored pasta sauce, you'll never miss the meat.

PENNE WITH MUSHROOM–FENNEL SAUCE

1   large fennel bulb, trimmed and coarsely chopped (1¾ cups)
8   ounces fresh mushrooms, quartered
1   19-ounce can fava beans, rinsed and drained
8   plum tomatoes, coarsely chopped (3½ cups)
¼   cup vegetable broth
1   tablespoon quick-cooking tapioca
1   teaspoon dried Italian seasoning, crushed
¼   teaspoon salt
¼   teaspoon freshly ground black pepper
6   ounces dried penne, cooked and drained
2   tablespoons pine nuts, toasted

Prep:
20 minutes

Cook:
Low 8 hours, High 4 hours

Makes:
4 servings

Slow Cooker Size:
3 ½- to 4-quart

1. In a 3½- to 4- quart slow cooker combine fennel, mushrooms, drained fava beans, tomatoes, and broth. Sprinkle with tapioca, Italian seasoning, salt, and pepper; stir to combine.

2. Cover and cook on low-heat setting for 8 to 9 hours or on high-heat setting for 4 to 4½ hours.

3. Toss penne with vegetable mixture. Sprinkle with pine nuts.

Nutrition Facts per serving: 342 cal., 5 g total fat (1 g sat. fat), 0 mg chol., 658 mg sodium, 61 g carbo., 17 g fiber, 18 g pro.
Daily Values: 26% vit. A, 49% vit. C, 10% calcium, 15% iron
Exchanges: 3 Vegetable, 3 Starch, 1 Very Lean Meat

Eggplant, with its mild flavor and spongy texture, soaks up flavors from foods. In this recipe, chunks of eggplant (a low-calorie alternative to ground beef or sausage) cook in a traditional spaghetti sauce.

PASTA WITH EGGPLANT SAUCE

Prep:
20 minutes

Cook:
Low 7 hours,
High 3 ½ hours

Makes:
6 servings

Slow Cooker Size:
3 ½- to 5 ½-quart

1	medium eggplant
½	cup chopped onion (1 medium)
1	28-ounce can Italian-style tomatoes, undrained and cut up
1	6-ounce can Italian-style tomato paste
1	4-ounce can (drained weight) sliced mushrooms, drained
2	cloves garlic, minced
¼	cup dry red wine
¼	cup water
1 ½	teaspoons dried oregano, crushed
⅓	cup pitted kalamata olives or pitted ripe olives, sliced
2	tablespoons snipped fresh parsley
4	cups hot cooked penne
¼	cup grated or shredded Parmesan cheese
2	tablespoons toasted pine nuts (optional)

1. Peel eggplant, if desired; cut eggplant into 1-inch cubes. In a 3½- to 5½-quart slow cooker combine eggplant, onion, undrained tomatoes, tomato paste, drained mushrooms, garlic, wine, water, and oregano.

2. Cover and cook on low-heat setting for 7 to 8 hours or on high-heat setting for 3½ to 4 hours. Stir in olives and parsley. Season to taste with salt and ground black pepper. Serve over pasta; sprinkle with Parmesan cheese. If desired, garnish with pine nuts.

Nutrition Facts per serving: 243 cal., 3 g total fat (1 g sat. fat), 3 mg chol., 647 mg sodium, 45 g carbo., 6 g fiber, 9 g pro.
Daily Values: 6% vit. A, 45% vit. C, 13% calcium, 23% iron
Exchanges: 3 Vegetable, 2 Starch

For a heartier main dish, brown a little ground beef in a skillet, drain off the fat, and add the browned meat to the tomato mixture before cooking.

HERBED MUSHROOM–TOMATO SAUCE

2	14½-ounce cans whole tomatoes, undrained and cut up
3	cups sliced fresh mushrooms
1	6-ounce can tomato paste
½	cup chopped onion (1 medium)
2	cloves garlic, minced
2	tablespoons grated Parmesan cheese
2	teaspoons dried oregano, crushed
2	teaspoons packed brown sugar
1½	teaspoons dried basil, crushed
½	teaspoon salt
½	teaspoon fennel seeds, crushed
¼	teaspoon crushed red pepper (optional)
1	bay leaf
12	ounces spaghetti, linguine, or other pasta, cooked and drained
	Grated Parmesan cheese (optional)

Prep:
25 minutes

Cook:
Low 8 hours, High 4 hours

Makes:
6 servings

Slow Cooker Size:
3½- to 4-quart

1. In a 3½- to 4-quart slow cooker combine undrained tomatoes, mushrooms, tomato paste, onion, garlic, 2 tablespoons Parmesan cheese, oregano, brown sugar, basil, salt, fennel seeds, crushed red pepper (if desired), and bay leaf.

2. Cover and cook on low-heat setting for 8 to 10 hours or on high-heat setting for 4 to 5 hours.

3. Remove and discard bay leaf. Serve sauce over pasta. If desired, top with Parmesan cheese.

Nutrition Facts per serving: 302 cal., 2 g total fat (1 g sat. fat), 1 mg chol., 679 mg sodium, 59 g carbo., 4 g fiber, 11 g pro.
Daily Values: 15% vit. A, 50% vit. C, 12% calcium, 20% iron
Exchanges: 2½ Vegetable, 3 Starch

A versatile sauce, this classic also is good over baked potatoes. Use the delayed-start feature on your oven to bake the potatoes while you're away. Then everything will be ready to put on the table when you arrive home.

MARINARA SAUCE

Prep:
20 minutes

Cook:
Low 8 hours, High 4 hours

Makes:
6 servings

Slow Cooker Size:
3 ½- to 4-quart

1	28-ounce can whole Italian-style tomatoes, undrained and cut up
2	cups coarsely chopped carrots (4 medium)
1½	cups sliced celery (3 stalks)
1	cup chopped onion (1 large)
1	cup chopped green sweet pepper (1 large)
1	6-ounce can tomato paste
½	cup water
3	cloves garlic, minced
2	teaspoons sugar
2	teaspoons dried Italian seasoning, crushed
1	teaspoon salt
¼	teaspoon ground black pepper
1	bay leaf
12	ounces dried pasta, cooked and drained

1. In a 3½- to 4-quart slow cooker combine undrained tomatoes, carrots, celery, onion, sweet pepper, tomato paste, water, garlic, sugar, Italian seasoning, salt, black pepper, and bay leaf.

2. Cover and cook on low-heat setting for 8 to 10 hours or on high-heat setting for 4 to 5 hours.

3. Remove and discard bay leaf. Serve sauce over pasta.

Nutrition Facts per serving: 308 cal., 1 g total fat (0 g sat. fat), 0 mg chol., 636 mg sodium, 64 g carbo., 6 g fiber, 11 g pro. Daily Values: 224% vit. A, 82% vit. C, 9% calcium, 20% iron Exchanges: 2 Vegetable, 3 Starch, ½ Other Carbo.

A variety of textures and flavors makes this an exotic main dish. Look for the optional chutney accompaniment in the condiment aisle of the supermarket.

CURRIED RICE AND VEGETABLES

3	cups medium potatoes cut into ½-inch chunks (3 medium)
2	cups carrots cut into ¼-inch slices (4 medium)
1	cup red onion cut into strips (1 large)
1¼	cups apple juice
2	tablespoons quick-cooking tapioca
2	teaspoons curry powder
1	teaspoon grated fresh ginger
½	teaspoon salt
½	teaspoon ground cardamom
1	cup uncooked regular brown rice
1	12.3-ounce package extra-firm tofu (fresh bean curd), drained, if necessary, and cut into ¾-inch cubes
1	medium zucchini, halved lengthwise and cut into ½-inch slices
1	cup frozen peas
⅓	cup golden raisins
	Chutney (optional)

Prep:
15 minutes

Cook:
Low 8 hours, High 4 hours; plus 30 minutes on High

Makes:
6 servings

Slow Cooker Size:
3½- to 4-quart

1. In a 3½- to 4-quart slow cooker combine potatoes, carrots, onion, apple juice, tapioca, curry powder, ginger, salt, and cardamom.

2. Cover and cook on low-heat setting for 8 to 10 hours or on high-heat setting for 4 to 5 hours.

3. Cook rice according to package directions. If using low-heat setting, turn to high-heat setting. Add tofu, zucchini, peas, and raisins to cooker. Cover and cook for 30 minutes more. Serve vegetable mixture over rice. If desired, serve with chutney.

Nutrition Facts per serving: 326 cal., 3 g total fat (0 g sat. fat), 0 mg chol., 262 mg sodium, 65 g carbo., 7 g fiber, 11 g pro.
Daily Values: 33% vit. C, 7% calcium, 17% iron
Exchanges: 2 Vegetable, 1 Fruit, 2½ Starch, ½ Very Lean Meat

If you love taco salad, you'll welcome this easy version loaded with vegetables and plenty of zing. For dessert, serve with fresh papaya slices or apple wedges.

LENTIL TACO SALAD

Prep:
20 minutes

Cook:
Low 10 hours, High 5 hours;
plus 15 minutes on High

Makes:
8 servings

Slow Cooker Size:
3 ½-quart

2 cups coarsely chopped red and/or green sweet peppers (2 large)
1 cup dry brown lentils, rinsed and drained
1 cup chopped onion (1 large)
½ cup uncooked regular brown rice
3 cloves garlic, minced
2 teaspoons chili powder
¼ teaspoon salt
2 14-ounce cans vegetable broth
1 medium yellow summer squash, quartered lengthwise and sliced ½-inch thick (1½ cups)
8 cups tortilla chips, broken
2 cups shredded lettuce
2 cups chopped tomatoes
½ cup dairy sour cream

1. In a 3½-quart slow cooker combine sweet peppers, lentils, onion, rice, garlic, chili powder, and salt. Pour broth over vegetables.

2. Cover and cook on low-heat setting for 10 to 12 hours or on high-heat setting for 5 to 6 hours.

3. If using low-heat setting, turn to high-heat setting. Stir in squash. Cover and cook for 15 minutes more.

4. To serve, arrange tortilla chips on 8 dinner plates. Spoon lentil mixture over chips. Top with lettuce and tomatoes and add a dollop of sour cream.

Nutrition Facts per serving: 324 cal., 11 g total fat (3 g sat. fat), 5 mg chol., 669 mg sodium, 49 g carbo., 12 g fiber, 12 g pro.
Daily Values: 163% vit. A, 130% vit. C, 9% calcium, 18% iron
Exchanges: 2½ Vegetable, 2½ Starch, 1½ Fat

The seasonings give the meatless filling a sausagelike taste. You'll even notice a hotness in the pepper filling; reduce the crushed red pepper if your family prefers milder flavors.

STUFFED PEPPERS

4   medium green, red, or yellow sweet peppers
1   cup converted rice, cooked according to package directions
1   12-ounce package frozen cooked and crumbled ground meat substitute (soy protein)
1   cup shredded reduced-fat mozzarella cheese (4 ounces)
1   teaspoon fennel seeds, crushed
½   teaspoon crushed red pepper
½   teaspoon dried thyme, crushed
½   teaspoon paprika
½   teaspoon ground black pepper
2   cups light spaghetti sauce
¼   cup water

Prep:
15 minutes

Cook:
Low 6 hours, High 3 hours

Makes:
4 servings

Slow Cooker Size:
5- to 6-quart

1. Remove tops, membranes, and seeds from sweet peppers. In a medium bowl stir together rice, ground meat substitute, ½ cup of the cheese, the fennel seeds, crushed red pepper, thyme, paprika, and black pepper. Spoon rice mixture into peppers. Pour spaghetti sauce and water into a 5- to 6-quart slow cooker. Place peppers, filled sides up, in cooker.

2. Cover and cook on low-heat setting for 6 to 6½ hours or on high-heat setting for 3 to 3½ hours. Transfer peppers to a serving platter. Spoon sauce over peppers and sprinkle peppers with remaining ½ cup cheese.

Nutrition Facts per serving: 434 cal., 5 g total fat (3 g sat. fat), 10 mg chol., 568 mg sodium, 69 g carbo., 11 g fiber, 32 g pro. Daily Values: 18% vit. A, 153% vit. C, 38% calcium, 28% iron Exchanges: 1 Vegetable, 2½ Starch, 1½ Other Carbo., 2½ Very Lean Meat

Nutritious, crisp-tender vegetables star in this colorful, curry-flavored mixture.

VEGETABLE AND GARBANZO CURRY

Prep:
15 minutes

Cook:
Low 5 hours,
High 2 1/2 hours

Makes:
4 to 6 servings

Slow Cooker Size:
3 1/2- to 4-quart

3 cups cauliflower florets
1 cup frozen cut green beans
1 cup sliced carrots (2 medium)
1/2 cup chopped onion (1 medium)
1 15-ounce can garbanzo beans (chickpeas), rinsed and drained
1 14-ounce can vegetable broth
2 to 3 teaspoons curry powder
1 14-ounce can light coconut milk
1/4 cup shredded fresh basil leaves

1. In a 3 1/2- to 4-quart slow cooker combine cauliflower, green beans, carrots, onion, and drained garbanzo beans. Stir in broth and curry powder.

2. Cover and cook on low-heat setting for 5 to 6 hours or on high-heat setting for 2 1/2 to 3 hours. Stir in coconut milk and basil.

Nutrition Facts per serving: 219 cal., 7 g total fat (4 g sat. fat), 0 mg chol., 805 mg sodium, 32 g carbo., 9 g fiber, 8 g pro.
Daily Values: 81% vit. A, 71% vit. C, 9% calcium, 16% iron
Exchanges: 1 1/2 Vegetable, 1 Starch, 1/2 Other Carbo., 1/2 Very Lean Meat, 1 Fat

Chapter 6

SOUPS
&
Stews

Not familiar with barley? Look for it next to the rice at your local supermarket.

BEEF AND BARLEY SOUP

Prep:
15 minutes

Cook:
Low 7 hours,
High 3 1/2 hours

Makes:
4 main-dish servings

Slow Cooker Size:
3 1/2- to 4 1/2-quart

Nonstick cooking spray
12 ounces boneless beef chuck roast, cut into 1/2-inch pieces
4 cups water
1 10 1/2-ounce can condensed French onion soup
1 cup shredded carrots (2 medium)
1/2 cup regular barley
1 teaspoon dried thyme or oregano, crushed
Salt
Ground black pepper

1. Lightly coat a large skillet with nonstick cooking spray. Heat skillet over medium heat. Brown meat in hot skillet; drain off fat.

2. In a 3 1/2- to 4 1/2-quart slow cooker combine meat, water, soup, carrots, barley, and thyme.

3. Cover and cook on low-heat setting for 7 to 8 hours or on high-heat setting for 3 1/2 to 4 hours. Season to taste with salt and pepper.

Nutrition Facts per serving: 252 cal., 5 g total fat (1 g sat. fat), 52 mg chol., 684 mg sodium, 29 g carbo., 5 g fiber, 22 g pro. Daily Values: 156% vit. A, 7% vit. C, 4% calcium, 18% iron Exchanges: 1 Vegetable, 1 1/2 Starch, 2 Lean Meat

Shredded reduced-fat cheddar cheese and/or light dairy sour cream make great low-fat toppers for this cold-weather favorite.

HEARTY BEEF CHILI

1½	pounds beef chuck roast, cut into 1-inch cubes
2	cups low-sodium vegetable juice or tomato juice
2	cups chopped onions (2 large)
2	15- to 16-ounce cans black, red kidney, and/or garbanzo beans (chickpeas), rinsed and drained
1	14½-ounce can no-salt-added diced tomatoes, undrained
1½	cups chopped green sweet peppers (2 medium)
1	10-ounce can diced tomatoes and green chile peppers, undrained
1	teaspoon ground chipotle chile pepper
1	teaspoon ground cumin
1	teaspoon dried oregano, crushed
3	cloves garlic, minced

Prep:
20 minutes

Cook:
Low 9 hours,
High 4 ½ hours

Makes:
8 to 10 main-dish servings

Slow Cooker Size:
4 ½- to 6-quart

1. In a 4½- to 6-quart slow cooker combine meat, vegetable juice, onions, drained beans, undrained tomatoes, sweet peppers, undrained tomatoes and green chile peppers, ground chipotle chile pepper, cumin, oregano, and garlic.

2. Cover and cook on low-heat setting for 9 to 10 hours or on high-heat setting for 4½ to 5 hours.

Nutrition Facts per serving: 226 cal., 4 g total fat (1 g sat. fat), 50 mg chol., 467 mg sodium, 27 g carbo., 8 g fiber, 26 g pro.
Daily Values: 23% vit. A, 70% vit. C, 9% calcium, 23% iron
Exchanges: 2 Vegetable, 1 Starch, 3 Very Lean Meat

Beer is a prominent ingredient in this hearty soup. If you want a lighter beer flavor, use a pale beer. Use a darker beer for a more pronounced beer taste.

BEEF AND BEER VEGETABLE SOUP

Prep:
25 minutes

Cook:
Low 10 hours, High 5 hours

Makes:
6 main-dish servings

Slow Cooker Size:
5- to 6-quart

3   medium onions, sliced
4   cups sliced, peeled parsnips (4 medium)
2½ cups sliced carrots (5 medium)
2   bay leaves
2   tablespoons quick-cooking tapioca
1   tablespoon snipped fresh thyme or 1 teaspoon dried thyme, crushed
¾   teaspoon salt
½   teaspoon ground black pepper
4   cloves garlic, minced
1½ pounds beef stew meat, cut into 1-inch cubes
1   14-ounce can beef broth
1   12-ounce can beer

1. In a 5- to 6-quart slow cooker place onions, parsnips, carrots, and bay leaves. Sprinkle with tapioca, dried thyme (if using), salt, pepper, and garlic. Add meat to cooker. Pour the beef broth and beer over all.

2. Cover and cook on low-heat setting for 10 to 12 hours or on high-heat setting for 5 to 6 hours. Remove and discard bay leaves. Stir in the fresh thyme, if using.

Nutrition Facts per serving: 344 cal., 7 g total fat (2 g sat. fat), 54 mg chol., 637 mg sodium, 38 g carbo., 7 g fiber, 29 g pro.
Daily Values: 341% vit. A, 37% vit. C, 8% calcium, 20% iron
Exchanges: 3 Vegetable, 1½ Starch, 3 Very Lean Meat, 1 Fat

Make this into a lamb soup by substituting lamb stew meat for the beef and replacing the thyme and basil with ³⁄₄ teaspoon dried rosemary and ³⁄₄ teaspoon dried mint.

BEEF AND RICE SOUP

1½ pounds beef stew meat, cut into 1-inch cubes
1 tablespoon cooking oil
2 medium yellow summer squash, halved lengthwise and cut into ½-inch slices (2½ cups)
1 cup sliced carrots (2 medium)
1 cup chopped onion (1 large)
¾ teaspoon dried thyme, crushed
¾ teaspoon dried basil, crushed
1 clove garlic, minced
6 cups reduced-sodium beef broth
¼ cup dry red or white wine (optional)
2 cups chopped fresh spinach
½ cup uncooked instant rice

1. In a large skillet brown meat, half at a time, in hot oil; drain fat.

2. Meanwhile, in a 4- to 6-quart slow cooker place squash, carrots, and onion. Add meat to cooker. Sprinkle with thyme, basil, and garlic. Pour broth and, if desired, wine over all.

3. Cover and cook on low-heat setting for 8 to 10 hours or on high-heat setting for 4 to 5 hours. Stir in spinach and rice. Cover and cook for 5 to 10 minutes more or until rice is tender.

Nutrition Facts per serving: 260 cal., 7 g total fat (2 g sat. fat), 67 mg chol., 541 mg sodium, 19 g carbo., 2 g fiber, 29 g pro. Daily Values: 66% vit. A, 22% vit. C, 5% calcium, 21% iron Exchanges: 1 Vegetable, 1 Starch, 3 Lean Meat

Prep:
20 minutes
Cook:
Low 8 hours, High 4 hours; plus 5 minutes
Makes:
6 main-dish servings
Slow Cooker Size:
4- to 6-quart

This soup derives its name from the marriage of meat and greens. Its many versions are based on the local availability of ingredients.

ITALIAN WEDDING SOUP

Prep:
30 minutes

Cook:
Low 8 hours, High 4 hours; plus 15 minutes on High

Makes:
8 main-dish servings

Slow Cooker Size:
5-quart

1　large onion
1　egg, slightly beaten
¼　cup fine dry bread crumbs
3　oil-packed dried tomatoes, drained and finely chopped
1　teaspoon dried Italian seasoning, crushed
1　pound lean ground beef
2　teaspoons olive oil
1　large fennel bulb (1 pound), trimmed and cut into thin wedges
1　teaspoon dried Italian seasoning, crushed
½　teaspoon ground white pepper
6　cloves garlic, minced
4　14-ounce cans reduced-sodium chicken broth
1　cup dried orzo
5　cups shredded fresh spinach

1. Finely chop ⅓ of the onion. Thinly slice the remaining onion; set sliced onion aside. In a bowl combine the chopped onion, egg, bread crumbs, dried tomatoes, and 1 teaspoon Italian seasoning. Add ground beef; mix well. Shape into 16 meatballs. In a large skillet cook meatballs in hot oil until brown; drain off fat.

2. In a 5-quart slow cooker place meatballs, reserved sliced onion, and fennel. Sprinkle with the remaining 1 teaspoon Italian seasoning, the white pepper, and garlic. Pour broth over all.

3. Cover and cook on low-heat setting for 8 to 10 hours or on high-heat setting for 4 to 5 hours.

4. If using low-heat setting, turn to high-heat setting. Gently stir orzo into cooker. Cover; cook for 15 minutes more. Stir in spinach.

Nutrition Facts per serving: 239 cal., 8 g total fat (3 g sat. fat), 62 mg chol., 619 mg sodium, 24 g carbo., 2 g fiber, 17 g pro.
Daily Values: 36% vit. A, 18% vit. C, 6% calcium, 16% iron
Exchanges: 1 Vegetable, 1 Starch, 2 Lean Meat, ½ Fat

This full-flavored soup calls for surprisingly few ingredients. If desired, you could substitute ground turkey for the ground beef.

EASY VEGETABLE–BEEF SOUP

1 pound lean ground beef
1 14½-ounce can tomatoes, cut up and undrained
1 14-ounce can reduced sodium beef broth
1 10¾-ounce can reduced-fat and reduced-sodium condensed tomato soup
1 10-ounce package frozen mixed vegetables
1¼ cups water
1 tablespoon dried minced onion
1 teaspoon dried Italian seasoning, crushed
¼ teaspoon garlic powder

1. In a large skillet cook beef until brown; drain off fat.

2. In a 3½- to 4-quart slow cooker combine beef, undrained tomatoes, broth, soup, frozen vegetables, water, dried onion, Italian seasoning, and garlic powder.

3. Cover and cook on low-heat setting for 7 to 8 hours or on high-heat setting for 3½ to 4 hours.

Nutrition Facts per serving: 311 cal., 12 g total fat (5 g sat. fat), 71 mg chol., 666 mg sodium, 26 g carbo., 5 g fiber, 25 g pro.
Daily Values: 79% vit. A, 36% vit. C, 7% calcium, 23% iron
Exchanges: 1 Vegetable, 1½ Other Carbo., 3 Lean Meat

Prep:
20 minutes

Cook:
Low 7 hours,
High 3 ½ hours

Makes:
4 to 6 main-dish servings

Slow Cooker Size:
3 ½- to 4-quart

Beef or pork stew meat substitutes deliciously for the lamb in this chunky soup.

LAMB AND BARLEY VEGETABLE SOUP

Prep:
25 minutes

Cook:
Low 6 hours, High 3 hours

Makes:
8 main-dish servings

Slow Cooker Size:
3 1/2- to 6-quart

1 1/2   pounds lamb stew meat, cut into 1-inch cubes
  2   cups sliced fresh mushrooms
  1   cup chopped onion (1 large)
  1   cup chopped, peeled parsnip (1 large)
  1/2   cup chopped carrot (1 medium)
  1/2   cup regular barley
  1   bay leaf
  1   teaspoon dried marjoram, crushed
  1/2   teaspoon salt
  1/4   teaspoon ground black pepper
  2   cloves garlic, minced
  4   cups beef broth
  1   14 1/2-ounce can Italian-style stewed tomatoes, undrained

1. In a 3 1/2- to 6-quart slow cooker place meat, mushrooms, onion, parsnip, carrot, barley, and bay leaf. Sprinkle with marjoram, salt, pepper, and garlic. Pour broth and undrained tomatoes over all.

2. Cover and cook on low-heat setting for 6 to 8 hours or on high-heat setting for 3 to 4 hours. Remove and discard bay leaf.

Nutrition Facts per serving: 212 cal., 4 g total fat (1 g sat. fat), 53 mg chol., 643 mg sodium, 20 g carbo., 4 g fiber, 23 g pro.
Daily Values: 39% vit. A, 8% vit. C, 4% calcium, 16% iron
Exchanges: 1 Vegetable, 1 Starch, 2 1/2 Very Lean Meat, 1/2 Fat

Balsamic vinegar and roasted red peppers add a new Italian angle to this utterly up-to-date soup. Both were once hard-to-find ingredients that are now widely available in the supermarket.

PORK AND RED PEPPER SOUP

1½ pounds boneless pork shoulder roast, cut into 1-inch cubes

2 14-ounce cans reduced-sodium beef broth

1 14½-ounce can diced tomatoes with basil, oregano, and garlic, undrained

1 cup roasted red sweet peppers, drained and cut into bite-size strips

½ cup chopped onion (1 medium)

2 tablespoons balsamic vinegar

¼ teaspoon ground black pepper

2 medium zucchini, halved lengthwise and cut into ¼-inch slices

Prep:
25 minutes

Cook:
Low 6 hours, High 3 hours; plus 15 minutes on High

Makes:
6 main-dish servings

Slow Cooker Size:
3 ½- to 4-quart

1. In a 3½- to 4-quart slow cooker combine meat, broth, undrained tomatoes, sweet peppers, onion, vinegar, and pepper.

2. Cover and cook on low-heat setting for 6 to 8 hours or on high-heat setting for 3 to 4 hours.

3. If using low-heat setting, turn to high-heat setting. Stir in zucchini. Cover and cook about 15 minutes more or until zucchini is crisp-tender.

Nutrition Facts per serving: 224 cal., 8 g total fat (3 g sat. fat), 76 mg chol., 689 mg sodium, 12 g carbo., 2 g fiber, 25 g pro. Daily Values: 10% vit. A, 137% vit. C, 7% calcium, 16% iron Exchanges: 1 Vegetable, ½ Other Carbo., 3 Lean Meat

Combine pork, hominy, and chili powder to make a flavorful rendition of posole. Hominy, dried corn that has had the hulls removed, is found in the canned vegetable section of supermarkets.

PORK AND HOMINY SOUP

Prep:
30 minutes

Cook:
Low 8 hours, High 4 hours

Makes:
6 main-dish servings

Slow Cooker Size:
3 ½- to 4-quart

1   pound boneless pork shoulder roast, cut into 1-inch cubes
1   tablespoon cooking oil
2   14½-ounce cans golden hominy, drained
¾   cup chopped red or green sweet pepper (1 medium)
½   cup chopped tomato (1 medium)
½   cup chopped onion (1 medium)
1   4-ounce can diced green chile peppers, undrained
1   tablespoon chili powder
½   teaspoon dried oregano, crushed
4   cloves garlic, minced
2   14-ounce cans reduced-sodium chicken broth
    Tortilla chips (optional)
    Light dairy sour cream (optional)

1. In a large skillet brown pork, half at a time, in hot oil; drain fat.

2. In a 3½- to 4-quart slow cooker place pork, drained hominy, sweet pepper, tomato, onion, and undrained chile peppers. Sprinkle with chili powder, oregano, and garlic. Pour broth over all.

3. Cover and cook on low-heat setting for 8 to 10 hours or on high-heat setting for 4 to 5 hours. If desired, serve with tortilla chips and sour cream.

Nutrition Facts per serving: 257 cal., 9 g total fat (2 g sat. fat), 49 mg chol., 732 mg sodium, 25 g carbo., 5 g fiber, 19 g pro.
Daily Values: 27% vit. A, 82% vit. C, 6% calcium, 13% iron
Exchanges: ½ Vegetable, 1½ Starch, 2 Lean Meat, ½ Fat

Put autumn's apple harvest to good use. In this recipe the apples dissolve to help thicken and sweeten the beef broth.

PORK, LENTIL, AND APPLE SOUP

Nonstick cooking spray
1 pound lean boneless pork, cut into ½-inch pieces
2 14-ounce cans reduced-sodium beef broth
3 cooking apples, peeled, cored, and cut up
1 cup brown lentils, rinsed and drained
1 teaspoon dried marjoram, crushed

1. Lightly coat a 12-inch skillet with nonstick cooking spray. Heat skillet over medium heat. Brown meat in hot skillet; drain off fat.

2. In a 3½-quart slow cooker combine meat, broth, apples, lentils, and marjoram.

3. Cover and cook on low-heat setting for 6 to 8 hours or on high-heat setting for 3 to 4 hours.

Nutrition Facts per serving: 394 cal., 8 g total fat (3 g sat. fat), 62 mg chol., 421 mg sodium, 42 g carbo., 17 g fiber, 40 g pro. Daily Values: 2% vit. A, 12% vit. C, 4% calcium, 27% iron Exchanges: 1 Fruit, 2 Starch, 5 Very Lean Meat

Prep:
20 minutes

Cook:
Low 6 hours, High 3 hours

Makes:
4 main-dish servings

Slow Cooker Size:
3 ½-quart

This sophisticated and tasty soup is packed full of winter vegetables. Fresh spinach added prior to serving provides a touch of color and a boost of nutrition.

SPICY PORK AND VEGETABLE SOUP

Prep:
30 minutes

Cook:
Low 10 hours, High 5 hours

Makes:
6 main-dish servings

Slow Cooker Size:
3 ½- to 4-quart

1   pound pork or beef stew meat, cut into ½-inch pieces
1   tablespoon cooking oil
½   cup chopped onion (1 medium)
1   teaspoon paprika
2   cloves garlic, minced
1½ cups chopped, peeled parsnips or carrots
     (2 or 3 medium)
1½ cups chopped, peeled winter squash (8 ounces)
1   cup chopped, peeled sweet potato (1 medium)
1   8¾-ounce can whole kernel corn, undrained
4   teaspoons instant beef bouillon granules
¼   teaspoon cayenne pepper
3   cups water
2   cups torn fresh spinach

1. In a large skillet brown half of the meat in hot oil. Remove meat; set aside. Brown remaining meat with onion, paprika, and minced garlic.

2. Meanwhile, in a 3½- to 4-quart slow cooker place parsnips, squash, sweet potato, and undrained corn. Add all of the meat and onion mixture to cooker. Sprinkle with bouillon granules and cayenne pepper. Pour water over all.

3. Cover and cook on low-heat setting for 10 to 11 hours or on high-heat setting for 5 to 5½ hours. Just before serving, add spinach to cooker; stir until slightly wilted.

Nutrition Facts per serving: 231 cal., 7 g total fat (2 g sat. fat), 41 mg chol., 681 mg sodium, 22 g carbo., 4 g fiber, 19 g pro.
Daily Values: 103% vit. A, 29% vit. C, 5% calcium, 8% iron
Exchanges: 1 Vegetable, 1 Starch, 2 Lean Meat

Unlike dry beans, lentils simmer to perfection in the slow cooker without precooking. In this soup, lemon peel and spinach enhance the nutty flavor of lentils.

HAM AND LENTIL SOUP

1 cup brown lentils, rinsed and drained
1 cup chopped celery (2 stalks)
1 cup sliced carrots (2 medium)
½ cup chopped onion (1 medium)
4 cups water
1½ teaspoons instant chicken bouillon granules
½ teaspoon finely shredded lemon peel
⅛ to ¼ teaspoon cayenne pepper
2 cloves garlic, minced
1 cup chopped cooked low-fat, reduced-sodium ham
2 cups chopped fresh spinach

Prep:
15 minutes

Cook:
Low 7 hours,
High 3 ½ hours;
plus 10 minutes on High

Makes:
4 to 6 main-dish servings

Slow Cooker Size:
3 ½- to 4-quart

1. In a 3½- to 4-quart slow cooker combine lentils, celery, carrots, and onion. Stir in water, bouillon granules, lemon peel, cayenne pepper, and garlic.

2. Cover and cook on low-heat setting for 7 to 8 hours or on high-heat setting for 3½ to 4 hours. If using low-heat setting, turn to high-heat setting. Add ham to cooker. Cover and cook for 10 minutes more. Stir in spinach.

Nutrition Facts per serving: 230 cal., 2 g total fat (1 g sat. fat), 15 mg chol., 785 mg sodium, 35 g carbo., 17 g fiber, 21 g pro.
Daily Values: 105% vit. A, 36% vit. C, 7% calcium, 29% iron
Exchanges: 1 Vegetable, 2 Starch, 2 Very Lean Meat

Slices of mushrooms, slivers of bok choy, and chunks of turkey mingle in a soy- and ginger-scented broth, giving stir-fry flavors to this savory soup.

ASIAN TURKEY AND RICE SOUP

Prep:
25 minutes

Cook:
Low 7 hours,
High 3 ½ hours;
plus 10 minutes on High

Makes:
6 main-dish servings

Slow Cooker Size:
3 ½- to 4-quart

1 pound turkey breast tenderloin or skinless, boneless chicken breast halves, cut into 1-inch pieces
2 cups sliced fresh mushrooms, such as shiitake or button
2 14-ounce cans reduced-sodium chicken broth
1½ cups water
1 cup carrots cut into thin bite-size strips (2 medium)
½ cup chopped onion (1 medium)
2 tablespoons reduced-sodium soy sauce
2 teaspoons grated fresh ginger
4 cloves garlic, minced
1½ cups sliced bok choy
1 cup uncooked instant brown rice

1. In a 3½- to 4-quart slow cooker combine turkey, mushrooms, broth, water, carrots, onion, soy sauce, ginger, and garlic.

2. Cover and cook on low-heat setting for 7 to 8 hours or on high-heat setting for 3½ to 4 hours. If using low-heat setting, turn to high-heat setting. Stir in bok choy and rice. Cover and cook for 10 to 15 minutes more or until rice is tender.

Nutrition Facts per serving: 166 cal., 2 g total fat (0 g sat. fat), 45 mg chol., 572 mg sodium, 15 g carbo., 2 g fiber, 22 g pro.
Daily Values: 60% vit. A, 17% vit. C, 5% calcium, 8% iron
Exchanges: 1 Vegetable, 1 Starch, 1 Very Lean Meat

Basic, comforting flavor and thick texture make this chowder a nice choice any night of the week.

NACHO CHEESE CHICKEN CHOWDER

1 pound skinless, boneless chicken breast halves, cut into ½-inch pieces
2 14½-ounce cans Mexican-style stewed tomatoes, undrained
1 10¾-ounce can condensed nacho cheese soup
1 10-ounce package frozen whole kernel corn
⅓ cup shredded taco cheese or cheddar cheese

1. In a 3½- to 4-quart slow cooker combine chicken, undrained tomatoes, soup, and corn.

2. Cover; cook on low-heat setting for 4 to 5 hours or on high-heat setting for 2 to 2½ hours. Sprinkle each serving with cheese.

Nutrition Facts per serving: 244 cal., 6 g total fat (3 g sat. fat), 55 mg chol., 647 mg sodium, 24 g carbo., 2 g fiber, 23 g pro.
Daily Values: 24% vit. A, 8% vit. C, 12% calcium, 6% iron
Exchanges: 2 Vegetable, 1 Starch, 2 Very Lean Meat, 1 Fat

Prep:
10 minutes

Cook:
Low 4 hours, High 2 hours

Makes:
6 main-dish servings

Slow Cooker Size:
3½- to 4-quart

All the world loves the comforting, restorative quality of chicken noodle soup. Why not expand your horizons and your health—next time, try it Asian style.

ASIAN CHICKEN SOUP WITH NOODLES

Prep:
20 minutes

Cook:
Low 8 hours, High 4 hours

Makes:
6 main-dish servings

Slow Cooker Size:
3 ½- to 4-quart

2 cups sliced fresh mushrooms. such as shiitake or button
1 cup bias-sliced carrots (2 medium)
1 medium onion, cut into thin wedges
1 pound skinless, boneless chicken breast halves, cut into 1-inch pieces
2 14-ounce cans reduced-sodium chicken broth
2 tablespoons reduced-sodium soy sauce
2 teaspoons grated fresh ginger
2 cloves garlic, minced
3 cups shredded Swiss chard or shredded fresh spinach
8 ounces Chinese egg noodles or rice sticks
   Fresh cilantro leaves (optional)
   Chili oil (optional)

1. In a 3½- to 4-quart slow cooker place mushrooms, carrots, and onion. Add chicken to cooker. Combine broth, soy sauce, ginger, and garlic. Pour over all.

2. Cover and cook on low-heat setting for 8 to 10 hours or on high-heat setting for 4 to 5 hours. Stir in Swiss chard. Cover and cook 5 minutes more.

3. Meanwhile, cook egg noodles according to package directions. Divide cooked noodles among serving bowls. Ladle soup over noodles. If desired, top each serving with cilantro leaves and sprinkle with chili oil.

Nutrition Facts per serving: 270 cal., 3 g total fat (1 g sat. fat), 80 mg chol., 605 mg sodium, 33 g carbo., 2 g fiber, 26 g pro. Daily Values: 67% vit. A, 13% vit. C, 4% calcium, 14% iron Exchanges: 1 Vegetable, 1½ Starch, 3 Very Lean Meat, ½ Fat

You can count on old basic favorites like this one to please time after time. The thyme lends an aromatic garden quality.

CHUNKY CHICKEN–VEGETABLE SOUP

1¼ pounds skinless, boneless chicken thighs, cut into
     ½- to ¾-inch pieces
1   20-ounce package refrigerated diced potatoes with
     onions
1   16-ounce package frozen loose-pack broccoli,
     cauliflower, and carrots
2   14-ounce cans reduced-sodium chicken broth
1¾   cups water
1   10¾-ounce can reduced-fat and reduced-sodium
     condensed cream of chicken soup
1   teaspoon dried thyme, crushed

1. In a 4½- to 6-quart slow cooker combine chicken, potatoes, frozen vegetables, broth, water, soup, and thyme.

2. Cover and cook on low-heat setting for 7 to 8 hours or on high-heat setting for 3½ to 4 hours.

Nutrition Facts per serving: 201 cal., 3 g total fat (1 g sat. fat), 60 mg chol., 662 mg sodium, 22 g carbo., 3 g fiber, 19 g pro. Daily Values: 25% vit. A, 39% vit. C, 7% calcium, 8% iron Exchanges: 1 Vegetable, 1 Starch, 2 Very Lean Meat, ½ Fat

Prep:
15 minutes

Cook:
Low 7 hours,
High 3 ½ hours

Makes:
8 main-dish servings

Slow Cooker Size:
4 ½- to 6-quart

This streamlined soup version of the classic French specialty is delicious served with crusty bread.

EASY CASSOULET SOUP

Prep:
20 minutes

Cook:
Low 7 hours,
High 3 ½ hours

Makes:
6 to 8 main-dish servings

Slow Cooker Size:
3 ½- to 5-quart

1   cup chopped carrots (2 medium)
1   cup chopped onion (1 large)
¾   cup chopped red or green sweet pepper (1 medium)
2   15-ounce cans white kidney beans (cannellini beans) or Great Northern beans, rinsed and drained
8   ounces skinless, boneless chicken thighs, cut into 1-inch pieces
8   ounces cooked smoked turkey sausage, halved lengthwise and cut into ½-inch slices
1   bay leaf
1   tablespoon snipped fresh parsley
1   teaspoon dried thyme, crushed
⅛   to ¼ teaspoon cayenne pepper
3   cloves garlic, minced
1   14½-ounce can Italian-style stewed tomatoes, undrained
1½ cups reduced-sodium chicken broth
½   cup dry white wine or reduced-sodium chicken broth

1. In a 3½- to 5-quart slow cooker place carrots, onion, and sweet pepper. Add drained beans, chicken, sausage, and bay leaf to cooker. Sprinkle with parsley, thyme, cayenne pepper, and garlic. Combine undrained tomatoes, broth, and wine. Pour over all.

2. Cover and cook on low-heat setting for 7 to 8 hours or on high-heat setting for 3½ to 4 hours. Remove and discard bay leaf.

Nutrition Facts per serving: 260 cal., 6 g total fat (1 g sat. fat), 56 mg chol., 890 mg sodium, 31 g carbo., 9 g fiber, 23 g pro.
Daily Values: 64% vit. A, 73% vit. C, 8% calcium, 18% iron
Exchanges: 1 Vegetable, 1 Starch, ½ Other Carbo., 2½ Lean Meat

Biscuits and a crisp green salad topped with citrus slices and your favorite vinaigrette round out a meal nicely.

SPINACH, CHICKEN, AND WILD RICE SOUP

3 cups water
1 14-ounce can chicken broth
1 10¾-ounce can condensed cream of chicken soup
⅔ cup uncooked wild rice, rinsed and drained
½ teaspoon dried thyme, crushed
¼ teaspoon ground black pepper
3 cups chopped cooked chicken or turkey
2 cups shredded fresh spinach

1. In a 3½- to 4-quart slow cooker combine water, broth, soup, wild rice, thyme, and pepper.

2. Cover and cook on low-heat setting for 7 to 8 hours or on high-heat setting for 3½ to 4 hours. Just before serving, stir in chicken and spinach.

Nutrition Facts per serving: 263 cal., 9 g total fat (3 g sat. fat), 66 mg chol., 741 mg sodium, 19 g carbo., 2 g fiber, 25 g pro.
Daily Values: 19% vit. A, 5% vit. C, 4% calcium, 10% iron
Exchanges: ½ Vegetable, 1 Starch, 3 Very Lean Meat, 1½ Fat

Prep:
15 minutes

Cook:
Low 7 hours,
High 3 ½ hours

Makes:
6 main-dish servings

Slow Cooker Size:
3 ½- to 4-quart

This easy fix-up will please the entire family. If desired, you could substitute 10 ounces frozen cut broccoli for the mixed vegetables.

CREAMY CHICKEN NOODLE SOUP

Prep:
15 minutes

Cook:
Low 6 hours, High 3 hours;
plus 20 minutes on High

Makes:
6 to 8 main-dish servings

Slow Cooker Size:
3 1/2- to 4-quart

5   cups water
2   10¾-ounce cans reduced-fat and reduced-sodium condensed cream of chicken soup
2   cups chopped cooked chicken
1   10-ounce package frozen mixed vegetables
1   teaspoon seasoned pepper or garlic-pepper seasoning
1½   cups dried egg noodles

1. In a 3½- to 4-quart slow cooker gradually stir or whisk the water into the soup until smooth. Stir in chicken, frozen vegetables, and seasoned pepper.

2. Cover and cook on low-heat setting for 6 to 8 hours or on high-heat setting for 3 to 4 hours.

3. If using low-heat setting, turn to high-heat setting. Stir in noodles. Cover and cook for 20 to 30 minutes more or until noodles are just tender.

Nutrition Facts per serving: 215 cal., 6 g total fat (1 g sat. fat), 60 mg chol., 502 mg sodium, 23 g carbo., 2 g fiber, 18 g pro.
Daily Values: 44% vit. A, 7% vit. C, 2% calcium, 9% iron
Exchanges: ½ Vegetable, 1 Other Carbo., 2 Very Lean Meat, 1 Fat

This hearty recipe can easily be made into a tasty meatless version by omitting the cooked chicken.

BEAN SOUP WITH CHICKEN AND VEGGIES

1	cup dry Great Northern beans
6	cups water
1⅓	cups chopped fennel (1 medium)
1	cup chopped onion (1 medium)
1	cup chopped carrots (2 medium)
1	teaspoon dried thyme, crushed
1	teaspoon dried marjoram, crushed
¼	teaspoon ground black pepper
2	cloves garlic, minced
3	14-ounce cans reduced-sodium chicken broth
2½	cups chopped cooked chicken
1	14½-ounce can diced tomatoes, undrained
2	tablespoons snipped fresh parsley

Prep:
30 minutes

Stand:
1 hour

Cook:
Low 8 hours, High 4 hours; plus 30 minutes on High

Makes:
6 main-dish servings

Slow Cooker Size:
4- to 5-quart

1. Rinse beans; place in a large saucepan. Add water. Bring to boiling; reduce heat. Simmer, uncovered, for 10 minutes. Remove from heat. Cover and let stand for 1 hour. Drain and rinse beans.

2. Meanwhile, in a 4- to 5-quart slow cooker place fennel, onion, and carrots. Sprinkle with thyme, marjoram, pepper, and garlic. Add drained beans to cooker. Pour broth over all.

3. Cover and cook on low-heat setting for 8 to 10 hours or on high-heat setting for 4 to 5 hours.

4. If using low-heat setting, turn to high-heat setting. Stir in chicken and undrained tomatoes. Cover and cook for 30 minutes more. Stir in parsley.

Nutrition Facts per serving: 273 cal., 5 g total fat (1 g sat. fat), 52 mg chol., 666 mg sodium, 30 g carbo., 8 g fiber, 26 g pro.
Daily Values: 48% vit. A, 26% vit. C, 11% calcium, 17% iron
Exchanges: 1 Vegetable, 1½ Starch, 3 Very Lean Meat, ½ Fat

Just drop the already seasoned and cooked chicken strips into the hot soup to heat through. The torn tortillas take the place of pasta or rice.

TEX-MEX CHICKEN SOUP

Prep:
20 minutes

Cook:
Low 8 hours, High 4 hours;
plus 15 minutes on High

Makes:
8 main-dish servings

Slow Cooker Size:
3 1/2- to 4-quart

2	cups water
1	14½-ounce can diced tomatoes, undrained
1	14-ounce can beef broth
1	8-ounce can tomato sauce
½	cup chopped onion (1 medium)
1	4-ounce can diced green chile peppers, undrained
1	teaspoon ground cumin
1	teaspoon chili powder
1	teaspoon Worcestershire sauce
½	teaspoon garlic powder
1	9-ounce package frozen cooked Southwestern-flavor chicken breast strips, thawed
8	to 10 corn tortillas, torn into 1- to 2-inch pieces
¾	cup shredded cheddar cheese or Monterey Jack cheese with jalapeño peppers (3 ounces)

1. In a 3½- to 4-quart slow cooker combine water, undrained tomatoes, broth, tomato sauce, onion, undrained chile peppers, cumin, chili powder, Worcestershire sauce, and garlic powder.

2. Cover and cook on low-heat setting for 8 to 10 hours or on high-heat setting for 4 to 5 hours.

3. If using low-heat setting, turn to high-heat setting. Stir in chicken strips. Cover and cook for 15 minutes more. Stir in tortilla pieces. Serve immediately. Sprinkle each serving with cheese.

Nutrition Facts per serving: 189 cal., 6 g total fat (3 g sat. fat), 26 mg chol., 615 mg sodium, 22 g carbo., 2 g fiber, 13 g pro.
Daily Values: 5% vit. A, 20% vit. C, 16% calcium, 14% iron
Exchanges: 1 Vegetable, 1 Starch, 1 Lean Meat, ½ Fat

Leaner ground turkey stands in for ground beef in this veggie-filled soup.

HEARTY TURKEY AND VEGETABLE SOUP

1	pound uncooked ground turkey
1	cup chopped celery (2 stalks)
½	cup thinly sliced carrot (1 medium)
2½	cups reduced-sodium tomato juice
1	14½-ounce can French-cut green beans, drained
1	cup sliced fresh mushrooms
½	cup chopped tomato (1 medium)
1	tablespoon dried minced onion
1½	teaspoons Worcestershire sauce
1	teaspoon dried basil, crushed
1	teaspoon dried oregano, crushed
½	teaspoon garlic powder
½	teaspoon sugar
¼	teaspoon salt
¼	teaspoon ground black pepper
1	bay leaf

Prep:
25 minutes

Cook:
Low 6 hours,
High 2 ½ hours

Makes:
4 to 6 main-dish servings

Slow Cooker Size:
3 ½- to 4-quart

1. In a large skillet cook turkey, celery, and carrot until turkey is no longer pink; drain off fat.

2. In a 3½- to 4-quart slow cooker combine turkey mixture, tomato juice, drained green beans, mushrooms, tomato, onion, Worcestershire sauce, basil, oregano, garlic powder, sugar, salt, pepper, and bay leaf.

3. Cover and cook on low-heat setting for 6 hours or on high-heat setting for 2½ to 3 hours. Remove and discard bay leaf.

Nutrition Facts per serving: 238 cal., 10 g total fat (3 g sat. fat), 90 mg chol., 662 mg sodium, 15 g carbo., 5 g fiber, 23 g pro.
Daily Values: 47% vit. A, 36% vit. C, 7% calcium, 17% iron
Exchanges: 2 Vegetable, 2½ Lean Meat, 1 Fat

Instead of ordering out, declare clam chowder a Friday-night tradition at your house. Fragrant dill gives this mild soup a colorful presentation. Serve the chowder in warm bowls.

CREAMY CLAM CHOWDER

Prep:
10 minutes

Cook:
Low 6 hours, High 3 hours;
plus 15 minutes on High

Makes:
6 main-dish servings

Slow Cooker Size:
3 1/2- to 4-quart

3   6½-ounce cans minced clams
3   cups chopped, peeled potatoes (3 medium)
1   10¾-ounce can condensed cream of onion soup
½   teaspoon dried dill
2   to 3 cups fat-free half-and-half or light cream

1. Drain clams, reserving liquid. Cover clams and refrigerate until needed. If necessary, add water to clam liquid to equal 1¾ cups.

2. In a 3½- to 4-quart slow cooker combine clam liquid and potatoes. Stir in soup and dill.

3. Cover and cook on low-heat setting for 6 to 8 hours or on high-heat setting for 3 to 4 hours. If using low-heat setting, turn to high-heat setting. Stir in clams and enough half-and-half to make desired consistency. Cover and cook for 15 minutes more or until heated through.

Nutrition Facts per serving: 280 cal., 4 g total fat (1 g sat. fat), 68 mg chol., 547 mg sodium, 28 g carbo., 1 g fiber, 28 g pro. Daily Values: 13% vit. A, 47% vit. C, 14% calcium, 146% iron Exchanges: 1 Starch, 1 Other Carbo., 3 Very Lean Meat, ½ Fat

To save time and retain nutrients, don't peel the potatoes. Just scrub them well.

MANHATTAN-STYLE CLAM CHOWDER

2 6½-ounce cans minced clams or one 10-ounce can baby clams

2 cups chopped, peeled potatoes (2 medium)

1 14½-ounce can Italian-style stewed tomatoes, undrained

1½ cups hot-style tomato juice or hot-style vegetable juice

1 cup chopped onion (1 large)

1 cup chopped celery (2 stalks)

½ cup chopped green sweet pepper (1 small)

½ teaspoon dried thyme, crushed

1 bay leaf

4 slices bacon, crisp-cooked, drained, and crumbled, or ¼ cup cooked bacon pieces

Prep:
20 minutes

Cook:
Low 8 hours, High 4 hours; plus 5 minutes on High

Makes:
4 main-dish servings

Slow Cooker Size:
3 ½- to 4-quart

1. Drain clams, reserving liquid. Cover clams; refrigerate until needed.

2. In a 3½- to 4-quart slow cooker combine reserved clam liquid, potatoes, undrained tomatoes, tomato juice, onion, celery, sweet pepper, thyme, and bay leaf. Cover and cook on low-heat setting for 8 to 10 hours or on high-heat setting for 4 to 5 hours.

3. If using low-heat setting, turn to high-heat setting. Stir in clams. Cover and cook for 5 minutes more. Remove and discard bay leaf. Sprinkle each serving with bacon.

Nutrition Facts per serving: 238 cal., 5 g total fat (1 g sat. fat), 34 mg chol., 719 mg sodium, 30 g carbo., 4 g fiber, 17 g pro.
Daily Values: 19% vit. A, 92% vit. C, 10% calcium, 78% iron
Exchanges: 3 Vegetable, 1 Starch, 1 Very Lean Meat, 1 Fat

Thick and chunky, this chowder measures up. Halibut and haddock are fine substitutes for the cod.

HEARTY FISH CHOWDER

Prep:
25 minutes

Cook:
Low 6 hours, High 3 hours;
plus 1 hour on High

Makes:
6 main-dish servings

Slow Cooker Size:
3 1/2- to 4-quart

1   pound fresh or frozen skinless cod or other whitefish
    fillets
2   cups finely chopped potatoes (2 medium)
1 1/2   cups reduced-sodium chicken broth
1   10¾-ounce can reduced-fat and reduced-sodium
    condensed cream of celery soup
1   10-ounce package frozen whole kernel corn
1   10-ounce package frozen baby lima beans
1   cup chopped onion (1 large)
⅓   cup dry white wine or reduced-sodium chicken broth
1   teaspoon lemon-pepper seasoning
2   cloves garlic, minced
1   14½-ounce can stewed tomatoes, undrained
⅓   cup nonfat dry milk powder

1. Thaw fish, if frozen. Rinse fish; pat dry. Cover fish and refrigerate until needed.

2. In a 3½- to 4-quart slow cooker combine potatoes, broth, soup, corn, lima beans, onion, wine, lemon-pepper seasoning, and garlic.

3. Cover and cook on low-heat setting for 6 to 7 hours or on high-heat setting for 3 to 3½ hours. If using low-heat setting, turn to high-heat setting. Place fish on soup mixture in cooker. Cover and cook for 1 hour more.

4. Add undrained tomatoes and dry milk powder to cooker, stirring gently to break up the fish.

Nutrition Facts per serving: 291 cal., 3 g total fat (1 g sat. fat), 35 mg chol., 707 mg sodium, 43 g carbo., 6 g fiber, 22 g pro.
Daily Values: 5% vit. A, 28% vit. C, 15% calcium, 14% iron
Exchanges: 1 Vegetable, 2 Starch, ½ Other Carbo., 2 Very Lean Meat

Combine lentils with vegetables to make a thick and satisfying soup that is perfect for a cold-weather meal.

LENTIL–VEGGIE SOUP

1	cup brown lentils, rinsed and drained
1	cup chopped carrots (2 medium)
1	cup chopped celery (2 stalks)
1	cup chopped onion (1 large)
1	bay leaf
½	teaspoon dried basil, crushed
½	teaspoon dried oregano, crushed
¼	teaspoon dried thyme, crushed
2	cloves garlic, minced
2	14-ounce cans vegetable broth or chicken broth
1½	cups water
1	14½-ounce can Italian-style stewed tomatoes, undrained
¼	cup snipped fresh parsley

Prep:
20 minutes

Cook:
Low 12 hours, High 5 hours

Makes:
6 main-dish servings

Slow Cooker Size:
3 ½- to 4-quart

1. In a 3½- to 4-quart slow cooker place lentils, carrots, celery, onion, and bay leaf. Sprinkle with basil, oregano, thyme, and garlic. Combine broth, water, and undrained tomatoes. Pour over all.

2. Cover and cook on low-heat setting for 12 hours or on high-heat setting for 5 to 6 hours. Remove and discard bay leaf. Stir in parsley.

Nutrition Facts per serving: 165 cal., 1 g total fat (0 g sat. fat), 0 mg chol., 713 mg sodium, 30 g carbo., 12 g fiber, 11 g pro.
Daily Values: 126% vit. A, 20% vit. C, 7% calcium, 20% iron
Exchanges: 1½ Vegetable, 1½ Starch, ½ Very Lean Meat

A small amount of sour cream heightens the flavor of this main-dish soup. Add a dollop to each bowl prior to serving.

CREAMY–STYLE LENTIL SOUP

Prep:
15 minutes

Cook:
Low 6 hours,
High 3 1/2 hours

Makes:
4 main-dish servings

Slow Cooker Size:
3 1/2- to 4-quart

3 cups water
1 10¾-ounce can reduced-fat and reduced-sodium condensed cream of mushroom soup
1 cup sliced carrots (2 medium)
1 cup sliced celery (1 stalk)
¾ cup brown lentils, rinsed and drained
½ cup chopped onion (1 medium)
1 teaspoon instant beef bouillon granules
¼ cup snipped fresh parsley
¼ cup dairy sour cream

1. In a 3½- to 4-quart slow cooker combine water, soup, carrots, celery, lentils, onion, and bouillon granules.

2. Cover and cook on low-heat setting for 6 to 8 hours or on high-heat setting for 3½ to 4½ hours. Stir in parsley. Top each serving with sour cream.

Nutrition Facts per serving: 215 cal., 4 g total fat (2 g sat. fat), 8 mg chol., 560 mg sodium, 33 g carbo., 13 g fiber, 12 g pro.
Daily Values: 84% vit. A, 17% vit. C, 6% calcium, 8% iron
Exchanges: ½ Vegetable, 1½ Starch, ½ Other Carbo., 1 Very Lean Meat, ½ Fat

The blend of spices in garam masala can include cinnamon, nutmeg, cloves, coriander, cumin, cardamom, pepper, chiles, fennel, and mace.

BUTTERNUT SQUASH AND LENTIL SOUP

2½ cups coarsely chopped butternut squash
1 cup brown lentils, rinsed and drained
½ cup chopped onion (1 medium)
½ cup chopped carrot (1 medium)
½ cup chopped celery (1 stalk)
1 teaspoon garam masala
2 cloves garlic, minced
4 cups chicken broth or vegetable broth

1. In a 3½- to 4-quart slow cooker place squash, lentils, onion, carrot, and celery. Sprinkle with garam masala and garlic. Pour broth over all.

2. Cover and cook on low-heat setting for 8 to 9 hours or on high-heat setting for 4 to 4½ hours.

Nutrition Facts per serving: 199 cal., 2 g total fat (0 g sat. fat), 0 mg chol., 639 mg sodium, 31 g carbo., 13 g fiber, 16 g pro.
Daily Values: 107% vit. A, 17% vit. C, 6% calcium, 22% iron
Exchanges: 1 Vegetable, 1½ Starch, 1½ Very Lean Meat

Prep:
25 minutes

Cook:
Low 8 hours, High 4 hours

Makes:
5 to 6 main-dish servings

Slow Cooker Size:
3½- to 4-quart

Control the level of heat in this chunky chili by choosing a mild or spicy salsa. Serve with warm cornmeal biscuits.

VEGETARIAN CHILI

Prep:
25 minutes

Cook:
Low 8 hours, High 4 hours

Makes:
6 main-dish servings

Slow Cooker Size:
3 ½- to 5-quart

1 15-ounce can black beans, rinsed and drained
2 14½-ounce cans diced tomatoes, undrained
1 10-ounce package frozen whole kernel corn
1 medium zucchini, halved lengthwise and cut into ½-inch slices
1 cup bottled salsa
¾ cup coarsely chopped green sweet pepper (1 medium)
½ cup chopped onion (1 medium)
½ cup sliced celery (1 stalk)
2 to 3 teaspoons chili powder
1 teaspoon dried oregano, crushed
½ teaspoon ground cumin
¾ cup shredded cheddar cheese (3 ounces)
⅓ cup light dairy sour cream

1. In a 3½- to 5-quart slow cooker combine drained beans, undrained tomatoes, corn, zucchini, salsa, sweet pepper, onion, celery, chili powder, oregano, and cumin.

2. Cover and cook on low-heat setting for 8 to 10 hours or on high-heat setting for 4 to 5 hours. Top each serving with cheese and sour cream.

Nutrition Facts per serving: 220 cal., 7 g total fat (4 g sat. fat), 19 mg chol., 609 mg sodium, 33 g carbo., 7 g fiber, 12 g pro.
Daily Values: 18% vit. A, 67% vit. C, 23% calcium, 13% iron
Exchanges: 2 Vegetable, 1½ Starch, ½ Very Lean Meat, 1 Fat

Finely chop the onion to ensure that it is fully cooked when you're ready to serve this family-style supper.

VEGETABLE CHILI WITH PASTA

1   15-ounce can garbanzo beans (chickpeas), rinsed and drained
1   15-ounce can red kidney beans, rinsed and drained
2   14½-ounce cans no-salt-added diced tomatoes, undrained
1   8-ounce can tomato sauce
1   cup finely chopped onion (1 large)
½   cup chopped green or yellow sweet pepper (1 small)
2   to 3 teaspoons chili powder
½   teaspoon dried oregano, crushed
⅛   teaspoon cayenne pepper (optional)
2   cloves garlic, minced
1   cup dried wagon wheel macaroni or elbow macaroni
    Shredded cheddar cheese (optional)

1. In a 3½- to 4-quart slow cooker combine drained garbanzo beans, drained kidney beans, undrained tomatoes, tomato sauce, onion, sweet pepper, chili powder, oregano, cayenne pepper (if desired), and garlic.

2. Cover and cook on low-heat setting for 4 to 5 hours or on high-heat setting for 2 to 2½ hours.

3. Meanwhile, cook pasta according to package directions; drain. Stir in pasta. If desired, sprinkle each serving with cheese.

Nutrition Facts per serving: 294 cal., 2 g total fat (0 g sat. fat), 0 mg chol., 692 mg sodium, 59 g carbo., 13 g fiber, 15 g pro.
Daily Values: 20% vit. A, 41% vit. C, 10% calcium, 19% iron
Exchanges: 1½ Vegetable, 2 Starch, 1½ Other Carbo., 1 Very Lean Meat

Prep:
20 minutes
Cook:
Low 4 hours, High 2 hours
Makes:
5 main-dish servings
Slow Cooker Size:
3 ½- to 4-quart

To reduce the amount of heat in this south-of-the-border soup, use Monterey Jack cheese without the jalapeño peppers.

SPICY BEAN SOUP

Prep:
15 minutes

Cook:
Low 8 hours, High 4 hours

Makes:
8 main-dish servings

Slow Cooker Size:
3 1/2- to 6-quart

1   15-ounce can red kidney beans, rinsed and drained
1   15-ounce can garbanzo beans (chickpeas), rinsed and drained
1   15-ounce can navy beans, rinsed and drained
2   14-ounce cans reduced-sodium beef broth
1   10-ounce package frozen lima beans
1   9-ounce package frozen cut green beans
1   cup chopped onion (1 large)
3/4   cup water
4   teaspoons chili powder
1 1/2   teaspoons dried basil, crushed
1/2   teaspoon dried oregano, crushed
1   cup shredded Monterey Jack cheese with jalapeño peppers (4 ounces)

1. In a 3 1/2- to 6-quart slow cooker combine drained kidney beans, drained garbanzo beans, drained navy beans, broth, lima beans, green beans, onion, water, chili powder, basil, and oregano.

2. Cover and cook on low-heat setting for 8 to 9 hours or on high-heat setting for 4 to 4 1/2 hours. Stir in cheese until melted.

Nutrition Facts per serving: 281 cal., 6 g total fat (3 g sat. fat), 12 mg chol., 846 mg sodium, 42 g carbo., 12 g fiber, 19 g pro.
Daily Values: 12% vit. A, 7% vit. C, 19% calcium, 18% iron
Exchanges: 1/2 Vegetable, 2 1/2 Starch, 2 Very Lean Meat

Set out an assortment of toppings—sour cream, chopped avocado, sliced green onions, and/or chopped tomatoes—and warm corn bread to accompany this soup.

BLACK BEAN SOUP

1	pound dry black beans
12	cups water
1	cup coarsely chopped carrots (2 medium)
1	cup coarsely chopped onion (1 large)
1	cup coarsely chopped celery (2 stalks)
2	large* vegetable bouillon cubes
2	teaspoons ground cumin
2	teaspoons ground coriander
2	teaspoons dried savory, crushed
1	teaspoon chili powder
½	teaspoon ground black pepper
2	cloves garlic, minced
1	cup half-and-half or light cream

Prep:
25 minutes

Stand:
1 hour

Cook:
Low 12 hours, High 6 hours

Makes:
6 to 8 main-dish servings

Slow Cooker Size:
4- to 5 ½-quart

1. Rinse beans; place in a large saucepan. Add 6 cups of the water. Bring to boiling; reduce heat. Simmer, uncovered, for 10 minutes. Remove from heat. Cover and let stand for 1 hour. Drain; rinse beans.

2. In a 4- to 5½-quart slow cooker combine drained beans, the remaining 6 cups water, carrots, onion, celery, bouillon cubes, cumin, coriander, savory, chili powder, pepper, and garlic.

3. Cover and cook on low-heat setting for 12 to 14 hours or on high-heat setting for 6 to 7 hours. Just before serving, mash beans slightly. Stir in half-and-half.

*Note: Each large bouillon cube makes 2 cups broth.

Nutrition Facts per serving: 346 cal., 6 g total fat (3 g sat. fat), 15 mg chol., 706 mg sodium, 56 g carbo., 14 g fiber, 19 g pro. Daily Values: 110% vit. A, 8% vit. C, 17% calcium, 24% iron Exchanges: 1 Vegetable, 3½ Starch, 1 Very Lean Meat

Pair this full-flavored barley and vegetable soup with your family's favorite sandwich for a complete meal.

BARLEY–VEGETABLE SOUP

Prep:
20 minutes

Cook:
Low 8 hours, High 4 hours

Makes:
8 side-dish servings

Slow Cooker Size:
3 ½- to 5-quart

4	cups low-sodium tomato juice
2½	cups chopped zucchini (2 medium)
2	14-ounce cans reduced-sodium chicken broth
1½	cups coarsely chopped yellow and/or red sweet peppers (2 medium)
1	cup chopped onion (1 large)
½	cup regular barley
¼	teaspoon salt
¼	teaspoon ground black pepper
3	cloves garlic, minced

1. In a 3½- to 5-quart slow cooker combine tomato juice, zucchini, broth, sweet peppers, onion, barley, salt, black pepper, and garlic.

2. Cover and cook on low-heat setting for 8 to 9 hours or on high-heat setting for 4 to 4½ hours.

Nutrition Facts per serving: 100 cal., 0 g total fat (0 g sat. fat), 0 mg chol., 385 mg sodium, 20 g carbo., 4 g fiber, 4 g pro.
Daily Values: 11% vit. A, 205% vit. C, 3% calcium, 7% iron
Exchanges: 2 Vegetable, ½ Starch

If you have an immersion blender, use it to puree the soup mixture in the slow cooker instead of using a blender or food processor. Boost the protein in the meal with a chicken sandwich on whole wheat bread.

CURRIED WINTER VEGETABLE SOUP

4 cups chopped, peeled celeriac (2 pounds)
3 cups chopped, peeled butternut squash (1 pound)
2 14-ounce cans reduced-sodium chicken broth
½ cup chopped onion (1 medium)
2 tablespoons dry sherry
1 tablespoon grated fresh ginger
2 teaspoons curry powder
2 cloves garlic, minced
½ cup whipping cream
¼ cup sliced green onions (2)

Prep:
30 minutes

Cook:
Low 6 hours, High 3 hours

Makes:
8 to 10 side-dish servings

Slow Cooker Size:
3 ½- to 4-quart

1. In a 3½- to 4-quart slow cooker combine celeriac, squash, broth, onion, sherry, ginger, curry powder, and garlic. Cover and cook on low-heat setting for 6 to 8 hours or on high-heat setting for 3 to 4 hours.

2. Stir in cream. Transfer half of the soup mixture to a blender or food processor. Cover and blend or process until smooth. Repeat with remaining soup mixture. Sprinkle each serving with sliced green onions.

Nutrition Facts per serving: 126 cal., 6 g total fat (4 g sat. fat), 21 mg chol., 342 mg sodium, 15 g carbo., 3 g fiber, 3 g pro.
Daily Values: 15% vit. A, 19% vit. C, 7% calcium, 6% iron
Exchanges: ½ Vegetable, ½ Starch, ½ Other Carbo., 1 Fat

The bounty here is fresh veggies—tomatoes plus your choice of carrots, celery, sweet peppers, fennel, and onion. A classic grilled cheese sandwich is the perfect accompaniment.

GARDEN BOUNTY TOMATO SOUP

Prep:
25 minutes

Cook:
Low 6 hours, High 3 hours

Makes:
8 to 10 side-dish servings

Slow Cooker Size:
3 1/2- to 4-quart

2 pounds plum tomatoes, chopped
2 cups finely chopped fresh vegetables, such as carrots, celery, sweet peppers, fennel, and/or onion
2 14-ounce cans reduced-sodium beef broth
1 6-ounce can tomato paste
1 to 2 teaspoons sugar

1. In a 3½- to 4-quart slow cooker combine tomatoes, vegetables, broth, tomato paste, and sugar.

2. Cover and cook on low-heat setting for 6 to 8 hours or on high-heat setting for 3 to 4 hours.

Nutrition Facts per serving: 58 cal., 0 g total fat (0 g sat. fat), 0 mg chol., 221 mg sodium, 12 g carbo., 3 g fiber, 3 g pro.
Daily Values: 92% vit. A, 33% vit. C, 2% calcium, 4% iron
Exchanges: 2 Vegetable

This stew contains ingredients that are trademarks of the cooking in southeastern France—garlic, olives, and onions.

PROVENÇAL BEEF STEW

8 tiny new potatoes
1 16-ounce package fresh peeled baby carrots
1 cup coarsely chopped shallots or onion
½ cup pitted green or ripe olives
1½ pounds boneless beef chuck roast, cut into 2-inch cubes
1 tablespoon quick-cooking tapioca
1 teaspoon dried herbes de Provence, crushed
¼ teaspoon salt
¼ teaspoon cracked black pepper
4 to 6 cloves garlic, minced
1 cup beef broth
¼ cup dry red wine
Snipped fresh parsley (optional)
Capers (optional)

Prep:
20 minutes

Cook:
Low 10 hours, High 4 hours

Makes:
6 main-dish servings

Slow Cooker Size:
3 ½- to 4-quart

1. Peel a narrow strip from around the center of each potato. In a 3½- to 4-quart slow cooker place potatoes, carrots, shallots, and olives. Add meat to cooker. Sprinkle with tapioca, herbes de Provence, salt, pepper. and garlic. Pour broth over all.

2. Cover and cook on low-heat setting for 10 to 12 hours or on high-heat setting for 4 to 5 hours. Stir in wine during the last 30 minutes of cooking. If desired, sprinkle each serving with parsley and capers.

Nutrition Facts per serving: 198 cal., 5 g total fat (2 g sat. fat), 54 mg chol., 308 mg sodium, 16 g carbo., 3 g fiber, 20 g pro.
Daily Values: 293% vit. A, 17% vit. C, 4% calcium, 18% iron
Exchanges: 1½ Vegetable, ½ Starch, 2 Lean Meat

Mexican-style stewed tomatoes and salsa lend a south-of-the-border accent to this beef stew. Complete the meal with tortillas and a festive salad of romaine, orange sections, and avocado slices.

SALSA VERDE BEEF STEW

Prep:
30 minutes

Cook:
Low 8 hours, High 5 hours

Makes:
8 main-dish servings

Slow Cooker Size:
4 ½- to 6-quart

1 ½	pounds boneless beef chuck roast, cut into 1-inch cubes
1	tablespoon cooking oil
1 ½	pounds potatoes, cut into 1-inch pieces (4 medium)
1	15- to 16-ounce can pinto beans, rinsed and drained
1	cup coarsely chopped onion (1 large)
¾	cup chopped green sweet pepper (1 medium)
1	teaspoon ground cumin
2	cloves garlic, minced
1	14½-ounce can Mexican-style stewed tomatoes, undrained
1	cup bottled mild or medium green salsa
8	7- to 8-inch flour tortillas, warmed* (optional)

1. In a large skillet brown meat, half at a time, in hot oil; drain fat.

2. In a 4½- to 6-quart slow cooker place beef, potatoes, drained beans, onion, and sweet pepper. Sprinkle with cumin and garlic. Pour undrained tomatoes and salsa over all.

3. Cover and cook on low-heat setting for 8 to 9 hours or on high-heat setting for 5 to 6 hours. If desired, serve with tortillas.

*Note: To warm tortillas, wrap them in white microwave-safe paper towels; microwave on high for 15 to 30 seconds or until tortillas are softened. (Or preheat oven to 350°F. Wrap tortillas in foil. Heat in the oven for 10 to 15 minutes or until warmed.)

Nutrition Facts per serving: 249 cal., 5 g total fat (1 g sat. fat), 50 mg chol., 576 mg sodium, 27 g carbo., 5 g fiber, 24 g pro.
Daily Values: 1% vit. A, 50% vit. C, 5% calcium, 22% iron
Exchanges: 1 Vegetable, 1½ Starch, 2½ Very Lean Meat, ½ Fat

You'll want to serve this wonderful stew with some crusty Italian bread so you can soak up every drop.

BEEF STEW WITH RED WINE GRAVY

¼ cup all-purpose flour
2 teaspoons dried Italian seasoning, crushed
1 teaspoon salt
½ teaspoon ground black pepper
2 pounds boneless beef chuck roast, cut into 1-inch cubes
2 tablespoons olive oil
2 large onions, cut into thin wedges
8 ounces parsnips, quartered lengthwise and halved
8 ounces carrots, quartered lengthwise and halved
8 ounces Jerusalem artichokes, peeled and coarsely chopped
1 cup dry red wine or beef broth
½ cup beef broth
¼ cup tomato paste
   Chopped tomatoes, golden raisins, and/or red wine vinegar or balsamic vinegar (optional)

Prep:
30 minutes

Cook:
Low 12 hours, High 6 hours

Makes:
6 main-dish servings

Slow Cooker Size:
4 ½- to 6-quart

1. Place flour, Italian seasoning, salt, and pepper in a large self-sealing plastic bag. Add meat cubes to bag, a few at a time, shaking to coat meat. In a 12-inch skillet brown meat, half at a time, in hot oil; drain off fat.

2. Meanwhile, in a 4½- to 6-quart slow cooker place onions, parsnips, carrots, and Jerusalem artichokes. Add meat to cooker. Pour wine and broth over all.

3. Cover and cook on low-heat setting for 12 to 14 hours or on high-heat setting for 6 to 7 hours. Stir in tomato paste. If desired, sprinkle each serving with tomatoes, raisins, and/or vinegar.

Nutrition Facts per serving: 356 cal., 9 g total fat (2 g sat. fat), 90 mg chol., 601 mg sodium, 26 g carbo., 4 g fiber, 35 g pro.
Daily Values: 73% vit. A, 20% vit. C, 6% calcium, 33% iron
Exchanges: 2 Vegetable, 1 Starch, 4 Lean Meat

This inviting stew comes from a region of Switzerland near the border of Italy. Swiss cooking is among the heartiest in Europe—and the use of polenta is traditional.

BEEF STEW WITH POLENTA

Prep:
40 minutes

Cook:
Low 8 hours, High 4 hours

Makes:
8 main-dish servings

Slow Cooker Size:
3 ½- to 4-quart

¼ cup all-purpose flour
1 teaspoon dried thyme, crushed
1 teaspoon dried basil, crushed
½ teaspoon salt
½ teaspoon ground black pepper
2½ pounds boneless beef chuck steak, cut into 1-inch pieces
2 tablespoons olive oil
2 cups chopped carrots (4 medium)
8 ounces boiling onions, peeled
1 teaspoon snipped fresh rosemary or ¼ teaspoon dried rosemary, crushed
6 cloves garlic, minced
1 14-ounce can beef broth
1½ cups dry red wine
1 recipe Polenta
½ cup snipped fresh Italian (flat-leaf) parsley
¼ cup tomato paste

1. Place flour, thyme, basil, salt, and pepper in a large self-sealing plastic bag. Add meat pieces to bag, a few at a time, shaking to coat meat. In a 4-quart Dutch oven brown meat, half at a time, in hot oil; drain off fat. (Add more oil if necessary.)

2. In a 3½- to 4-quart slow cooker place carrots and onions. Add meat to cooker. Sprinkle with dried rosemary (if using) and garlic. Pour broth and wine over all. Cover and cook on low-heat setting for 8 to 10 hours or on high-heat setting for 4 to 5 hours.

3. Prepare Polenta. Just before serving, stir fresh rosemary (if using), parsley, and tomato paste into cooker. Serve stew in bowls with Polenta.

Polenta: In a large saucepan bring 2¾ cups water to boiling. Meanwhile, in a bowl combine 1 cup cornmeal, 1 cup cold water, and ½ teaspoon salt. Slowly add cornmeal mixture to boiling water, stirring constantly. Cook and stir until mixture returns to boiling. Reduce heat to low. Cook for 10 to 15 minutes or until mixture is very thick, stirring occasionally. Makes 3½ cups.

Nutrition Facts per serving: 365 cal., 10 g total fat (3 g sat. fat), 86 mg chol., 506 mg sodium, 26 g carbo., 4 g fiber, 33 g pro.
Daily Values: 199% vit. A, 19% vit. C, 5% calcium, 29% iron
Exchanges: 1 Vegetable, 1½ Starch, 3½ Lean Meat, ½ Fat

Look for Jerusalem artichokes, also called sunchokes, from fall through winter in the grocery store produce aisle.

SPICED BEEF AND SUNCHOKE STEW

1¼ pounds boneless beef chuck steak, cut into ¾-inch pieces
1 tablespoon olive oil or cooking oil
8 whole allspice
½ teaspoon dillseed
1 bay leaf
1 pound Jerusalem artichokes, red potatoes, or tiny new potatoes, cut ¼-inch thick
2 cups frozen pearl onions or 1 medium onion, cut into thin wedges
8 ounces fresh mushrooms, halved
¼ teaspoon celery salt
¼ teaspoon ground black pepper
2 cloves garlic, minced
1 14½-ounce can tomatoes, cut up and undrained
1 8-ounce can tomato sauce
2 tablespoons cider vinegar

Prep:
30 minutes

Cook:
Low 9 hours, High 4 hours

Makes:
5 main-dish servings

Slow Cooker Size:
3 ½- to 4-quart

1. In a large skillet brown meat, half at a time, in hot oil; drain fat.

2. Meanwhile, for spice bag, place allspice, dillseed, and bay leaf in the center of a square of 100-percent-cotton cheesecloth. Tie closed with clean cotton kitchen string. Set aside.

3. In a 3½- to 4-quart slow cooker place Jerusalem artichokes, onions, and mushrooms. Add meat and spice bag to cooker. Sprinkle with celery salt, pepper, and garlic. Combine undrained tomatoes, tomato sauce, and vinegar. Pour over all.

4. Cover and cook on low-heat setting for 9 to 10 hours or on high-heat setting for 4 to 5 hours. Remove and discard spice bag.

Nutrition Facts per serving: 296 cal., 12 g total fat (3 g sat. fat), 60 mg chol., 574 mg sodium, 23 g carbo., 3 g fiber, 26 g pro.
Daily Values: 9% vit. A, 33% vit. C, 8% calcium, 32% iron
Exchanges: 1½ Vegetable, 1 Starch, 3 Very Lean Meat, ½ Fat

The flavors of steak Diane, a classic French dish, translate well to this hearty stew that cooks up perfectly in a slow cooker.

MUSHROOM STEAK DIANE STEW

Prep:
20 minutes

Cook:
Low 8 hours, High 4 hours

Makes:
6 main-dish servings

Slow Cooker Size:
3 ½- to 4-quart

2	medium onions, cut into thin wedges
3	cups sliced fresh button mushrooms
1½	pounds boneless beef round steak, cut into 1-inch cubes
1	teaspoon dry mustard
½	teaspoon cracked black pepper
1	10¾-ounce can condensed golden mushroom soup
¼	cup tomato paste
2	teaspoons Worcestershire sauce
3	cups hot cooked noodles

1. In a 3½- to 4-quart slow cooker place onions and mushrooms. Add meat to cooker. Sprinkle with mustard and pepper. Combine soup, tomato paste, and Worcestershire sauce. Pour over all.

2. Cover and cook on low-heat setting for 8 to 10 hours or on high-heat setting for 4 to 5 hours. Serve over noodles.

Nutrition Facts per serving: 314 cal., 7 g total fat (2 g sat. fat), 92 mg chol., 569 mg sodium, 30 g carbo., 3 g fiber, 33 g pro.
Daily Values: 12% vit. A, 11% vit. C, 2% calcium, 25% iron
Exchanges: 1½ Vegetable, 1½ Starch, 3½ Lean Meat

For a change from Mom's old-fashioned beef stew, try this delicious variation. The green olives and raisins make it unique.

BEEF STEW WITH A TWIST

2 tablespoons all-purpose flour
1 pound beef stew meat, cut into 1-inch cubes
2 tablespoons cooking oil
2½ cups chopped carrots (5 medium)
1½ cups chopped, peeled parsnips (2 medium)
12 ounces boiling onions, peeled and halved
1 bay leaf
1 tablespoon snipped fresh thyme or 1 teaspoon dried thyme, crushed
¼ teaspoon ground black pepper
2 cloves garlic, minced
1 14½-ounce can diced tomatoes, undrained
1 14-ounce can reduced-sodium beef broth
½ cup pimiento-stuffed green olives
⅓ cup golden raisins

Prep:
35 minutes

Cook:
Low 8 hours, High 4 hours

Makes:
4 main-dish servings

Slow Cooker Size:
3 ½- to 4-quart

1. Place flour in a large self-sealing plastic bag. Add meat cubes to bag, a few at a time, shaking to coat meat. In a large skillet brown meat, half at a time, in hot oil; drain off fat.

2. Meanwhile, in a 3½- to 4-quart slow cooker place carrots, parsnips, onions, and bay leaf. Add meat to cooker. Sprinkle with dried thyme (if using), pepper, and garlic. Pour undrained tomatoes and broth over all.

3. Cover and cook on low-heat setting for 8 to 10 hours or on high-heat setting for 4 to 5 hours. Remove and discard bay leaf. Stir in fresh thyme (if using), olives, and raisins.

Nutrition Facts per serving: 402 cal., 14 g total fat (3 g sat. fat), 67 mg chol., 766 mg sodium, 43 g carbo., 9 g fiber, 29 g pro.
Daily Values: 193% vit. A, 44% vit. C, 11% calcium, 26% iron
Exchanges: 2½ Vegetable, 1 Fruit, 1 Starch, 3 Lean Meat, 1 Fat

A ragout is a rich, well-seasoned stew. Beans and beef star in this tasty version.

BEEF AND BEAN RAGOUT

Prep:
10 minutes

Cook:
Low 8 hours, High 4 hours

Makes:
6 main-dish servings

Slow Cooker Size:
3 1/2- to 4-quart

1   pound beef stew meat, cut into 1-inch cubes
1   16-ounce can kidney beans, rinsed and drained
1   15-ounce can tomato sauce with onion and garlic
1   14½-ounce can Italian-style stewed tomatoes, undrained
½   of a 28-ounce package (about 4 cups) frozen loose-pack diced hash brown potatoes with onion and peppers

1. In a 3½- to 4-quart slow cooker combine meat, drained beans, tomato sauce, undrained tomatoes, and frozen potatoes.

2. Cover and cook on low-heat setting for 8 to 10 hours or on high-heat setting for 4 to 5 hours.

Nutrition Facts per serving: 247 cal., 4 g total fat (1 g sat. fat), 45 mg chol., 634 mg sodium, 31 g carbo., 6 g fiber, 23 g pro.
Daily Values: 14% vit. C, 4% calcium, 20% iron
Exchanges: 1½ Vegetable, 1½ Starch, 2 Very Lean Meat, ½ Fat

When peeling fresh beets, wear latex gloves to prevent your hands from being stained. Don't forget to serve the stew with sour cream, a traditional ingredient in this classic Russian dish.

BEEF AND BORSCHT STEW

1 pound beef stew meat, cut into 1-inch cubes
1 tablespoon cooking oil
4 medium beets, peeled and cut into ½-inch pieces, or one 16-ounce can diced beets, drained
2 cups chopped, peeled potatoes (2 medium)
1 cup coarsely chopped tomatoes (2 medium)
1 cup shredded carrots (2 medium)
½ cup chopped onion (1 medium)
3 cloves garlic, minced
1 bay leaf
4 cups reduced-sodium beef broth
1 6-ounce can tomato paste
2 tablespoons red wine vinegar
1 tablespoon packed brown sugar
½ teaspoon salt
½ teaspoon dried dill
¼ teaspoon ground black pepper
3 cups shredded cabbage
Light dairy sour cream or plain yogurt (optional)

Prep:
40 minutes

Cook:
Low 8 hours, High 4 hours; plus 30 minutes on High

Makes:
6 to 8 main-dish servings

Slow Cooker Size:
4- to 5-quart

1. In a large skillet brown meat, half at a time, in hot oil; drain fat.

2. Meanwhile, in a 4- to 5-quart slow cooker place beets, potatoes, tomatoes, carrots, onion, garlic, and bay leaf. Add meat to cooker.

3. In a large bowl combine broth, tomato paste, vinegar, brown sugar, salt, dill, and pepper. Pour over all.

4. Cover and cook on low-heat setting for 8 to 10 hours or on high-heat setting for 4 to 4½ hours. If using low-heat setting, turn to high-heat setting. Stir in cabbage. Cover and cook for 30 minutes more. Remove and discard bay leaf. If desired, top each serving with sour cream.

Nutrition Facts per serving: 248 cal., 5 g total fat (2 g sat. fat), 45 mg chol., 623 mg sodium, 29 g carbo., 5 g fiber, 22 g pro.
Daily Values: 53% vit. A, 59% vit. C, 6% calcium, 22% iron
Exchanges: 1 Vegetable, ½ Starch, 1 Other Carbo., 2½ Lean Meat

A can of your favorite beer gives this stew a zesty foundation. To keep preparation time quick and simple, use purchased shredded cabbage.

BEEF AND CABBAGE STEW

Prep:
10 minutes

Cook:
Low 7 hours,
High 3 ½ hours

Makes:
4 main-dish servings

Slow Cooker Size:
3 ½- to 4-quart

1　pound beef stew meat, cut into 1-inch cubes
4　cups packaged shredded cabbage with carrot (coleslaw mix)
3　tablespoons quick-cooking tapioca
1　envelope (½ of a 2½-ounce package) onion soup mix
3　cups water
1　12-ounce can beer

1. In a 3½- to 4-quart slow cooker place beef and cabbage. Sprinkle with tapioca and soup mix. Pour water and beer over all.

2. Cover and cook on low-heat setting for 7 to 8 hours or on high-heat setting for 3½ to 4 hours.

Nutrition Facts per serving: 242 cal., 4 g total fat (1 g sat. fat), 67 mg chol., 476 mg sodium, 19 g carbo., 2 g fiber, 26 g pro.
Daily Values: 2% vit. A, 38% vit. C, 5% calcium, 18% iron
Exchanges: 2 Vegetable, ½ Starch, 3 Very Lean Meat, 1 Fat

Instead of pricier stew meat, purchase a beef chuck or shoulder roast and cut it into 1-inch cubes.

SUPERSIMPLE BEEF STEW

1 pound beef stew meat, cut into 1-inch cubes
2 cups quartered small red potatoes (12 ounces)
2 cups chopped carrots (4 medium)
1 small red onion, cut into wedges
½ teaspoon dried marjoram or thyme, crushed
1 10¾-ounce can reduced-fat and reduced-sodium condensed cream of mushroom or cream of celery soup
1 cup reduced-sodium beef broth
1 9-ounce package frozen cut green beans, thawed

1. In a 3½- to 4-quart slow cooker place meat, potatoes, carrots, and onion. Sprinkle with marjoram. Combine soup and broth. Pour over all.

2. Cover and cook on low-heat setting for 8 to 9 hours or on high-heat setting for 4 to 4½ hours. If using low-heat setting, turn to high-heat setting. Stir in green beans. Cover and cook for 10 to 15 minutes more.

Nutrition Facts per serving: 298 cal., 6 g total fat (1 g sat. fat), 70 mg chol., 545 mg sodium, 32 g carbo., 5 g fiber, 29 g pro.
Daily Values: 138% vit. A, 38% vit. C, 7% calcium, 28% iron
Exchanges: 1 Vegetable, 1 Starch, 1 Other Carbo., 3 Very Lean Meat, 1 Fat

Prep:
15 minutes

Cook:
Low 8 hours, High 4 hours; plus 10 minutes on High

Makes:
4 main-dish servings

Slow Cooker Size:
3 ½- to 4-quart

Ginger, molasses, and raisins provide pleasant sweetness to this flavorful stew. Serve the stew with a salad of greens, grapes, and a sprinkling of toasted walnuts.

SWEET 'N' SNAPPY BEEF STEW

Prep:
35 minutes

Cook:
Low 8 hours, High 4 hours

Makes:
8 main-dish servings

Slow Cooker Size:
3 1/2- to 6-quart

2   pounds beef stew meat, cut into 1-inch cubes
2   cups sliced carrots (4 medium)
2   cups sliced, peeled parsnips (2 medium)
1   medium onion, sliced
1/2   cup sliced celery (1 stalk)
1/4   cup quick-cooking tapioca
1   tablespoon grated fresh ginger or 1/2 teaspoon ground ginger
1   teaspoon salt
1/2   teaspoon ground black pepper
1   14 1/2-ounce can diced tomatoes, undrained
1/4   cup cider vinegar
1/4   cup molasses
1/2   cup raisins

1. In a 3 1/2- to 6-quart slow cooker place meat, carrots, parsnips, onion, and celery. Sprinkle with tapioca, ginger, salt, and pepper. Combine undrained tomatoes, vinegar, and molasses. Pour over all.

2. Cover and cook on low-heat setting for 8 to 9 hours or on high-heat setting for 4 to 4 1/2 hours. Stir in raisins. Cover and cook for 30 minutes more.

Nutrition Facts per serving: 302 cal., 7 g total fat (2 g sat. fat), 54 mg chol., 486 mg sodium, 34 g carbo., 4 g fiber, 27 g pro.
Daily Values: 155% vit. A, 20% vit. C, 7% calcium, 20% iron
Exchanges: 1 Vegetable, 1/2 Fruit, 1 1/2 Other Carbo., 3 1/2 Very Lean Meat, 1 Fat

Luscious dried apricots, peaches, and cherries impart a bit of sweetness to this savory, thick stew.

FRUITED BEEF STEW

1   16-ounce package frozen loose-pack stew vegetables, thawed
1   8-ounce package mixed dried fruit
1   pound beef stew meat, cut into 1-inch cubes
2   tablespoons quick-cooking tapioca
2   14-ounce cans beef broth

1. Cut up any large pieces of stew vegetables and dried fruit. In a 3½- to 4½-quart slow cooker place vegetables, fruit, and meat. Sprinkle with tapioca. Pour broth over all.

2. Cover and cook on low-heat setting for 7 to 8 hours or on high-heat setting for 3½ to 4 hours.

Nutrition Facts per serving: 231 cal., 3 g total fat (1 g sat. fat), 45 mg chol., 546 mg sodium, 32 g carbo., 3 g fiber, 19 g pro.
Daily Values: 90% vit. A, 4% vit. C, 2% calcium, 16% iron
Exchanges: 1½ Vegetable, 1 Fruit, ½ Starch, 2 Lean Meat

Prep:
10 minutes

Cook:
Low 7 hours,
High 3 ½ hours

Makes:
6 main-dish servings

Slow Cooker Size:
3 ½- to 4 ½-quart

The flavors of India emerge when you mix lamb, potatoes, and tomatoes with garam masala. You'll find garam masala—an Indian spice mix—at ethnic grocers, but most supermarkets stock it too.

INDIAN-FLAVORED LAMB STEW

Prep:
15 minutes

Cook:
Low 8 hours, High 4 hours

Makes:
6 main-dish servings

Slow Cooker Size:
3 1/2- to 4-quart

2　pounds lamb stew meat, cut into 1-inch cubes
1　tablespoon garam masala
3　cups chopped, peeled potatoes (3 medium)
¼　teaspoon salt
¼　teaspoon ground black pepper
1　14½-ounce can diced tomatoes with garlic and onion, undrained
¼　cup water
¾　cup plain yogurt (optional)

1. In a bowl toss lamb with garam masala. In a 3½- to 4-quart slow cooker place seasoned meat and potatoes. Sprinkle with salt and pepper. Pour undrained tomatoes and water over all.

2. Cover and cook on low-heat setting for 8 to 10 hours or on high-heat setting for 4 to 5 hours. If desired, top each serving with yogurt.

Nutrition Facts per serving: 282 cal., 8 g total fat (3 g sat. fat), 97 mg chol., 538 mg sodium, 18 g carbo., 1 g fiber, 33 g pro.
Daily Values: 23% vit. C, 4% calcium, 23% iron
Exchanges: ½ Vegetable, 1 Starch, 4 Very Lean Meat, 1 Fat

In Persian stews like this one, yellow split peas are a classic ingredient. During cooking, the peas soften and fall apart, giving the stew a thick consistency.

PERSIAN-STYLE STEW

1½ to 2 pounds lamb or beef stew meat, cut into 1-inch cubes
1 tablespoon cooking oil
3 leeks, cut into 1-inch pieces
1 cup chopped onion (1 large)
½ cup dry yellow split peas, rinsed and drained
2 bay leaves
1 tablespoon snipped fresh oregano or 1 teaspoon dried oregano, crushed
1½ teaspoons ground cumin
¼ teaspoon ground black pepper
4 cloves garlic, minced
3 cups chicken broth
⅓ cup raisins
2 tablespoons lemon juice
3 cups hot cooked bulgur or rice

Prep:
25 minutes

Cook:
Low 8 hours, High 4 hours; plus 10 minutes on High

Makes:
6 to 8 main-dish servings

Slow Cooker Size:
3½- to 5-quart

1. In a large skillet brown meat, half at a time, in hot oil; drain off fat. In a 3½- to 5-quart slow cooker place meat, leeks, onion, split peas, and bay leaves. Sprinkle with dried oregano (if using), cumin, pepper, and garlic. Pour broth over all.

2. Cover and cook on low-heat setting for 8 to 10 hours or on high-heat setting for 4 to 5 hours.

3. If using low-heat setting, turn to high-heat setting. Stir in raisins. Cover and cook for 10 minutes more. Remove and discard bay leaves. Stir in fresh oregano (if using) and lemon juice. Serve with bulgur.

Nutrition Facts per serving: 358 cal., 7 g total fat (2 g sat. fat), 73 mg chol., 578 mg sodium, 44 g carbo., 10 g fiber, 32 g pro.
Daily Values: 16% vit. A, 18% vit. C, 7% calcium, 27% iron
Exchanges: ½ Fruit, 2 Starch, ½ Other Carbo., 3½ Very Lean Meat

If buffalo (bison) stew meat is unavailable, use a 1½-pound buffalo (bison) pot roast, cut into 1-inch cubes. Of course, beef stew meat works equally well.

BUFFALO STEW

Prep:
25 minutes

Cook:
Low 10 hours, High 5 hours

Makes:
6 main-dish servings

Slow Cooker Size:
4- to 5-quart

4   cups chopped red potatoes (4 medium)
2   cups packaged fresh peeled baby carrots
1   cup coarsely chopped onion (large)
½   cup sliced celery (1 stalk)
1   pound buffalo (bison) or beef stew meat, cut into
    1-inch cubes
2   tablespoons quick-cooking tapioca
1   tablespoon sugar
1   tablespoon dried Italian seasoning, crushed (optional)
1   teaspoon salt
½   teaspoon ground black pepper
2   14½-ounce cans stewed tomatoes, cut up and undrained

1. In a 4- to 5-quart slow cooker place potatoes, carrots, onion, and celery. Add meat to cooker. Sprinkle with tapioca, sugar, Italian seasoning (if desired), salt, and pepper. Pour undrained tomatoes over all.

2. Cover and cook on low-heat setting for 10 to 12 hours or on high-heat setting for 5 to 6 hours.

Nutrition Facts per serving: 263 cal., 3 g total fat (1 g sat. fat), 47 mg chol., 702 mg sodium, 39 g carbo., 5 g fiber, 21 g pro.
Daily Values: 206% vit. A, 37% vit. C, 7% calcium, 24% iron
Exchanges: 3 Vegetable, 1½ Starch, 1½ Very Lean Meat, ½ Fat

If you haven't thought of using parsnips lately, it's time to give this nutty-tasting root a try. Look for small to medium parsnips that are firm with fairly smooth skin and few rootlets.

AUTUMN HARVEST STEW

2	cups chopped, peeled sweet potatoes (2 medium)
1¾	cups chopped, peeled parsnips (2 medium)
1¾	cups sliced apples (2 small)
½	cup chopped onion (1 medium)
1	pound boneless pork shoulder roast, cut into 1-inch cubes
¾	teaspoon dried thyme, crushed
½	teaspoon dried rosemary, crushed
½	teaspoon salt
¼	teaspoon ground black pepper
2	cups apple cider or apple juice

1. In a 3½- to 4-quart slow cooker place sweet potatoes, parsnips, apples, and onion. Add meat to cooker. Sprinkle with thyme, rosemary, salt, and pepper. Pour apple cider over all.

2. Cover and cook on low-heat setting for 7 to 8 hours or on high-heat setting for 3½ to 4 hours.

Nutrition Facts per serving: 395 cal., 7 g total fat (2 g sat. fat), 73 mg chol., 411 mg sodium, 47 g carbo., 6 g fiber, 25 g pro. Daily Values: 166% vit. A, 91% vit. C, 7% calcium, 17% iron Exchanges: ½ Vegetable, 1½ Fruit, 1½ Starch, 3 Lean Meat

Prep:
25 minutes

Cook:
Low 7 hours,
High 3½ hours

Makes:
4 main-dish servings

Slow Cooker Size:
3½ to 4-quart

Pork and apples are perfect complements in this hearty dish that you'll want to enjoy time and again. The deep, nutty kick comes from a sprinkling of caraway.

PORK CIDER STEW

Prep:
20 minutes

Cook:
Low 10 hours, High 5 hours

Makes:
8 main-dish servings

Slow Cooker Size:
3 ½- to 6-quart

2 pounds pork shoulder roast, cut into 1-inch cubes
3 cups chopped potatoes (3 medium)
2 medium onions, sliced
1½ cups chopped carrots (3 medium)
⅔ cup coarsely chopped apple (1 medium)
½ cup chopped celery (1 stalk)
3 tablespoons quick-cooking tapioca
1 teaspoon salt
1 teaspoon caraway seeds
¼ teaspoon ground black pepper
2 cups apple cider or apple juice

1. In a 3½- to 6-quart slow cooker place meat, potatoes, onions, carrots, apple, and celery. Sprinkle with tapioca, salt, caraway seeds, and pepper. Pour apple cider over all.

2. Cover and cook on low-heat setting for 10 to 12 hours or on high-heat setting for 5 to 6 hours.

Nutrition Facts per serving: 273 cal., 8 g total fat (3 g sat. fat), 76 mg chol., 395 mg sodium, 26 g carbo., 3 g fiber, 24 g pro.
Daily Values: 116% vit. A, 22% vit. C, 4% calcium, 14% iron
Exchanges: 1 Vegetable, ½ Fruit, 1 Starch, 2½ Lean Meat

The few extra minutes it takes to brown the pork are well spent. Browning brings out the flavor of the meat and adds appealing color.

GREEN CHILE STEW

2 pounds boneless pork sirloin or shoulder roast, cut into ½-inch pieces
1 tablespoon cooking oil
½ cup chopped onion (1 medium)
4 cups chopped, peeled potatoes (4 medium)
1 15-ounce can hominy or whole kernel corn, drained
2 4-ounce cans diced green chile peppers, undrained
2 tablespoons quick-cooking tapioca
1 teaspoon garlic salt
½ teaspoon ground black pepper
½ teaspoon ground cumin
⅛ teaspoon dried oregano, crushed
3 cups water
Snipped fresh cilantro (optional)

Prep:
25 minutes

Cook:
Low 7 hours, High 4 hours

Makes:
6 main-dish servings

Slow Cooker Size:
3 ½- to 4 ½-quart

1. In a large skillet brown half of the pork in hot oil. Transfer meat to a 3½- to 4½-quart slow cooker. Brown remaining meat with onion; drain off fat and transfer meat and onion to the cooker.

2. Add potatoes, drained hominy, and undrained chile peppers. Sprinkle with tapioca, garlic salt, black pepper, cumin, and oregano. Pour water over all.

3. Cover and cook on low-heat setting for 7 to 8 hours or on high-heat setting for 4 to 5 hours. If desired, garnish each serving with cilantro.

Nutrition Facts per serving: 370 cal., 12 g total fat (3 g sat. fat), 95 mg chol., 499 mg sodium, 29 g carbo., 3 g fiber, 35 g pro.
Daily Values: 2% vit. A, 41% vit. C, 9% calcium, 14% iron
Exchanges: 2 Starch, 4 Lean Meat

This stew's light sage-infused sauce makes it an elegant evening meal. Ladle it over rice, egg noodles, or your favorite fluffy mashed potatoes.

PORK AND MUSHROOM STEW

Prep:
25 minutes

Cook:
Low 6 hours, High 3 hours

Makes:
5 main-dish servings

Slow Cooker Size:
3 ½- to 4-quart

Nonstick cooking spray
1 ½ pounds lean boneless pork, cut into ¾-inch pieces
1 16-ounce package frozen small whole onions, thawed
12 ounces whole fresh mushrooms, quartered
1 10¾-ounce can condensed cream of mushroom soup with roasted garlic
½ teaspoon ground sage

1. Lightly coat a 12-inch skillet with nonstick cooking spray. Heat skillet over medium heat. Brown meat, half at a time, in hot skillet; drain off fat.

2. In a 3½- to 4-quart slow cooker place meat, onions, and mushrooms. Combine soup and sage. Add to cooker.

3. Cover and cook on low-heat setting for 6 to 7 hours or on high-heat setting for 3 to 3½ hours.

Nutrition Facts per serving: 271 cal., 9 g total fat (3 g sat. fat), 77 mg chol., 481 mg sodium, 15 g carbo., 3 g fiber, 33 g pro.
Daily Values: 7% vit. C, 13% calcium, 8% iron
Exchanges: 1½ Vegetable, ½ Other Carbo., 4 Very Lean Meat, 1 Fat

Try this hearty stew that features some familiar Southern standbys—collard greens, black-eyed peas, okra, and hominy.

DIXIE HAM STEW

1½ cups dry black-eyed peas, rinsed and drained
8½ cups water
2 cups chopped cooked ham
1 15-ounce can white hominy, rinsed and drained
1 10-ounce package frozen cut okra
1 cup chopped onion (1 large)
1 to 2 teaspoons Cajun or Creole seasoning
¼ teaspoon ground black pepper
4 cloves garlic, minced
4 cups chopped collard greens or fresh spinach
1 14½-ounce can stewed tomatoes, undrained

Prep:
20 minutes

Cook:
Low 8 hours, High 4 hours; plus 10 minutes on High

Makes:
8 main-dish servings

Slow Cooker Size:
3 ½- to 6-quart

1. In a large saucepan combine peas and 4 cups of the water. Bring to boiling; reduce heat. Simmer, uncovered, for 10 minutes. Drain and rinse peas.

2. In a 3½- to 6-quart slow cooker combine drained peas, ham, drained hominy, okra, onion, Cajun seasoning, pepper, and garlic. Stir in the remaining 4½ cups water. Cover and cook on low-heat setting for 8 to 10 hours or on high-heat setting for 4 to 5 hours.

3. If using low-heat setting, turn to high-heat setting. Stir in collard greens and undrained tomatoes. Cover and cook for 10 minutes more.

Nutrition Facts per serving: 191 cal., 4 g total fat (1 g sat. fat), 19 mg chol., 709 mg sodium, 25 g carbo., 7 g fiber, 10 g pro. Daily Values: 91% vit. A, 34% vit. C, 18% calcium, 9% iron Exchanges: 1½ Vegetable, 1 Starch, 1 Lean Meat

Watch the cornmeal dumplings through the transparent cooker lid as they cook. Lifting the lid during cooking causes them to cook slowly.

VEGETABLE STEW WITH DUMPLINGS

Prep:
25 minutes

Cook:
Low 8 hours, High 4 hours;
plus 50 minutes on High

Makes:
6 main-dish servings

Slow Cooker Size:
3 1/2- to 4-quart

3 cups chopped, peeled butternut or acorn squash
2 cups sliced fresh mushrooms
1 15-ounce can Great Northern beans, rinsed and drained
2 14½-ounce cans diced tomatoes, undrained
1 cup water
1 teaspoon dried Italian seasoning, crushed
¼ teaspoon ground black pepper
4 cloves garlic, minced
½ cup all-purpose flour
⅓ cup cornmeal
2 tablespoons grated Parmesan cheese
1 tablespoon snipped fresh parsley
1 teaspoon baking powder
¼ teaspoon salt
1 egg, beaten
2 tablespoons milk
2 tablespoons cooking oil
1 9-ounce package frozen Italian green beans or
   frozen cut green beans
   Paprika

1. In a 3½- to 4-quart slow cooker combine squash, mushrooms, drained beans, undrained tomatoes, water, Italian seasoning, pepper, and garlic.

2. Cover and cook on low-heat setting for 8 to 10 hours or on high-heat setting for 4 to 5 hours.

3. Meanwhile, for dumplings, in a medium bowl stir together flour, cornmeal, Parmesan cheese, parsley, baking powder, and salt. Combine egg, milk, and oil; add to flour mixture. Stir with a fork just until combined.

4. If using low-heat setting, turn to high-heat setting. Stir in frozen green beans. Drop dumpling mixture by tablespoons onto stew; sprinkle with paprika. Cover and cook for 50 minutes more, leaving the lid on during the entire cooking time.

Nutrition Facts per serving: 288 cal., 7 g total fat (2 g sat. fat), 37 mg chol., 442 mg sodium, 45 g carbo., 7 g fiber, 12 g pro.
Daily Values: 51% vit. A, 50% vit. C, 21% calcium, 21% iron
Exchanges: 3 Vegetable, 2 Starch, 1 Fat

1½-QUART Recipes

If you can't find a roast this small in the meat case, ask the butcher to cut one for you.

CRANBERRY–CHIPOTLE BEEF

Prep:
10 minutes

Cook:
Low 6 hours, High 3 hours

Makes:
2 servings

Slow Cooker Size:
1½-quart

1   small onion, cut into thin wedges
12   ounces beef chuck roast
⅛   teaspoon salt
⅛   teaspoon ground black pepper
1   clove garlic, minced
½   of a 16-ounce can (about ¾ cup) whole cranberry sauce
½   to 1 teaspoon finely chopped canned chipotle peppers in adobo sauce
1   cup uncooked instant brown rice

1. In a 1½-quart slow cooker place onion. If necessary, cut beef to fit into cooker; add to cooker. Sprinkle with salt, black pepper, and garlic. In a small bowl combine cranberry sauce and chipotle peppers. Pour over all.

2. Cover and cook on low-heat setting for 6 to 8 hours or on high-heat setting for 3 to 4 hours. If no heat setting is available, cook for 4½ to 5½ hours.

3. Meanwhile, cook rice according to package directions, omitting salt and butter. Serve beef mixture with rice.

Nutrition Facts per serving: 506 cal., 7 g total fat (2 g sat. fat), 101 mg chol., 296 mg sodium, 71 g carbo., 4 g fiber, 40 g pro.
Daily Values: 4% vit. C, 2% calcium, 25% iron
Exchanges: 2 Starch, 3 Other Carbo., 5 Very Lean Meat

In mid-January, when temperatures plunge, there's nothing better than a bowl of chunky beef stew.

BEEF STEW FOR TWO

8 ounces beef chuck roast, cut into 1-inch cubes
1 cup low-sodium tomato juice
½ cup reduced-sodium chicken broth
½ cup chopped potato (1 small)
½ cup chopped carrot (1 medium)
½ cup frozen cut green beans
½ cup chopped celery (1 stalk)
2 teaspoons quick-cooking tapioca
½ teaspoon dried thyme, crushed
⅛ teaspoon salt
⅛ teaspoon ground black pepper
1 clove garlic, minced

Prep:
25 minutes

Cook:
Low 11 hours,
High 5 ½ hours

Makes:
2 servings

Slow Cooker Size:
1 ½-quart

1. In a 1½-quart slow cooker combine cubes of beef, tomato juice, broth, potato, carrot, green beans, celery, tapioca, thyme, salt, pepper, and garlic.

2. Cover and cook on low-heat setting for 11 to 12 hours or on high-heat setting for 5½ to 6 hours. If no heat setting is available, cook for 9 to 10 hours.

Nutrition Facts per serving: 246 cal., 4 g total fat (1 g sat. fat), 67 mg chol., 486 mg sodium, 22 g carbo., 4 g fiber, 28 g pro.
Daily Values: 79% vit. A, 66% vit. C, 6% calcium, 24% iron
Exchanges: 1½ Vegetable, 1 Starch, 3 Very Lean Meat, ½ Fat

To get the best flavor from your pasta, cook it only until al dente, which means it is still slightly firm and a little chewy.

BEEFY PASTA SAUCE

Prep:
20 minutes

Cook:
Low 4 hours, High 2 hours

Makes:
2 servings

Slow Cooker Size:
1½-quart

8 ounces lean ground beef
¼ cup chopped onion
1 clove garlic, minced
1 cup chopped tomatoes (2 medium)
1 4-ounce can (drained weight) sliced mushrooms, drained
¼ cup tomato paste
½ teaspoon dried Italian seasoning, crushed
¼ teaspoon salt
⅛ teaspoon ground black pepper
3 ounces dried spaghetti or fettuccine
1 tablespoon finely shredded Parmesan cheese

1. In a medium skillet cook beef, onion, and garlic until meat is brown and onion is tender; drain off fat.

2. In a 1½-quart slow cooker combine tomatoes, mushrooms, tomato paste, Italian seasoning, salt, and pepper. Stir meat mixture into cooker.

3. Cover and cook on low-heat setting for 4 to 5 hours or on high-heat setting for 2 to 2½ hours. If no heat setting is available, cook for 3 to 4 hours.

4. Cook pasta according to package directions, omitting salt; drain pasta. Serve sauce over pasta. Sprinkle each serving with cheese.

Nutrition Facts per serving: 430 cal., 13 g total fat (5 g sat. fat), 73 mg chol., 643 mg sodium, 48 g carbo., 5 g fiber, 31 g pro.
Daily Values: 21% vit. A, 39% vit. C, 8% calcium, 27% iron
Exchanges: 1½ Vegetable, 2 Starch, ½ Other Carbo., 3 Lean Meat, 1 Fat

Fresh mint and feta cheese infuse Mediterranean flavors into this ground meat and vegetable soup.

MEDITERRANEAN SOUP

6	ounces lean ground beef or lamb
¼	cup chopped onion
1¼	cups reduced-sodium chicken broth
¾	cup coarsely chopped zucchini
½	cup coarsely chopped tomato
2	teaspoons lemon juice
⅛	teaspoon ground black pepper
1	clove garlic, minced
1	tablespoon snipped fresh mint
2	tablespoons crumbled feta cheese

1. In a medium skillet cook meat and onion until meat is brown and onion is tender; drain off fat.

2. In a 1½-quart slow cooker combine meat mixture, broth, zucchini, tomato, lemon juice, pepper, and garlic.

3. Cover and cook on low-heat setting for 4 to 5 hours or on high-heat setting for 2 to 2½ hours. If no heat setting is available, cook for 3 to 4 hours. Stir in the fresh mint. Sprinkle each serving with feta cheese.

Nutrition Facts per serving: 201 cal., 10 g total fat (5 g sat. fat), 62 mg chol., 498 mg sodium, 8 g carbo., 2 g fiber, 19 g pro.
Daily Values: 13% vit. A, 33% vit. C, 7% calcium, 13% iron
Exchanges: 1 Vegetable, 2½ Lean Meat, 1 Fat

Prep:
20 minutes

Cook:
Low 4 hours, High 2 hours

Makes:
2 servings

Slow Cooker Size:
1½-quart

Serve this white chili in bread bowls if your supermarket bakery sells them or spoon it over corn bread squares.

CHICKEN CHILI

Prep:
25 minutes

Cook:
Low 5 hours,
High 2 ½ hours

Makes:
2 servings

Slow Cooker Size:
1 ½-quart

Nonstick cooking spray
8 ounces skinless, boneless chicken breast halves, cut into 1-inch pieces
1 15-ounce can white kidney beans (cannellini beans) or Great Northern beans, rinsed and drained
1 ¼ cups reduced-sodium chicken broth
¼ cup chopped onion
⅓ cup chopped green sweet pepper
½ of a small fresh jalapeño chile pepper, seeded and finely chopped*
¼ teaspoon ground cumin
¼ teaspoon dried oregano, crushed
⅛ teaspoon ground white pepper
1 clove garlic, minced
¼ cup shredded Monterey Jack cheese (1 ounce) (optional)

1. Lightly coat a medium skillet with nonstick cooking spray. Heat skillet over medium-high heat. Brown chicken in the hot skillet; drain off fat.

2. In a 1 ½-quart slow cooker combine chicken, drained beans, broth, onion, sweet pepper, chile pepper, cumin, oregano, white pepper, and garlic.

3. Cover and cook on low-heat setting for 5 to 6 hours or on high-heat setting for 2 ½ to 3 hours. If no heat setting is available, cook for 4 to 5 hours. If desired, sprinkle each serving with cheese.

*Note: Because chile peppers contain volatile oils that can burn your skin and eyes, avoid direct contact with them as much as possible. When working with chile peppers, wear plastic or rubber gloves. If your bare hands do touch the peppers, wash your hands and nails well with soap and warm water.

Nutrition Facts per serving: 275 cal., 2 g total fat (0 g sat. fat), 66 mg chol., 750 mg sodium, 33 g carbo., 11 g fiber, 40 g pro.
Daily Values: 3% vit. A, 45% vit. C, 8% calcium, 19% iron
Exchanges: 1 Vegetable, 1 ½ Starch, 4 ½ Very Lean Meat

Red sweet pepper pieces, cilantro, and corn make this a colorful south-of-the-border homestyle soup.

MEXICAN CHICKEN SOUP

Nonstick cooking spray
2 skinless, boneless chicken thighs, cut into 1-inch pieces (6 ounces)
1 small skinless, boneless chicken breast half, cut into 1-inch pieces (4 ounces)
1¼ cups reduced-sodium chicken broth
¾ cup coarsely chopped red or green sweet pepper (1 medium)
½ cup frozen whole kernel corn
¼ cup chopped onion
1 small fresh jalapeño chile pepper, seeded and finely chopped*
½ teaspoon ground cumin
⅛ teaspoon salt
⅛ teaspoon ground black pepper
1 clove garlic, minced
1 tablespoon snipped fresh cilantro
2 tablespoons shredded Monterey Jack cheese or Monterey Jack cheese with jalapeño peppers

Prep:
25 minutes
Cook:
Low 5 hours,
High 2 ½ hours
Makes:
2 servings
Slow Cooker Size:
1½-quart

1. Lightly coat a medium skillet with nonstick cooking spray. Heat skillet over medium-high heat. Brown chicken in the hot skillet; drain off fat.

2. In a 1½-quart slow cooker combine chicken, broth, sweet pepper, corn, onion, jalapeño chile pepper, cumin, salt, black pepper, and garlic.

3. Cover and cook on low-heat setting for 5 to 6 hours or on high-heat setting for 2½ to 3 hours. If no heat setting is available, cook for 4 to 5 hours. Stir in cilantro. Sprinkle each serving with cheese.

*Note: Because chile peppers contain volatile oils that can burn your skin and eyes, avoid direct contact with them as much as possible. When working with chile peppers, wear plastic or rubber gloves. If your bare hands do touch the peppers, wash your hands and nails well with soap and warm water.

Nutrition Facts per serving: 271 cal., 7 g total fat (3 g sat. fat), 107 mg chol., 634 mg sodium, 16 g carbo., 3 g fiber, 36 g pro.
Daily Values: 42% vit. A, 196% vit. C, 9% calcium, 11% iron
Exchanges: 1 Vegetable, ½ Starch, 4½ Very Lean Meat, 1 Fat

Use easy-to-find white button mushrooms in this classic one-dish meal.

CHICKEN MARSALA

Prep:
20 minutes

Cook:
Low 5 hours,
High 2 ½ hours

Makes:
2 servings

Slow Cooker Size:
1 ½-quart

1 ½	cups fresh mushrooms, quartered
4	chicken thighs, skinned
¼	teaspoon salt
¼	teaspoon dried marjoram or thyme, crushed
⅛	teaspoon ground black pepper
1	clove garlic, minced
¼	cup dry Marsala or dry sherry
3	ounces dried linguine or fettuccine
1	tablespoon cold water
2	teaspoons cornstarch

1. In a 1 ½-quart slow cooker place mushrooms. Add chicken to cooker. Sprinkle with salt, marjoram, pepper, and garlic. Pour Marsala over all.

2. Cover and cook on low-heat setting for 5 to 6 hours or on high-heat setting for 2 ½ to 3 hours. If no heat setting is available, cook for 4 to 5 hours.

3. Cook pasta according to package directions, omitting salt; drain. Divide pasta between 2 shallow bowls. Transfer chicken to bowls with pasta, reserving liquid in cooker. Cover chicken; keep warm.

4. For sauce, transfer cooking liquid and mushrooms from cooker to a small saucepan. Stir together water and cornstarch; stir into saucepan. Cook and stir until thickened and bubbly. Cook and stir for 2 minutes more. Spoon sauce over chicken and pasta.

Nutrition Facts per serving: 395 cal., 7 g total fat (2 g sat. fat), 114 mg chol., 392 mg sodium, 39 g carbo., 2 g fiber, 35 g pro.
Daily Values: 1% vit. A, 1% vit. C, 3% calcium, 19% iron
Exchanges: 1 ½ Vegetable, 2 Starch, 4 Very Lean Meat, 1 Fat

Serve with a salad of torn mixed greens, shredded carrots, and sliced fresh mushrooms; drizzle salad with reduced-calorie Italian salad dressing.

CREAMY LEMON CHICKEN

2 chicken breast halves with skin and bone (about 1 pound)

1 9-ounce package frozen cut green beans

½ of a small onion, cut into very thin wedges

⅛ teaspoon ground black pepper

1 clove garlic, minced

¼ cup reduced-sodium chicken broth

2 ounces reduced-fat cream cheese (Neufchâtel), cubed

½ teaspoon finely shredded lemon peel

Prep:
15 minutes

Cook:
Low 4 hours, High 2 hours

Makes:
2 servings

Slow Cooker Size:
1½-quart

1. Skin chicken; set aside. In a 1½-quart slow cooker place green beans and onion. Add chicken to cooker. Sprinkle with pepper and garlic. Pour broth over all.

2. Cover and cook on low-heat setting for 4 to 5 hours or on high-heat setting for 2 to 2½ hours. If no heat setting is available, cook for 3½ to 4 hours. Transfer chicken and vegetables from cooker to 2 serving plates. Cover chicken and vegetables; keep warm.

3. For sauce, in a small bowl beat cream cheese and lemon peel with an electric mixer on low speed until smooth. Slowly add cooking liquid, beating on low speed until combined. Spoon sauce over chicken and vegetables.

Nutrition Facts per serving: 288 cal., 9 g total fat (5 g sat. fat), 107 mg chol., 266 mg sodium, 13 g carbo., 4 g fiber, 40 g pro. Daily Values: 19% vit. A, 33% vit. C, 10% calcium, 12% iron Exchanges: 1½ Vegetable, 5 Very Lean Meat, 1½ Fat

You may have to trim a larger turkey breast tenderloin to 8 ounces. Wrap and store the remaining turkey in the freezer for another meal.

HOISIN–SAUCED TURKEY TENDERLOIN

Prep:
20 minutes

Cook:
Low 3 hours,
High 1½ hours

Makes:
2 servings

Slow Cooker Size:
1½-quart

½ of a medium red sweet pepper, cut into thin
    bite-size strips
½ of a small onion, cut into thin wedges
8 ounces turkey breast tenderloin, halved crosswise
⅛ teaspoon salt
⅛ teaspoon ground black pepper
1 clove garlic, minced
2 tablespoons orange juice
2 tablespoons hoisin sauce
¾ cup uncooked instant brown rice
1 tablespoon chopped almonds, toasted
2 tablespoons sliced green onion (1)

1. In a 1½-quart slow cooker place sweet pepper and onion. Add turkey to cooker. Sprinkle with salt, black pepper, and garlic. Combine orange juice and hoisin sauce. Pour over all.

2. Cover and cook on low-heat setting for 3 to 4 hours or on high-heat setting for 1½ to 2 hours. If no heat setting is available, cook for 2 to 3 hours.

3. Cook rice according to package directions, omitting salt and butter. Serve turkey mixture with rice. Sprinkle each serving with almonds and green onion.

Nutrition Facts per serving: 325 cal., 5 g total fat (1 g sat. fat), 68 mg chol., 408 mg sodium, 37 g carbo., 4 g fiber, 32 g pro. Daily Values: 23% vit. A, 112% vit. C, 6% calcium, 12% iron
Exchanges: ½ Vegetable, 2 Starch, 3½ Very Lean Meat, ½ Fat

Chopped green onion sprinkled on top of this meatless chili adds a colorful touch.

VEGETABLE CHILI

1	15-ounce can black beans, rinsed and drained
1½	cups low-sodium tomato juice
1	cup frozen whole kernel corn
¾	cup coarsely chopped zucchini or yellow summer squash
⅓	cup coarsely chopped red or yellow sweet pepper
¼	cup chopped onion
1	teaspoon chili powder
¼	teaspoon dried oregano, crushed
⅛	teaspoon salt
1	clove garlic, minced
2	tablespoons light dairy sour cream

Prep:
20 minutes

Cook:
Low 6 hours, High 3 hours

Makes:
2 servings

Slow Cooker Size:
1½-quart

1. In a 1½-quart slow cooker combine beans, tomato juice, corn, zucchini, sweet pepper, onion, chili powder, oregano, salt, and garlic.

2. Cover and cook on low-heat setting for 6 to 8 hours or on high-heat setting for 3 to 4 hours. If no heat setting is available, cook for 5 to 6 hours. Ladle into bowls. Top with sour cream.

Nutrition Facts per serving: 291 cal., 3 g total fat (1 g sat. fat), 5 mg chol., 800 mg sodium, 60 g carbo., 14 g fiber, 20 g pro. Daily Values: 39% vit. A, 172% vit. C, 14% calcium, 21% iron Exchanges: 4 Vegetable, 2½ Starch

Bake some corn muffins to serve with this classic soup. You can freeze the leftover muffins for up to three months.

LENTIL–HAM SOUP

Prep:
20 minutes

Cook:
Low 7 hours,
High 3 ½ hours

Makes:
2 servings

Slow Cooker Size:
1 ½-quart

1   cup reduced-sodium chicken broth
1   cup water
½   of a small onion, cut into thin wedges
½   cup chopped celery (1 stalk)
½   cup thinly sliced carrot (1 medium)
⅓   cup brown lentils, rinsed and drained
⅓   cup diced cooked ham (2 ounces)
½   teaspoon dried thyme, crushed
1   cup shredded fresh spinach
1   tablespoon finely shredded Parmesan cheese

1. In a 1 ½-quart slow cooker combine broth, water, onion, celery, carrot, lentils, ham, and thyme.

2. Cover and cook on low-heat setting for 7 to 8 hours or on high-heat setting for 3 ½ to 4 hours. If no heat setting is available, cook for 5 ½ to 6 hours.

3. Stir in spinach. Ladle into bowls. Sprinkle each serving with Parmesan cheese.

Nutrition Facts per serving: 193 cal., 3 g total fat (1 g sat. fat), 15 mg chol., 795 mg sodium, 25 g carbo., 12 g fiber, 17 g pro.
Daily Values: 106% vit. A, 16% vit. C, 10% calcium, 22% iron
Exchanges: 1 Vegetable, 1 ½ Starch, 1 ½ Very Lean Meat

Ready-to-use coconut milk, made from pressed coconuts, is readily available in specialty stores and many supermarkets.

THAI–STYLE VEGETABLE RICE

1¼   cups reduced-sodium chicken broth
1   cup frozen sweet soybeans (edamame)
1   small sweet potato, peeled and cut into 1-inch pieces
     (1 cup)
½   cup thinly sliced carrot (1 medium)
½   teaspoon curry powder
¼   teaspoon ground cumin
⅛   teaspoon ground ginger
1   clove garlic, minced
1   cup uncooked instant brown rice
¼   cup reduced-fat unsweetened coconut milk
1   tablespoon snipped fresh cilantro
2   tablespoons chopped cashews

Prep:
20 minutes

Cook:
Low 4 ½ hours,
High 2 hours;
plus 10 minutes on High

Makes:
2 servings

Slow Cooker Size:
1 ½-quart

1. In a 1½-quart slow cooker combine broth, soybeans, sweet potato, carrot, curry powder, cumin, ginger, and garlic.

2. Cover and cook on low-heat setting for 4½ to 5 hours or on high heat setting for 2 to 2½ hours. If no heat setting is available, cook for 4 to 4½ hours.

3. If using a cooker with heat settings, turn to high-heat setting. Stir in rice. Cover and cook for 10 to 15 minutes more or until rice is tender and most of the liquid is absorbed. Stir in coconut milk and cilantro. Sprinkle each serving with cashews.

Nutrition Facts per serving: 345 cal., 9 g total fat (2 g sat. fat), 0 mg chol., 406 mg sodium, 52 g carbo., 12 g fiber, 15 g pro. Daily Values: 271% vit. A, 45% vit. C, 10% calcium, 18% iron Exchanges: 3½ Starch, ½ Very Lean Meat, 1 Fat

Peeling the eggplant is strictly a personal choice—it's just fine to leave the peel on.

RATATOUILLE WITH PARMESAN TOAST

Prep:
25 minutes

Cook:
Low 4½ hours,
High 2 hours

Broil
30 seconds

Makes:
2 servings

Slow Cooker Size:
1½-quart

1½ cups cubed, peeled (if desired) eggplant
½ cup coarsely chopped yellow summer squash or zucchini
½ cup coarsely chopped tomato
½ of an 8-ounce can no-salt-added tomato sauce
⅓ cup coarsely chopped red or green sweet pepper
¼ cup finely chopped onion
¼ teaspoon salt
⅛ teaspoon ground black pepper
1 clove garlic, minced
4 ½-inch slices baguette-style French bread
1 teaspoon olive oil
3 tablespoons finely shredded Parmesan cheese
1 tablespoon snipped fresh basil

1. In a 1½-quart slow cooker combine eggplant, squash, tomato, tomato sauce, sweet pepper, onion, salt, black pepper, and garlic.

2. Cover and cook on low-heat setting for 4½ to 5 hours or on high-heat setting for 2 to 2½ hours. If no heat setting is available, cook for 4 to 4½ hours.

3. For Parmesan toast, brush one side of each slice of bread with olive oil. Place bread, oiled sides up, on a baking sheet. Broil 3 to 4 inches from heat about 15 seconds or until toasted (watch carefully to avoid burning). Sprinkle bread slices with 1 tablespoon of the Parmesan cheese. Broil about 15 seconds more or until cheese is melted.

4. Stir basil into cooker. Serve vegetable mixture in shallow bowls with Parmesan toast. Sprinkle servings with the remaining 2 tablespoons Parmesan cheese.

Nutrition Facts per serving: 248 cal., 6 g total fat (2 g sat. fat), 5 mg chol., 739 mg sodium, 39 g carbo., 6 g fiber, 10 g pro.
Daily Values: 33% vit. A, 112% vit. C, 17% calcium, 14% iron
Exchanges: 2 Vegetable, 2 Starch, 1 Fat

Chapter 8

SIDE DISHES
&
Desserts

Like eggplant Parmesan? Transfer the same basic idea to zucchini or yellow summer squash for this zesty side dish.

ITALIAN–STYLE ZUCCHINI

Prep:
15 minutes

Cook:
Low 4 hours, High 2 hours

Makes:
8 to 10 servings

Slow Cooker Size:
3 ½- to 4-quart

2½ to 3 pounds zucchini and/or yellow summer squash, halved or quartered lengthwise and cut into 1-inch pieces

2   14½-ounce cans Italian-style stewed tomatoes, drained

1   tablespoon quick-cooking tapioca, crushed

2   teaspoons sugar

½   teaspoon dried basil, crushed

2   cloves garlic, minced

½   cup shredded provolone or mozzarella cheese (2 ounces)

1. In a very large bowl stir together squash, drained tomatoes, tapioca, sugar, basil, and garlic. Transfer mixture to a 3½- to 4-quart slow cooker.

2. Cover and cook on low-heat setting for 4 to 5 hours or on high-heat setting for 2 to 2½ hours. Transfer to a serving dish; sprinkle with cheese.

Nutrition Facts per serving: 97 cal., 3 g total fat (1 g sat. fat), 5 mg chol., 285 mg sodium, 13 g carbo., 3 g fiber, 4 g pro.
Daily Values: 11% vit. A, 23% vit. C, 10% calcium, 7% iron
Exchanges: 2½ Vegetable, ½ Fat

Serve these veggies alongside grilled chicken breasts and accompany with crisp salad greens tossed with a reduced-fat dressing.

CARAMELIZED ONIONS AND POTATOES

2	large sweet onions, thinly sliced
1½	pounds tiny new potatoes, halved
½	cup reduced-sodium beef broth
2	tablespoons butter or margarine, melted
2	tablespoons packed brown sugar
¼	teaspoon salt
¼	teaspoon ground black pepper

1. In a 3½- to 4-quart slow cooker combine onions and potatoes.

2. In a small bowl combine broth, butter, brown sugar, salt, and pepper. Pour mixture over onions and potatoes in cooker.

3. Cover and cook on low-heat setting for 6 to 7 hours or on high-heat setting for 3 to 3½ hours. Stir gently before serving. Serve with a slotted spoon.

Nutrition Facts per serving: 154 cal., 4 g total fat (2 g sat. fat), 11 mg chol., 173 mg sodium, 27 g carbo., 3 g fiber, 3 g pro.
Daily Values: 3% vit. A, 34% vit. C, 3% calcium, 10% iron
Exchanges: 1½ Starch, 1 Fat

Prep:
15 minutes

Cook:
Low 6 hours, High 3 hours

Makes:
6 servings

Slow Cooker Size:
3 ½- to 4-quart

Remember this dish, red cabbage lightly coated with a creamy sauce, when planning a holiday dinner.

CARAWAY CABBAGE IN CREAM

Prep:
10 minutes

Cook:
Low 6 hours, High 3 hours

Makes:
8 servings

Slow Cooker Size:
4- to 5-quart

1   large head red cabbage (about 2 pounds), coarsely chopped (12 cups)
2   teaspoons caraway seeds, crushed
½   teaspoon salt
¼   teaspoon ground black pepper
½   cup whipping cream
¼   cup chicken broth

1. Place cabbage in a 4- to 5-quart slow cooker. Sprinkle with caraway seeds, salt, and pepper. In a small bowl stir together cream and broth. Pour over cabbage.

2. Cover and cook on low-heat setting for 6 hours or on high-heat setting for 3 hours.

Nutrition Facts per serving: 79 cal., 6 g total fat (3 g sat. fat), 21 mg chol., 201 mg sodium, 7 g carbo., 3 g fiber, 2 g pro.
Daily Values: 8% vit. A, 48% vit. C, 6% calcium, 4% iron
Exchanges: 1½ Vegetable, 1 Fat

Brilliantly colored fruits and vegetables sparkle in this tart-tangy side dish, which is packed with nutritive value. Some call it beauty food.

CRANBERRY–ORANGE SAUCED BEETS

2 pounds medium beets, peeled and quartered
½ teaspoon ground nutmeg
1 cup cranberry juice
1 teaspoon finely shredded orange peel
2 tablespoons butter
2 tablespoons sugar
4 teaspoons cornstarch

1. Place beets in a 3½- to 4-quart slow cooker. Sprinkle nutmeg on beets. Add cranberry juice and orange peel; dot with butter.

2. Cover and cook on low-heat setting for 6 to 7 hours or on high-heat setting for 3 to 3½ hours or until beets are tender.

3. If using low-heat setting, turn to high-heat setting. In a small bowl combine sugar and cornstarch. Remove ½ cup of the cooking liquid from the cooker and stir into the cornstarch mixture; stir mixture into beets and liquid in cooker. Cover and cook for 15 to 30 minutes more or until sauce is thickened.

Nutrition Facts per serving: 127 cal., 4 g total fat (3 g sat. fat), 11 mg chol., 117 mg sodium, 22 g carbo., 2 g fiber, 2 g pro.
Daily Values: 4% vit. A, 31% vit. C, 2% calcium, 5% iron
Exchanges: 2½ Vegetable, ½ Other Carbo., 1 Fat

Prep:
25 minutes

Cook:
Low 6 hours, High 3 hours; plus 15 minutes on High

Makes:
6 servings

Slow Cooker Size:
3 ½- to 4-quart

Curry powder used to flavor the sauce is a mild-to-hot combination of many herbs and spices that's often used in Indian and Asian cooking.

CURRIED EGGPLANT AND ZUCCHINI

Prep:
15 minutes

Cook:
Low 5 hours,
High 2 1/2 hours;
plus 15 minutes on High

Makes:
8 to 10 servings

Slow Cooker Size:
3 1/2- to 4-quart

1	medium eggplant, peeled and cut into 1-inch cubes
1	medium zucchini, cut into 1-inch cubes
1	medium onion, cut into thin wedges
1	cup sliced fresh mushrooms
1	clove garlic, minced
1/2	cup chicken broth
1	tablespoon curry powder
1/2	teaspoon salt
1/4	teaspoon ground black pepper
1	tablespoon cornstarch
1	tablespoon cold water

1. In a 3½- to 4-quart slow cooker stir together eggplant, zucchini, onion, mushrooms, and garlic. In a small bowl stir together broth, curry powder, salt, and pepper. Pour over vegetables.

2. Cover and cook on low-heat setting for 5 to 6 hours or on high-heat setting for 2½ to 3 hours. Transfer vegetables to a serving dish, reserving cooking liquid in cooker. Cover vegetables with foil to keep warm.

3. If using low-heat setting, turn to high-heat setting. For sauce, in a small bowl stir together cornstarch and water; stir into cooking liquid in cooker. Cover and cook for 15 minutes more. Spoon sauce over vegetables; toss to coat.

Nutrition Facts per serving: 30 cal., 0 g total fat (0 g sat. fat), 0 mg chol., 211 mg sodium, 6 g carbo., 2 g fiber, 1 g pro.
Daily Values: 1% vit. A, 10% vit. C, 2% calcium, 3% iron
Exchanges: 1 Vegetable

Serve this side dish in small bowls along with grilled burgers for a picnic-style meal.

SAUCY SUCCOTASH

1	16-ounce package frozen whole kernel corn, thawed
1	16-ounce package frozen lima beans, thawed
1	14¾-ounce can cream-style corn
1	cup chopped red sweet pepper
1	cup shredded smoked Gouda cheese (4 ounces)
½	cup chopped onion (1 medium)
2	teaspoons cumin seeds
¼	cup water
1	8-ounce carton light dairy sour cream

1. In a 3½- to 4-quart slow cooker combine whole kernel corn, lima beans, cream-style corn, sweet pepper, cheese, onion, and cumin seeds. Pour water over all.

2. Cover and cook on low-heat setting for 5 to 6 hours or on high-heat setting for 2½ to 3 hours. Gently stir in sour cream. Let stand for 10 minutes before serving.

Nutrition Facts per serving: 158 cal., 4 g total fat (3 g sat. fat), 14 mg chol., 282 mg sodium, 25 g carbo., 4 g fiber, 7 g pro. Daily Values: 12% vit. A, 59% vit. C, 11% calcium, 5% iron Exchanges: 1½ Starch, ½ Very Lean Meat, ½ Fat

Prep:
15 minutes

Cook:
Low 5 hours,
High 2 ½ hours

Cool:
10 minutes

Makes:
12 servings

Slow Cooker Size:
3 ½- to 4-quart

Choose two root veggies—turnips and parsnips—for a warming wintertime side.

TURNIPS AND PARSNIPS

Prep:
30 minutes

Cook:
Low 6 hours, High 3 hours

Makes:
8 to 10 servings

Slow Cooker Size:
3 ½- to 4-quart

2 pounds turnips, peeled and cut into 1-inch pieces
2 medium parsnips, peeled and cut into 1-inch pieces
2 medium onions, cut into thin wedges (1 cup)
1 10¾-ounce can reduced-fat and reduced-sodium condensed cream of celery soup
2 tablespoons water
1 teaspoon dried thyme, crushed
¼ teaspoon garlic salt
⅛ teaspoon ground black pepper

1. In a 3½- to 4-quart slow cooker combine turnips, parsnips, and onions. Add soup, water, thyme, garlic salt, and pepper; stir to coat.

2. Cover and cook on low-heat setting for 6 to 7 hours or on high-heat setting for 3 to 3½ hours.

Nutrition Facts per serving: 87 cal., 1 g total fat (0 g sat. fat), 2 mg chol., 248 mg sodium, 19 g carbo., 4 g fiber, 2 g pro.
Daily Values: 1% vit. A, 36% vit. C, 5% calcium, 4% iron
Exchanges: 1½ Vegetable, ½ Other Carbo.

Deep orange mashed sweet potatoes are beautiful on the table and plate; the addition of a few parsnips makes the taste sophisticated.

MASHED SWEET POTATOES AND PARSNIPS

Nonstick cooking spray
1½ pounds sweet potatoes, peeled and cubed (about 4 cups)
3 medium parsnips, peeled and cubed (about 2½ cups)
½ cup chicken broth
2 tablespoons butter or margarine, melted
½ teaspoon ground sage
½ teaspoon onion salt

1. Lightly coat a 3½- to 4-quart slow cooker with nonstick cooking spray. Add sweet potatoes, parsnips, broth, butter, sage, and onion salt.

2. Cover and cook on low-heat setting for 7 to 8 hours or on high-heat setting for 3½ to 4 hours. Mash with potato masher.

Nutrition Facts per serving: 166 cal., 5 g total fat (3 g sat. fat), 11 mg chol., 273 mg sodium, 30 g carbo., 5 g fiber, 2 g pro.
Daily Values: 298% vit. A, 35% vit. C, 4% calcium, 4% iron
Exchanges: 1 Vegetable, 1½ Starch, ½ Fat

Prep:
20 minutes

Cook:
Low 7 hours,
High 3 ½ hours

Makes:
6 to 8 servings

Slow Cooker Size:
3 ½- to 4-quart

The flavors of this mixture go especially well with baked ham or roasted pork.

MAPLE–GINGER SWEET POTATOES

Prep:
15 minutes

Cook:
Low 5 hours,
High 2 ½ hours

Makes:
8 servings

Slow Cooker Size:
3 ½- to 4-quart

1 ½ pounds sweet potatoes, peeled and cut into bite-size pieces (about 5 cups)
2   medium tart cooking apples, such as Granny Smith, peeled, cored, and coarsely chopped (about 2 cups)
2   tablespoons dried cranberries, snipped
1 ½ teaspoons grated fresh ginger
½   teaspoon salt
½   teaspoon ground cinnamon
¼   teaspoon ground nutmeg
⅛   teaspoon ground black pepper
½   cup water
¼   cup light pancake and waffle syrup product

1. In a 3½- to 4-quart slow cooker combine sweet potatoes, apples, cranberries, ginger, salt, cinnamon, nutmeg, and pepper. Pour water and syrup over all.

2. Cover and cook on low-heat setting for 5 to 6 hours or on high-heat setting for 2½ to 3 hours.

Nutrition Facts per serving: 98 cal., 0 g total fat (0 g sat. fat), 0 mg chol., 179 mg sodium, 24 g carbo., 3 g fiber, 1 g pro.
Daily Values: 211% vit. A, 26% vit. C, 3% calcium, 3% iron
Exchanges: ½ Fruit, 1 Starch

Serve this salad as an accompaniment to pork or take it along to a potluck supper. Stirring in the bacon at the last minute keeps it crisp.

HOT GERMAN–STYLE POTATO SALAD

6	cups peeled potatoes cut into ¾-inch cubes
1	cup chopped onion (1 large)
1	cup water
⅔	cup cider vinegar
¼	cup sugar
2	tablespoons quick-cooking tapioca
¾	teaspoon salt
¼	teaspoon celery seeds
¼	teaspoon ground black pepper
4	slices bacon, crisp-cooked, drained, and crumbled

Prep:
25 minutes

Cook:
Low 8 hours, High 4 hours

Makes:
8 servings

Slow Cooker Size:
3 ½- to 4-quart

1. In a 3½- to 4-quart slow cooker combine potatoes and onion. In a bowl combine water, vinegar, sugar, tapioca, salt, celery seeds, and pepper; pour over potatoes.

2. Cover and cook on low-heat setting for 8 to 9 hours or on high-heat setting for 4 to 4½ hours. Stir in bacon.

Nutrition Facts per serving: 151 cal., 2 g total fat (1 g sat. fat), 3 mg chol., 291 mg sodium, 30 g carbo., 2 g fiber, 4 g pro.
Daily Values: 39% vit. C, 2% calcium, 10% iron
Exchanges: 2 Starch

Bits of dried apricot are sun-flavored jewels in this pretty, earthy side dish. Pair it with roasted chicken or broiled salmon and steamed broccoli for an easy and colorful meal.

CREAMY WILD RICE PILAF

Prep:
20 minutes

Cook:
Low 7 hours,
High 3 ½ hours

Makes:
12 servings

Slow Cooker Size:
3 ½- to 4-quart

1 cup wild rice, rinsed and drained
1 cup regular brown rice
1 cup shredded carrots (2 medium)
1 cup sliced fresh mushrooms
½ cup thinly sliced celery (1 stalk)
⅓ cup chopped onion (1 small)
¼ cup snipped dried apricots
1 teaspoon dried thyme, crushed
1 teaspoon poultry seasoning
½ teaspoon salt
½ teaspoon ground black pepper
5½ cups water
1 10¾-ounce can condensed cream of mushroom with
    roasted garlic or golden mushroom soup
½ cup light dairy sour cream

1. In a 3½- to 4-quart slow cooker combine uncooked wild rice, uncooked brown rice, carrots, mushrooms, celery, onion, apricots, thyme, poultry seasoning, salt, and pepper. Stir in water and soup.

2. Cover and cook on low-heat setting for 7 to 8 hours or on high-heat setting for 3½ to 4 hours. Stir in sour cream.

Nutrition Facts per serving: 150 cal., 2 g total fat (1 g sat. fat), 4 mg chol., 287 mg sodium, 29 g carbo., 2 g fiber, 5 g pro.
Daily Values: 29% vit. A, 2% vit. C, 4% calcium, 4% iron
Exchanges: 1 Vegetable, 1½ Starch

Not all bread pudding is served for dessert. Spoon a small serving of this herb-flavored side next to a slice of roast turkey breast. It's like a stuffing.

SAVORY BREAD PUDDING

Nonstick cooking spray
½ cup dried tomatoes (not oil-packed)
¾ cup boiling water
6 cups firm-textured wheat bread cubes (about 8 slices)
4 ounces Gruyère cheese, shredded (1 cup)
¼ cup pine nuts, toasted
2½ cups fat-free milk
4 eggs
1 tablespoon dried basil, crushed
1 teaspoon garlic salt
½ teaspoon onion powder
½ teaspoon ground black pepper

Prep:
25 minutes

Cook:
Low 4 hours, High 2 hours

Cool:
15 minutes

Makes:
15 servings

Slow Cooker Size:
3 ½- to 4-quart

1. Coat a 3½- to 4-quart slow cooker with nonstick cooking spray; set aside. Place tomatoes in a small bowl; add boiling water. Let stand 5 minutes; drain and snip tomatoes.

2. In a very large bowl combine snipped tomatoes, bread cubes, cheese, and pine nuts. In a medium bowl whisk together milk, eggs, basil, garlic salt, onion powder, and pepper. Add to bread mixture, tossing gently to coat. Pour into prepared cooker.

3. Cover and cook on low-heat setting for 4 to 5 hours or on high-heat setting for 2 to 2½ hours or until a knife inserted near the center comes out clean. Remove liner from cooker, if possible, or turn off cooker. Let stand for 15 to 30 minutes before serving (pudding will fall as it cools).

Nutrition Facts per serving: 147 cal., 7 g total fat (2 g sat. fat), 66 mg chol., 321 mg sodium, 15 g carbo., 2 g fiber, 8 g pro.
Daily Values: 5% vit. A, 1% vit. C, 14% calcium, 9% iron
Exchanges: ½ Starch, ½ Other Carbo., ½ Medium-Fat Meat, 1 Fat

This bread tastes great served with a baked bean casserole or a main-dish salad.

SLOW–BAKED BOSTON BROWN BREAD

Prep:
20 minutes

Cook:
High 2 hours

Cool:
10 minutes

Makes:
2 loaves
(6 servings per loaf)

Slow Cooker Size:
4- to 6-quart

½   cup whole wheat flour
⅓   cup all-purpose flour
¼   cup cornmeal
½   teaspoon baking powder
¼   teaspoon baking soda
⅛   teaspoon salt
1   egg, beaten
¾   cup buttermilk or sour milk*
¼   cup molasses
2   tablespoons packed brown sugar
1   tablespoon butter or margarine, melted
2   tablespoons raisins, finely chopped

1. Generously grease two 1-pint straight-sided wide-mouth canning jars; set aside. In a medium bowl stir together whole wheat flour, all-purpose flour, cornmeal, baking powder, soda, and salt.

2. In a small bowl combine egg, buttermilk, molasses, brown sugar, and butter. Add egg mixture to flour mixture, stirring just until combined. Stir in raisins.

3. Divide mixture between the prepared canning jars. Cover the jars tightly with greased foil, greased side in. Place the jars in a 4- to 6-quart slow cooker. Pour ½ cup warm water into the cooker around the jars.

4. Cover and cook on high-heat setting about 2 hours or until a long wooden skewer inserted near the centers comes out clean. Remove jars from cooker; cool for 10 minutes. Carefully remove bread from jars. Serve warm or cooled to room temperature.

*Note: To make ¾ cup sour milk, place 2 teaspoons lemon juice or vinegar in a glass measuring cup. Add enough milk to make ¾ cup liquid; stir. Let mixture stand for 5 minutes before using in a recipe.

Nutrition Facts per serving: 89 cal., 2 g total fat (1 g sat. fat), 21 mg chol., 102 mg sodium, 17 g carbo., 1 g fiber, 2 g pro.
Daily Values: 2% vit. A, 5% calcium, 5% iron
Exchanges: 1 Other Carbo.

Bread in the slow cooker? You bet. Serve the round slices of this sweet bread with soft-style cream cheese.

APPLE BREAD

1	cup all-purpose flour
1½	teaspoons baking powder
1	teaspoon apple pie spice
¼	teaspoon salt
½	cup packed brown sugar
½	cup applesauce
2	tablespoons cooking oil or melted butter
2	eggs, slightly beaten
½	cup chopped walnuts, toasted

1. Generously grease two 1-pint straight-sided wide-mouth canning jars; flour the greased jars. Set aside.

2. In a medium bowl combine flour, baking powder, apple pie spice, and salt. Make a well in center of the flour mixture; set aside.

3. In a small bowl combine brown sugar, applesauce, oil, and eggs; mix well. Add applesauce mixture all at once to the flour mixture. Stir just until moistened. Stir in walnuts.

4. Divide mixture between the prepared canning jars. Cover the jars tightly with greased foil, greased side in. Place the jars in a 4- to 6-quart slow cooker. Pour ½ cup warm water into the cooker around the jars.

5. Cover and cook on high-heat setting for 1¾ to 2 hours or until a long wooden skewer inserted near the centers comes out clean. Remove jars from cooker; cool for 10 minutes. Carefully remove bread from jars. Serve warm.

Nutrition Facts per serving: 146 cal., 7 g total fat (1 g sat. fat), 35 mg chol., 113 mg sodium, 20 g carbo., 1 g fiber, 3 g pro.
Daily Values: 1% vit. A, 1% vit. C, 5% calcium, 6% iron
Exchanges: 1½ Other Carbo., 1 Fat

Prep:
20 minutes

Cook:
High 1¾ hours

Cool:
10 minutes

Makes:
2 loaves
(6 servings per loaf)

Slow Cooker Size:
4- to 6-quart

Granny Smith apples are good choices for this homemade applesauce. Stash extras in the freezer for up to eight months.

APPLE-Y CHUNKY APPLESAUCE

Prep:
20 minutes

Cook:
Low 6 hours, High 3 hours

Makes:
10 servings

Slow Cooker Size:
3 ½- to 4-quart

3   pounds tart cooking apples, peeled, cored, and sliced
1   cup snipped dried apples
½   cup packed brown sugar
½   cup water
¼   cup frozen apple juice concentrate, thawed
1   teaspoon finely shredded lemon peel
3   tablespoons lemon juice
6   inches stick cinnamon, broken into 1-inch pieces

1. In a 3½- to 4-quart slow cooker combine sliced apples, dried apples, brown sugar, water, apple juice concentrate, lemon peel, lemon juice, and stick cinnamon. Cover and cook on low-heat setting for 6 to 8 hours or on high-heat setting for 3 to 4 hours. Remove and discard stick cinnamon. Using a potato masher, coarsely mash apples.

2. If storing applesauce for later use, cool slightly. Ladle into airtight containers; seal. Refrigerate for up to 1 week or freeze for up to 8 months.

Nutrition Facts per serving: 141 cal., 0 g total fat (0 g sat. fat), 0 mg chol., 14 mg sodium, 37 g carbo., 3 g fiber, 0 g pro.
Daily Values: 1% vit. A, 10% vit. C, 2% calcium, 3% iron
Exchanges: 1½ Fruit, 1 Other Carbo.

Slow-simmer your favorite fruits that are in season. A dollop of whipped topping is an option for this ginger-spiked dessert.

GINGER–SPICE FRUIT COMPOTE

6 cups assorted sliced fresh fruit, such as pitted nectarines, peeled and seeded mangoes, cored pears, and/or cored apples
1 7-ounce package mixed dried fruit bits
1 cup white grape-peach juice or white grape juice
2 tablespoons packed brown sugar
1 tablespoon quick-cooking tapioca
1 teaspoon finely shredded orange peel
1 teaspoon grated fresh ginger
Frozen fat-free or light whipped dessert topping, thawed (optional)

Prep:
25 minutes
Cook:
Low 4 hours, High 2 hours
Makes:
8 servings
Slow Cooker Size:
3 1/2- to 4-quart

1. In a 3½- to 4-quart slow cooker combine desired sliced fruit, dried fruit, juice, brown sugar, tapioca, orange peel, and ginger.

2. Cover and cook on low-heat setting for 4 to 5 hours or on high-heat setting for 2 to 2½ hours. Spoon compote into small dessert bowls. If desired, add a small dollop of whipped topping.

Nutrition Facts per serving: 155 cal., 0 g total fat (0 g sat. fat), 0 mg chol., 21 mg sodium, 39 g carbo., 2 g fiber, 2 g pro.
Daily Values: 7% vit. A, 23% vit. C, 2% calcium, 3% iron
Exchanges: 2½ Fruit

Serve this pretty and colorful fruit dessert either warm or chilled. It's a light and refreshing way to finish a meal.

BERRY COMPOTE

Prep:
10 minutes

Cook:
Low 8 hours, High 4 hours

Stand:
10 minutes

Makes:
10 servings

Slow Cooker Size:
3 ½- to 4-quart

2½ cups cranberry-raspberry drink or cranberry juice
1 7-ounce package mixed dried fruit, cut into 1-inch pieces
⅔ cup dried cranberries or raisins
⅓ cup packed brown sugar
3 inches stick cinnamon
1 12-ounce package loose-pack frozen red raspberries

1. In a 3½- to 4-quart slow cooker combine cranberry-raspberry drink, dried fruit, cranberries, brown sugar, and stick cinnamon.

2. Cover and cook on low-heat setting for 8 to 10 hours or on high-heat setting for 4 to 5 hours. Stir in frozen raspberries; let stand 10 minutes. Remove and discard cinnamon stick. Spoon compote into dessert bowls.

Nutrition Facts per serving: 149 cal., 0 g total fat (0 g sat. fat), 0 mg chol., 16 mg sodium, 38 g carbo., 3 g fiber, 1 g pro.
Daily Values: 10% vit. A, 3% vit. C, 2% calcium, 5% iron
Exchanges: 2 Fruit, ½ Other Carbo.

Show off this pretty dessert by ladling it into small glass bowls. Gently spiced with cinnamon, ginger, cloves, and nutmeg, it's versatile, too, and a nice accompaniment spooned over pork, pancakes, or waffles.

WINTER FRUIT SOUP

2	7-ounce packages mixed dried fruit bits (about 3 cups)
½	cup snipped pitted dates or snipped dried figs
½	cup dried cranberries or dried cherries
¼	cup granulated sugar
¼	cup packed brown sugar
2	tablespoons quick-cooking tapioca
1	medium orange, sliced
2	3-inch pieces stick cinnamon
1½	teaspoons finely chopped crystallized ginger
	Dash ground cloves
	Dash ground nutmeg
6	cups water

1. In a 3½- to 4-quart slow cooker combine fruit bits, dates, cranberries, granulated sugar, brown sugar, tapioca, orange slices, stick cinnamon, ginger, cloves, and nutmeg. Pour water over all and stir to mix.

2. Cover and cook on low-heat setting for 6 to 7 hours or on high-heat setting for 3 to 4 hours. Remove and discard orange slices and stick cinnamon before serving in dessert bowls.

Nutrition Facts per serving: 203 cal., 0 g total fat (0 g sat. fat), 0 mg chol., 36 mg sodium, 53 g carbo., 1 g fiber, 2 g pro.
Daily Values: 1% vit. C, 2% calcium, 4% iron
Exchanges: 2½ Fruit, 1 Other Carbo.

Prep:
15 minutes

Cook:
Low 6 hours, High 3 hours

Makes:
10 to 12 servings

Slow Cooker Size:
3½- to 4-quart

A light, fresh finish to a heavy meal, this cinnamon-scented soup is made with only five ingredients.

APRICOT–PEACH DESSERT SOUP

Prep:
15 minutes

Cook:
Low 5 hours,
High 2 ½ hours

Cool:
30 minutes

Makes:
10 servings

Slow Cooker Size:
3 ½- to 4-quart

4   cups orange-peach-mango juice or orange-tangerine juice
1   16-ounce package frozen unsweetened peach slices
1   7-ounce package dried apricots, cut into 1-inch pieces
1   6-ounce package dried cherries and golden raisins
2   3-inch pieces stick cinnamon

1. In a 3½- to 4-quart slow cooker combine juice, frozen peaches, apricots, cherries and raisins, and stick cinnamon.

2. Cover and cook on low-heat setting for 5 to 6 hours or on high-heat setting for 2½ to 3 hours. Remove liner from cooker, if possible, or turn off cooker. Let stand, uncovered, for 30 to 45 minutes to cool slightly before serving. Remove and discard stick cinnamon with a slotted spoon. To serve, spoon into dessert bowls.

Nutrition Facts per serving: 167 cal., 0 g total fat (0 g sat. fat), 0 mg chol., 11 mg sodium, 42 g carbo., 3 g fiber, 2 g pro.
Daily Values: 19% vit. A, 46% vit. C, 3% calcium, 4% iron
Exchanges: 3 Fruit

If you decide to serve this sauce over frozen yogurt or cake, a half-cup of soft-serve vanilla frozen yogurt adds 115 calories and a small slice of angel food cake adds 161.

STRAWBERRY–RHUBARB DESSERT SAUCE

Nonstick cooking spray
½ cup no-calorie, heat-stable granulated sugar substitute (Splenda®)
⅓ cup apple juice
2 tablespoons quick-cooking tapioca
1 16-ounce package frozen unsweetened whole strawberries or 4 cups fresh whole strawberries
1 16-ounce package frozen unsweetened sliced rhubarb or 4 cups fresh sliced rhubarb
Low-fat vanilla frozen yogurt or angel food cake slices (optional)

Prep:
5 minutes

Cook:
Low 5 hours,
High 2 ½ hours

Stand:
15 minutes

Cool:
1 hour

Makes:
8 servings

Slow Cooker Size:
3 ½- to 4-quart

1. Lightly coat a 3½- to 4-quart slow cooker with nonstick cooking spray. In prepared cooker combine sugar substitute, apple juice, and tapioca; let stand for 15 minutes. Let frozen fruit stand at room temperature for 15 minutes. Stir fruit into mixture in cooker.

2. Cover and cook on low-heat setting for 5 to 6 hours or on high-heat setting for 2½ to 3 hours. Remove liner from cooker, if possible, or turn off cooker. Let stand, uncovered, about 1 hour to cool slightly before serving. If desired, serve over frozen yogurt or cake slices.

Nutrition Facts per serving: 47 cal., 0 g total fat (0 g sat. fat),
0 mg chol., 3 mg sodium, 13 g carbo., 2 g fiber, 1 g pro.
Daily Values: 5% vit. A, 44% vit. C, 12% calcium, 3% iron
Exchanges: 1 Fruit

Amaretto adds just the right amount of almond flavor to the fruit sauce. Spoon about one-third cup of the sauce over each cake slice.

ANGEL CAKE WITH CHERRY SAUCE

Prep:
10 minutes

Cook:
Low 4 hours, High 2 hours

Cool:
30 minutes

Makes:
10 servings

Slow Cooker Size:
3 ½- to 4-quart

Nonstick cooking spray
2   16-ounce packages frozen unsweetened pitted dark
    sweet cherries
½   cup cherry apple cider, apple cider, or apple juice
¼   cup packed brown sugar
3   tablespoons amaretto
2   tablespoons quick-cooking tapioca
10   1-ounce slices angel food cake

1. Coat a 3½- to 4-quart slow cooker with cooking spray. In prepared cooker combine cherries, cider, brown sugar, amaretto, and tapioca.

2. Cover and cook on low-heat setting for 4 to 5 hours or on high-heat setting for 2 to 2½ hours. Remove liner from cooker, if possible, or turn off cooker. Let stand, uncovered, about 30 minutes to cool slightly. Spoon over cake slices placed on dessert plates.

Nutrition Facts per serving: 163 cal., 1 g total fat (0 g sat. fat), 0 mg chol., 216 mg sodium, 37 g carbo., 2 g fiber, 3 g pro. Daily Values: 16% vit. A, 11% vit. C, 6% calcium, 4% iron Exchanges: 1 Fruit, 1½ Other Carbo.

No added sugar is needed for this dessert. Grape juice and dried cranberries add all the sweetness that's needed.

POACHED PEARS AND CRANBERRIES

¾ cup dried cranberries
6 medium ripe pears, peeled, cored, and halved
1½ cups white grape juice
½ teaspoon almond extract (optional)
Fat-free or low-fat vanilla frozen yogurt (optional)

1. In a 3½- to 4-quart slow cooker place cranberries. Top with pear halves. Pour juice and almond extract (if using) over all.

2. Cover and cook on low-heat setting for 4 to 5 hours or on high-heat setting for 2 to 2½ hours.

3. To serve, use a slotted spoon to place 2 pear halves in each of 6 shallow dessert bowls. Spoon cranberry mixture over pears. If desired, serve with a small scoop of frozen yogurt.

Nutrition Facts per serving: 183 cal., 0 g total fat (0 g sat. fat), 0 mg chol., 8 mg sodium, 47 g carbo., 6 g fiber, 1 g pro.
Daily Values: 1% vit. A, 38% vit. C, 2% calcium, 3% iron
Exchanges: 3 Fruit

Prep:
20 minutes

Cook:
Low 4 hours, High 2 hours

Makes:
6 servings

Slow Cooker Size:
3 ½- to 4-quart

Prepare a classic, old-fashioned dessert in your slow cooker—a real family-pleaser.

STUFFED APPLES

Prep:
20 minutes

Cook:
Low 5 hours,
High 2 ½ hours

Makes:
4 servings

Slow Cooker Size:
3 ½- to 4-quart

4	medium, tart baking apples, such as Granny Smith
⅓	cup snipped dried figs, golden raisins, or raisins
¼	cup packed brown sugar
½	teaspoon apple pie spice or ground cinnamon
¼	cup apple juice
1	tablespoon butter or margarine, cut into 4 pieces

1. Core apples; peel a strip from the top of each. Place apples, top sides up, in a 3½- to 4-quart slow cooker. In a small bowl combine figs, brown sugar, and apple pie spice. Spoon mixture into centers of apples, patting in with a knife or thin metal spatula. Pour apple juice around apples in slow cooker. Top each with a piece of butter.

2. Cover and cook on low-heat setting for 5 hours or on high-heat setting for 2½ hours. Use a large spoon to transfer apples to shallow bowls or dessert dishes. Spoon juices over apples. Serve warm.

Nutrition Facts per serving: 200 cal., 3 g total fat (2 g sat. fat), 8 mg chol., 31 mg sodium, 45 g carbo., 5 g fiber, 1 g pro.
Daily Values: 3% vit. A, 9% vit. C, 5% calcium, 5% iron
Exchanges: 1½ Fruit, 1½ Other Carbo., ½ Fat

Your family will love the generous servings of this contemporary dessert.

FRENCH PEACH AND BLUEBERRY DESSERT

6 cups sliced, peeled fresh peaches or frozen unsweetened peach slices

1 3-ounce package dried blueberries (⅔ cup)

½ cup white grape-peach juice or white grape juice

¼ cup no-calorie, heat-stable granular sugar substitute (Splenda®)

1 tablespoon quick-cooking tapioca

1 teaspoon vanilla

24 frozen French toast sticks (one 18.8-ounce package) Frozen fat-free or light whipped dessert topping, thawed (optional)

Prep:
15 minutes

Cook:
Low 4 hours, High 2 hours

Cool:
30 minutes

Makes:
8 servings

Slow Cooker Size:
3 ½- to 4-quart

1. In a 3½- to 4-quart slow cooker combine peaches, blueberries, juice, sugar substitute, and tapioca.

2. Cover and cook on low-heat setting for 4 to 5 hours or on high-heat setting for 2 to 2½ hours. Remove liner from cooker, if possible, or turn off cooker. Stir in vanilla. Let stand, uncovered, about 30 minutes to cool slightly.

3. Prepare frozen French toast sticks according to package directions and separate into sticks. (Discard maple syrup cups or save for another use.) To serve, place 3 toasted sticks in each dessert dish. Spoon warm peach-blueberry mixture over the sticks. If desired, top with a small dollop of whipped topping.

Nutrition Facts per serving: 231 cal., 4 g total fat (1 g sat. fat), 3 mg chol., 236 mg sodium, 47 g carbo., 3 g fiber, 3 g pro.
Daily Values: 25% vit. A, 20% vit. C, 10% iron
Exchanges: 1½ Fruit, 1 Starch, ½ Other Carbo., ½ Fat

One reason this crisp is so easy is the "crisp" part. It's crushed graham crackers.

EASY FRUIT CRISP

Prep:
25 minutes

Cook:
Low 4 hours, High 2 hours

Makes:
6 to 8 servings

Slow Cooker Size:
3 1/2- to 4-quart

Nonstick cooking spray
8   cups sliced, peeled cooking apples and/or sliced, peeled ripe pears (about 8 medium)
½   cup dried tart cherries
3   tablespoons sugar
1   tablespoon apple or peach brandy or apple juice
¾   cup coarsely crushed graham crackers

1. Coat a 3½- to 4-quart slow cooker with nonstick cooking spray. In prepared cooker combine sliced fruit, cherries, sugar, and brandy.

2. Cover and cook on low-heat setting for 4 to 4½ hours or on high-heat setting for 2 to 2½ hours. Cool slightly before serving. Spoon into serving dishes. Sprinkle with crushed graham crackers.

Nutrition Facts per serving: 187 cal., 1 g total fat (0 g sat. fat), 0 mg chol., 59 mg sodium, 43 g carbo., 4 g fiber, 2 g pro.
Daily Values: 1% vit. A, 8% vit. C, 1% calcium, 3% iron
Exchanges: 2 Fruit, 1 Other Carbo.

With its intense berry flavor and muffinlike cake, cobbler wins a place on the list of classic summer fare. Using a slow cooker lets you enjoy the dessert without heating up the kitchen.

MIXED BERRY COBBLER

Nonstick cooking spray
1 14-ounce package frozen loose-pack mixed berries
1 21-ounce can blueberry pie filling
¼ cup sugar
1 6½-ounce package blueberry or triple-berry muffin mix
⅓ cup water
2 tablespoons cooking oil
Light or fat-free vanilla ice cream (optional)

1. Lightly coat a 3½- to 4-quart slow cooker with nonstick cooking spray; set aside.

2. In a bowl combine frozen mixed berries, pie filling, and sugar. Place berry mixture in the bottom of the prepared cooker.

3. Cover and cook on low-heat setting for 3 hours. Turn cooker to high-heat setting. In a medium bowl combine muffin mix, water, and oil; stir just until combined. Spoon muffin mixture over berry mixture. Cover and cook for 1 hour more or until a wooden toothpick inserted into center of muffin mixture comes out clean. Remove liner from cooker, if possible, or turn off cooker. Let stand, uncovered, for 30 to 45 minutes to cool slightly before serving.

4. To serve, spoon warm cobbler into dessert dishes. If desired, top with a small scoop of ice cream.

Nutrition Facts per serving: 200 cal., 5 g total fat (1 g sat. fat), 0 mg chol., 145 mg sodium, 39 g carbo., 4 g fiber, 1 g pro.
Daily Values: 5% iron
Exchanges: 1 Fruit, 1½ Other Carbo., 1 Fat

Prep:
15 minutes

Cook:
Low 3 hours;
plus 1 hour on High

Cool:
30 minutes

Makes:
10 servings

Slow Cooker Size:
3½- to 4-quart

No need to cut up apples for this dessert. It starts with canned pie filling, plus ruby red dried cranberries.

APPLE–CRANBERRY PUDDING CAKE

Prep:
20 minutes

Cook:
High 2 hours

Cool:
45 minutes

Makes:
8 servings

Slow Cooker Size:
3 1/2-quart

Nonstick cooking spray
1   20-ounce can no-sugar-added apple pie filling
½   cup dried cranberries
1   cup all-purpose flour
¼   cup no-calorie, heat-stable granular sugar substitute (Splenda®)
1   teaspoon baking powder
¼   teaspoon apple pie spice
½   cup fat-free milk
2   tablespoons butter or margarine, melted
1¼   cups apple juice
3   tablespoons packed brown sugar
1   tablespoon butter or margarine, melted
    Frozen fat-free or light whipped dessert topping, thawed (optional)

1. Lightly coat a 3½-quart slow cooker with nonstick cooking spray. In prepared cooker stir together pie filling and cranberries.

2. In a medium bowl stir together flour, sugar substitute, baking powder, and apple pie spice. Add milk and the 2 tablespoons butter; stir just until combined. Spread over apple mixture in cooker. In a medium bowl stir together apple juice, brown sugar, and the 1 tablespoon butter. Carefully pour apple juice mixture over batter in cooker.

3. Cover and cook on high-heat setting for 2 to 2½ hours or until a wooden toothpick inserted into center of cake comes out clean. Remove liner from cooker, if possible, or turn off cooker. Let stand, uncovered, for 45 to 60 minutes to cool slightly before serving. To serve, spoon warm cake and sauce into dessert dishes. If desired, top with a small dollop of whipped topping.

Nutrition Facts per serving: 184 cal., 5 g total fat (2 g sat. fat), 12 mg chol., 82 mg sodium, 34 g carbo., 1 g fiber, 2 g pro.
Daily Values: 5% vit. A, 1% vit. C, 4% calcium, 6% iron
Exchanges: 1 Fruit, ½ Starch, 1 Other Carbo., ½ Fat

Before beginning this recipe, check to make sure that the dish or casserole you plan to use fits into your slow cooker.

CRUSTLESS LEMONY LIGHT CHEESECAKE

Nonstick cooking spray

12 ounces reduced-fat cream cheese (Neufchatel), softened
½ cup no-calorie, heat-stable granulated sugar substitute (Splenda®)
2 teaspoons finely shredded lemon peel (set aside)
2 tablespoons lemon juice
1 tablespoon all-purpose flour
½ teaspoon vanilla
½ cup light dairy sour cream
⅔ cup refrigerated or frozen egg product, thawed
Fresh or frozen raspberries (optional)

Prep:
30 minutes

Cook:
Low 3 hours,
High 1½ hours

Cool:
1 hour

Chill:
4 hours

Makes:
10 servings

Slow Cooker Size:
3½- to 5-quart

1. Lightly coat a 1-quart soufflé dish or casserole with nonstick cooking spray. Tear off an 18×12-inch piece of heavy foil. Cut in half lengthwise. Fold each piece into thirds lengthwise. Crisscross the strips and place the dish in the center of the foil cross; set aside.

2. For filling, in a large mixing bowl beat cream cheese, sugar substitute, lemon juice, flour, and vanilla until combined. Beat in sour cream until smooth. Beat in egg product on low speed just until combined. Stir in lemon peel. Pour mixture into prepared dish. Cover dish tightly with foil.

3. Pour 1 cup warm water into a 3½- to 5-quart slow cooker. Bringing up the foil strips, lift the ends of the strips to transfer the dish and foil to the cooker. Leave foil strips under dish.

4. Cover cooker and cook on low-heat setting for 3 hours or on high-heat setting for 1½ hours. Carefully remove dish, using the foil strips. Discard foil strips. Cool completely on a wire rack. Chill, covered, at least 4 hours before serving. Spoon into small dessert dishes. If desired, serve with raspberries.

Nutrition Facts per serving: 116 cal., 9 g total fat (6 g sat. fat), 30 mg chol., 173 mg sodium, 4 g carbo., 0 g fiber, 6 g pro.
Daily Values: 16% vit. A, 3% vit. C, 6% calcium, 2% iron
Exchanges: ½ Very Lean Meat, 2 Fat

Studded with plump raisins, dried cranberries, or dried cherries, the homey dessert gets a new look to go with its comforting flavor.

OLD–FASHIONED RICE PUDDING

Prep:
10 minutes

Cook:
Low 2 hours

Makes:
12 to 14 servings

Slow Cooker Size:
3 ½- to 4-quart

Nonstick cooking spray
4   cups cooked rice
1   12-ounce can evaporated milk
1   cup milk
⅓   cup sugar
¼   cup water
1   cup raisins, dried cranberries, or dried cherries
3   tablespoons butter or margarine, softened
1   tablespoon vanilla
1   teaspoon ground cinnamon

1. Coat a 3½- to 4-quart slow cooker with nonstick cooking spray; set aside. In a large bowl combine rice, evaporated milk, milk, sugar, and water. Add raisins, butter, vanilla, and cinnamon. Stir well to combine. Transfer to prepared slow cooker.

2. Cover and cook on low-heat setting for 2 to 3 hours. Stir well before serving in dessert bowls.

Nutrition Facts per serving: 204 cal., 6 g total fat (3 g sat. fat), 18 mg chol., 73 mg sodium, 34 g carbo., 1 g fiber, 4 g pro.
Daily Values: 5% vit. A, 2% vit. C, 11% calcium, 6% iron
Exchanges: ½ Fruit, 1½ Starch, 1 Fat

This moist, homespun dessert is just right for small families. The caramel ice cream topping is optional and adds about 65 calories per tablespoon.

RAISIN BREAD PUDDING

Nonstick cooking spray
⅓ cup refrigerated or frozen egg product, thawed
⅓ cup no-calorie, heat-stable granular sugar substitute (Splenda®)
1 teaspoon ground cinnamon
1 teaspoon vanilla
⅛ teaspoon ground nutmeg
1 12-ounce can evaporated low-fat milk
3 cups dried French bread cubes*
⅓ cup raisins
Fat-free caramel ice cream topping (optional)

Prep:
25 minutes

Cook:
Low 3 hours

Cool:
30 minutes

Makes:
4 servings

Slow Cooker Size:
1½-quart

1. Coat a 1½-quart slow cooker with nonstick cooking spray. In a medium bowl combine egg product, sugar substitute, cinnamon, vanilla, and nutmeg. Whisk in evaporated milk. Gently stir in bread cubes and raisins. Pour mixture into prepared cooker.

2. Cover and cook on low-heat setting for 3 hours or until a knife inserted in center comes out clean. If no heat setting is available, cook for 2½ to 3 hours (high-heat setting is not recommended). Turn off cooker. Let bread pudding stand 30 minutes to 1 hour to cool slightly before serving in dessert dishes. Serve warm. If desired, drizzle with ice cream topping.

*Note: To make dry bread cubes, cut 3 to 4 ounces bread into cubes to make 4 cups. Spread cubes in a single layer in a 15×10×1-inch baking pan. Bake, uncovered, in a 300°F oven for 10 to 15 minutes or until dry, stirring twice; cool.

Nutrition Facts per serving: 187 cal., 2 g total fat (0 g sat. fat), 14 mg chol., 214 mg sodium, 32 g carbo., 1 g fiber, 10 g pro.
Daily Values: 9% vit. A, 1% vit. C, 21% calcium, 7% iron
Exchanges: 1 Milk, ½ Fruit, 1 Starch

INDEX

METRIC INFORMATION

The charts on this page provide a guide for converting measurements from the U.S. customary system, which is used throughout this book, to the metric system.

Product Differences

Most of the ingredients called for in the recipes in this book are available in most countries. However, some are known by different names. Here are some common American ingredients and their possible counterparts:

■ All-purpose flour is enriched, bleached or unbleached white household flour. When self-rising flour is used in place of all-purpose flour in a recipe that calls for leavening, omit the leavening agent (baking soda or baking powder) and salt.

■ Baking soda is bicarbonate of soda.

■ Cornstarch is cornflour.

■ Golden raisins are sultanas.

■ Green, red, or yellow sweet peppers are capsicums or bell peppers.

■ Light-colored corn syrup is golden syrup.

■ Powdered sugar is icing sugar.

■ Sugar (white) is granulated, fine granulated, or castor sugar.

■ Vanilla or vanilla extract is vanilla essence.

Volume and Weight

The United States traditionally uses cup measures for liquid and solid ingredients. The chart below shows the approximate imperial and metric equivalents. If you are accustomed to weighing solid ingredients, the following approximate equivalents will be helpful.

■ 1 cup butter, castor sugar, or rice = 8 ounces = ½ pound = 250 grams

■ 1 cup flour = 4 ounces = ¼ pound = 125 grams

■ 1 cup icing sugar = 5 ounces = 150 grams

Canadian and U.S. volume for a cup measure is 8 fluid ounces (237 ml), but the standard metric equivalent is 250 ml.

1 British imperial cup is 10 fluid ounces.

In Australia, 1 tablespoon equals 20 ml, and there are 4 teaspoons in the Australian tablespoon.

Spoon measures are used for smaller amounts of ingredients. Although the size of the tablespoon varies slightly in different countries, for practical purposes and for recipes in this book, a straight substitution is all that's necessary. Measurements made using cups or spoons always should be level unless stated otherwise.

Common Weight Range Replacements

Imperial / U.S.	Metric
½ ounce	15 g
1 ounce	25 g or 30 g
4 ounces (¼ pound)	115 g or 125 g
8 ounces (½ pound)	225 g or 250 g
16 ounces (1 pound)	450 g or 500 g
1¼ pounds	625 g
1½ pounds	750 g
2 pounds or 2¼ pounds	1,000 g or 1 Kg

Oven Temperature Equivalents

Fahrenheit Setting	Celsius Setting*	Gas Setting
300°F	150°C	Gas Mark 2 (very low)
325°F	160°C	Gas Mark 3 (low)
350°F	180°C	Gas Mark 4 (moderate)
375°F	190°C	Gas Mark 5 (moderate)
400°F	200°C	Gas Mark 6 (hot)
425°F	220°C	Gas Mark 7 (hot)
450°F	230°C	Gas Mark 8 (very hot)
475°F	240°C	Gas Mark 9 (very hot)
500°F	260°C	Gas Mark 10 (extremely hot)
Broil	Broil	Grill

*Electric and gas ovens may be calibrated using celsius. However, for an electric oven, increase celsius setting 10 to 20 degrees when cooking above 160°C. For convection or forced air ovens (gas or electric), lower the temperature setting 25°F/10°C when cooking at all heat levels.

Baking Pan Sizes

Imperial / U.S.

9×1½-inch round cake pan
Metric 22- or 23×4-cm (1.5 L)

9×1½-inch pie plate
Metric 22- or 23×4-cm (1 L)

8×8×2-inch square cake pan
Metric 20×5-cm (2 L)

9×9×2-inch square cake pan
Metric 22- or 23×4.5-cm (2.5 L)

11×7×1½-inch baking pan
Metric 28×17×4-cm (2 L)

2-quart rectangular baking pan
Metric 30×19×4.5-cm (3 L)

13×9×2-inch baking pan
Metric 34×22×4.5-cm (3.5 L)

15×10×1-inch jelly roll pan
Metric 40×25×2-cm

9×5×3-inch loaf pan
Metric 23×13×8-cm (2 L)

2-quart casserole
Metric 2 L

U.S. / Standard Metric Equivalents

⅛ teaspoon = 0.5 ml
¼ teaspoon = 1 ml
½ teaspoon = 2 ml
1 teaspoon = 5 ml
1 tablespoon = 15 ml
2 tablespoons = 25 ml
¼ cup = 2 fluid ounces = 50 ml
⅓ cup = 3 fluid ounces = 75 ml
½ cup = 4 fluid ounces = 125 ml
⅔ cup = 5 fluid ounces = 150 ml
¾ cup = 6 fluid ounces = 175 ml
1 cup = 8 fluid ounces = 250 ml
2 cups = 1 pint = 500 ml
1 quart = 1 litre

GUILT-FREE COMFORT FOOD?
★ yes! ★
Find It Here

Looking for family-pleasing, kid-friendly, healthy meals?
Look no further! Here you'll find delicious recipes for your slow cooker,
ways to prepare savory, quick-to-table meals, and even tempting and
appealing ways to help your kids eat healthy, too.